GILDAS

The Ruin of Britain
and other works

History from the Sources

GILDAS

The Ruin of Britain and other works

edited and translated by

MICHAEL WINTERBOTTOM

History from the Sources
General Editor: John Morris

PHILLIMORE

1978

Published by
PHILLIMORE & CO. LTD.
London and Chichester

Head Office: Shopwyke Hall,
Chichester, Sussex, England

©

Text and translation: Michael Winterbottom, 1978
History from the Sources series: Mrs. Susan Morris, 1978

ISBN 0 85033 295 8 (case)
ISBN 0 85033 296 6 (limp)

Printed and Bound in Great Britain by
Hartnolls Limited, Bodmin, Cornwall.

CONTENTS

HISTORICAL INTRODUCTION

Gildas wrote his main work, the 'Ruin of Britain', about 540 A.D. or just before, when he was forty three years old (26.1). It is a fierce denunciation of the rulers and churchmen of his day, prefaced by a brief explanation of how these evils came to be. This preface is the only surviving narrative history of fifth century Britain. But it was not written as history. Gildas names in the fifth century only one person, one place, and one date, which he misplaced (20.1 note). Just enough is known to make his narrative intelligible, two key dates from contemporary Europe, and isolated detail from other sources, chief among them a collection of historical documents assembled about 800 A.D., known by the name of Nennius.

At the beginning of the fifth century Britain had been a Roman province for nearly 400 years, and for 200 years all freeborn Britons had been Roman citizens; there was no more contrast between 'native' and 'Roman' than there is to-day between 'Yorkshireman' and 'Englishman'. Society was dominated by a landed nobility, whose splendid country mansions, abundant in the southern lowlands, were built and furnished on a scale not matched again until the 18th century. The rents that sustained them were drawn from a vigorous agriculture and industry, whose output was distributed along an intricate road system. But in the highland regions of the south-west, of Wales and the North, there was little comparable prosperity; poorer farmers supported no wealthy gentry. Beyond the frontier, northern border kingdoms were still uneasy allies of Roman authority, and beyond the Clyde and Forth lived the hostile barbarian Picts, ready allies of the Scots, the late Roman name for the inhabitants of Ireland, who raided when they could, and had established a number of colonies on the western coasts of Britain.

This sophisticated civilisation was destroyed long before Gildas was born. When he wrote, its realities were fast fading from men's memories; to Gildas, Romans were again foreigners, their empire a thing of the past. The Roman empire of the west was mortally wounded in 410, when the western Goths took Rome, though its ghost survived for two generations. The Goths obtained the right to settle in Roman territory under their own laws and rulers, with the status of federate allies, in 418. They were the first, but others soon followed, and when Gildas was young the western empire was divided between four Germanic kingdoms, in France, Spain, Italy and North Africa. Roman and German fused; German kings inherited the centralised authoritarian rule of Rome, and preserved the property and power of landlords.

1

The British differed. In 410 the emperor in Italy instructed them to provide their own defence and government. At first they were outstandingly successful, and kept their society undamaged for a generation. A strong sovereign emerged in the 420s (23.1 note) and survived for some 30 years. Later writers knew him by the name or title of Vortigern, which means 'superior ruler'; Gildas' word-play describes him as *superbus tyrannus*, proud tyrant. Invasion from Ireland and beyond the Forth, which had harassed previous Roman governments for centuries, was permanently ended; but to curb it he settled German federates. Romans, British and Irish called them Saxons, but in Britain they called themselves English; the two words mean the same people, in different languages.

In or about 441 the English rebelled. Gildas (24 and notes) condenses nearly twenty years' fighting, which ended with the destruction of a large part of the nobility of Britain, and the emigration of many of the survivors. The migration, to northern and central Gaul, is dated by contemporary Europeans (25.1 note) to 460, or a year or two before. At home, renewed resistance was begun under the leadership of Ambrosius Aurelianus (25.3 note) and continued, traditionally under the leadership of Arthur (26.3 note), for over thirty years until 'the final victory of our fatherland' (2.1), after the decisive battle at Badon Hill, probably near Bath (26.1 note), in the 490s.

Gildas asserts that the victors maintained orderly government for a generation, but that in recent years power had passed to regional warlords, whose mutual violence overrode law and convention and corrupted the church. But the British had won the war. The English were beaten, though not expelled, and were confined to partitioned reservations, chiefly in the east (10.2 note). Yet victory had come too late, at the cost of almost everything that the victors had striven to protect. Though Britain was 'calm' and 'secure', freed from 'external wars', Roman civilisation was destroyed. Industry and market agriculture perished as roads became unsafe; towns that lost their supplies became 'ruinous and unkempt'; country mansions not built for defence were abandoned to wind and rain. After more than fifty years of war, peace could not revive a dead society. The skills of the builder, the potter, the tool-maker and other crafts were buried with old men who had trained no apprentices; more important, the rents and taxes that had paid for them could no longer be collected or paid. The war-lords could compel a self-sufficient agriculture to maintain their men and horses, but not to rebuild the past. They maintained their power throughout Gildas' lifetime; but soon after his death the English rebelled again, and between 570 and 600 permanently subdued most of what is now England.

But Gildas did not write in vain. On the contrary, few books have had a more immediate and far-reaching impact than his. He uttered what tens of thousands felt. His readers did not reform political society.

They opted out. They had a precedent. Two hundred years earlier, in the eastern mediterranean lands, immense numbers had dropped out of a corrupt society to seek solitary communion with God in the deserts; but their sheer numbers forced them to form communities. Their western imitators had hitherto aroused little response; apart from the clergy of some cathedrals and a few high-powered seminaries, Latin monasticism was 'torpid' by 500 A.D. (26.4 note), and had inspired only a few pioneers in the British Isles when Gildas wrote. But within ten years monasticism had become a mass movement, in South Wales, Ireland, and northern Gaul. Its extensive literature reveres Gildas as its founding father,named more often than any other individual(65.2 note).

Most of this literature is a sickly stew of half-truths, distorted by the ignorance and bias of medieval pietism. But there is first hand evidence that reforming monks were many and popular in South Wales, Ireland and Brittany before the mid sixth century plague, rapidly increasing in numbers thereafter; and that Gildas was respected. In the 7th century the movement spread from Ireland through Northumbria to much of England, and also to eastern France; in the 8th century, English and Irish missionaries brought Christianity and monasticism to Germany. In time, many of these houses adopted a version of the Rule of Benedict of Nursia, and became the nucleus of the later Benedictine Order.

A few notices outline Gildas' life. He was born a northerner, in the kingdom of the Clyde (15.3 note), but is said to have been schooled in South Wales (36.1 note), where he clearly wrote, since it is only the rulers of Wales and the South-West that he denounced by name. In later years he said to have migrated to St. Gildas de Rhuys, in Morbihan, in southern Brittany. The Welsh Annals enter his death at 570, and report a visit to Ireland in 565. It is in these maturer years that the Letters were written. There is contemporary evidence (Letter 4, note) that some concerned Ireland, and others intervene in the dispute between ascetic extremists and milder monks which sharpened in the 560s (Letters 2 and 3, notes). The 'Penitential' or Monastic Rule ascribed to him deals with the same problems, and may well be his.

Gildas' reputation stood high among the early monks, but he is less esteemed by later and modern writers. Historians who have quarried his early chapters are understandably irritated that he did not provide a clear narrative with names and dates; and the extraordinary Latinity of his main invective seems tiresome, its purpose irrelevant to other ages.

The narrative is unclear because it was written from oral memory. The experience of our own age or any other defines the limits of oral memory. Most men over 60 today have learnt something from their fathers of the late 19th century; some listened in childhood to men who were born and schooled before Wellington died, and have heard of Waterloo. But, by word of mouth alone, they can have no understanding or time scale beyond their fathers' youth; they cannot know whether a Martello Tower is older or younger than a romanesque church. So it was with Gildas. In youth he knew older men who had lived through the wars, but few who were adult before they began. All he understood of the Roman past was that it was orderly; though he knew two northern walls, he knew nothing of when or why they were built. Oral memory took him back to the wars and a dateless Vortigern, but no further. But for all its obscurity his narrative remains our chief guide to the history of Britain between the Romans and the English. That period shaped the peculiarities of our future. The mid fourth century Roman frontier is still the border between England and Scotland; but behind it, Britain was the only western province where the newcomers met prolonged resistance. The conflict ended in permanent division. There was no fusion between German and Roman; Roman institutions and language disappeared; the Welsh and the English both perpetuate the languages that their ancestors had spoken in and before the Roman centuries. The present day consequences of these divisions are better understood when their origin is known.

Gildas' strange idiom served its purpose. He aimed to move men's emotions, and he succeeded. Where political society was vicious and insecure, their imagination was as ready to be fired as a drought-stricken heath. Gildas' manifesto provided the spark, for though many had pioneered monastic ideals before him, in Europe as in Britain and Ireland, none had inspired a mass-movement. That movement flared suddenly and swiftly immediately after he wrote, and spread far beyond Britain. But the idiom that moved Gildas' contemporaries is hard for later ages to comprehend, so that he is more often quoted than read. This edition aims to make his work accessible and intelligible.

University College
London   JOHN MORRIS

4

PREFACE

'There was a prophet of the people in the time of the Britons called Gildas. He wrote about their misdeeds, how they so angered God that in the end he caused the army of the English to conquer their land and utterly destroy the strength of the Britons. And that was the result of the irregularity of the clergy and the lawlessness of the laity'. So the homilist Wulfstan (ed. Napier, p.166) writing in the early eleventh century: he saw more clearly than some modern critics the essential purpose and unity of Gildas' book. Gildas was later to be called a writer of history[1]; and he himself (37.1) speaks of 'this tearful history, this complaint on the evils of the age'. But though he sketches the history of Britain, he gives it a moralizing framework, and subordinates it to moral aims.

One crisis of the past Gildas gives special stress, for its relevance to his own day. After the letter to Aëtius and the famine, there was a victory over the Picts and Scots and an unusual period of calm. 'The enemy retreated from the people, but the people did not retreat from their own sins' (20.3). Sin flourished, and in particular 'the hatred of truth...and the love of falsehood'. Gildas underlines the parallel with the present ('nowadays too' 21.3; 'then as now' 21.6); and we see why when he brings the story up to his own day. A second victory, at the Hill of Badon, had been followed by a period of freedom from foreign enemies. For a time, while men still remembered 'that storm', there was internal tranquillity. Later, a generation with experience only of the serenity of their own day lost their sense of truth and justice, and government broke down (26.1-3). The earlier period of sinful calm had been punished by God: the Saxons came. Gildas reminds his readers of the history of their island largely (I take it) to point this parallel, and to warn, by implication, that God doubtless had an equally crushing punishment in store for his own generation. The continental sources he relies on in the early chapters, Orosius and especially Rufinus[2], had told their story to demonstrate the working out of God's plan for the world. Gildas does the same; but, as well as historian, he is (as Wulfstan saw) a prophet, in the Old Testament sense[3]. And he has a good deal more to say of the present than of the past.

The structure of his book is firm and monumentally wrought. An elaborate preface describes his hesitations and his final decision to make his views known. There follows (2-26) the history of his

5

country from the coming of the Romans down to the victory at the Hill of Badon and the ensuing troubles. But this is only a preliminary - 'before I make good my promise' (2.1). What Gildas had promised was a warning ('admonitiuncula' 1.2) to his countrymen, and especially to two crucial sections of them, the kings and the clergy. The rest of the book consists of successive assaults on these two classes. The method in each case is similar, and the parallellism is consciously marked by the likeness of the openings and, particularly, of the first sentences: 'Britain has kings, but they are tyrants' (27.1) and 'Britain has priests, but they are fools' (66.1) words that take us back to the internal soliloquy reported in 1.14: 'Britain has her governors, she has her watchmen'. Against both kings and priests Gildas musters first his own denunciations (27-36, 66-8), then a series of extracts from the Bible. But whereas the kings are faced merely with instances from the Old Testament (37-61), rounded off with some passages from *Wisdom* (62-3) to present, as the positive side of the case, the virtues of the good ruler, Gildas marks the superior interest he feels in the morals of the clergy by a more elaborate treatment. First we have a high standard set for the better priests: good as they think they are, do they match up to the heroes of Old and New Testament and of church history (69-75)? Then Old and New Testaments are drawn upon afresh to document the denunciation of wicked priests (76-105). Finally, as in the earlier passages from *Wisdom,* a more positive note is sounded in a comparison of the practice of modern priests with the precepts read to them in the ordination ceremony (106-9)[4]. Gildas ends with a short prayer for the few remaining good pastors.

Even in the long series of extracts from the Bible, Gildas has a system. The prophets and the apostles lend him their authority in his attack on powerful persons, and at the same time they help to protect him from the criticisms of the envious (37.3). The passages are not chosen at random, nor arranged without order. Gildas works through Old and New Testament according to a fixed, though idiosyncratic, scheme[5]; and most of the passages he chooses are obviously to his point without his own added comment (see an important remark at 93.4 on his reluctance to indulge too freely in 'interpretation').

This is structure on the grand scale, conscious and calculated. And Gildas' style is of a piece with his structure. He thinks in paragraphs rather than sentences. Sometimes the paragraph is a sentence, long and intricate. Sometimes, where the basic units are short, there are devices to construct interlocking systems out of them; thus the word *quis* ('who') or a variant of it opens virtually every sentence from 69 to 75, clearly marking off the section which these chapters form. Gildas strives after the grand, even if in the process he falls in with the grandiose[6].

The effort may be seen most clearly where we possess the source Gildas was adapting. Rufinus (himself translating Eusebius) lets his style rise with his subject as he prepares to tell of the coming of Christ: it was suddenly as if 'caelitus lumen ostensum aut radius quidam solis erumpens totum orbem claritate superni luminis inlustraret'[7] (*Hist.|Eccl.* 2.3.1). From this material Gildas fashions the grand and elaborate sentence that makes up chapter 8: Britain, hidden away in the frozen north far from the visible sun, is vouchsafed his rays by Christ, the true sun, who shows his brilliant light to the whole globe, not from the temporal firmament but from the citadel of heaven that goes beyond time. The sentence, packed with conceits, trailing clouds of decorative adjectives and subordinate clauses, yet not lacking direction and finally ending triumphantly on the name 'Christus', is, in its shapeless splendour, wholly typical of its author.

Gildas' armoury is well stocked. The all pervading Biblical language is reinforced with borrowings from Vergil[8]. The vocabulary is lightly spiced with Greek and glossary words[9]. A vivid and even grotesque imagination sees the invading Picts and Scots as worms emerging from their holes into the spring sunshine (19.1), a violated altar as covered with purple cloaks of congealed blood (28.2). Constant alliterative effects add to the sarcastic invective[10]. Puns abound, not always capable of translation.

All this goes to make up a manner that is to a large extent unique: and it is easier to describe Gildas' style than to put it into a context. We can do no more than speculate about British contemporaries. If certain fifth-century Pelagian tracts are rightly ascribed to this island[11], they testify to the controlled and sophisticated rhetoric of British writing a century before Gildas; but that is a different matter. What then of continental writers of the sixth century? Gildas' Latin has nothing in common with that of Gregory of Tours a generation later. Gregory makes concessions to the vernacular of his day, and his style (for once) justifies the traditional protestations of *rusticitas*. Gildas, naturally, writes 'late' Latin, but he is not under the influence of a vernacular. Perhaps there was no such vernacular; perhaps Gildas is able to rise above it.

Hugh Williams was on the right lines in looking to a more exactly contemporary writer, Cassiodorus, for a parallel to the style of Gildas. The example he cites from a letter composed for Theoderic by Cassiodorus is given only in English[12]. The Latin proves a further point:

7

'Quae ergo talis mora, ut in tantis tranquillitatibus velocia

necdum fuerint destināta nāvĭgĭa, cum stellarum non

mergentium lucidus situs tendi carbasa festināntĕr ĭnvĭtĕt

et aeris sereni fides properantium nequeat vōtă tērrĕrĕ ?

Aut forte incumbente austro remigiisque iuvantibus meatus

navium echinais morsus inter undas liquidas āllĭgāvĭt:

aut Indici maris conchae simili potentia labiis suis navium

dōrsă fīxērūnt, quarum quietus tactus plus dicitur

retinere quam exagitata possunt elemēntă cōmpēllĕrĕ'

(Var. 1.35.2-3).

Tumid this certainly is; and it is a valid point that Gildas' pomposity is dependent on, or parallel to, a continental tradition of inflated rhetoric. But the contrast with Gildas is no less marked than the similarity. In Cassiodorus the cola are rigorously organised and marked - as Latin *Kunstprosa* after Cicero almost always was - by rhythmic cadences[13]. The effect of the whole is quite unlike that of Gildas' sprawling and elaborate sentences.

Nor is rhythm, and the organisation of sentences that goes with it, confined in the sixth century to Cassiodorus and the mandarin manner of court correspondence[14]. It is found in the rhetorical Ennodius, as one would expect, but also, at times, in more surprising surroundings: the barbarous historian Jordanes, the Rule of Saint Benedict, and even Gregory of Tours himself. Gildas knows nothing of this, or chooses to ignore it. He has cut himself off from something continental stylists had always prided themselves on. He has abandoned the practice of his own sources; he had certainly read the elegantly rhythmical Rufinus. And when he quotes the alleged words of the Letter to Aëtius, the old crisp declamatory manner contrasts weirdly with its baroque surroundings:-

'Repellunt barbari ad mare, repellĭt mărĕ ād bārbărōs; inter

haec duo genera funerum aut iugulāmŭr aūt mērgĭmŭr' (20.1)

Along with rhythm, Gildas abandoned the conventions of Latin word order. Continental writers could indulge in hyperbaton, particularly to facilitate rhythm: observe Cassiodorus' separation of *velocia* from *navigia* in the passage cited above. But their ingrained sense of the run of a Latin sentence excluded complex patterns of

8

words. Quintilian (9.4.28) laughed at Maecenas for writing 'inter sacra movit aqua fraxinos' instead of 'aqua sacra inter fraxinos (se) movit'. That sort of thing might do in verse (cf. Isidore *Etym.* 1.37.20). Gildas seems to be the first to think it could be a systematic ornament to prose. His word order, indeed, at times seems almost completely arbitrary.

He is especially ready to experiment with the positioning of adjectives, which he interweaves among the corresponding nouns with a conscious artistry. Hence a passage like 24.1 'cunctam paene exurens insulae superficiem *rubra* occidentalem *trucique* oceanum *lingua* delamberet'. Hence too a series of variations on the shape of the Golden Line. Ever since Catullus (e.g. 64.129 'mollia nudatae tollentem tegmina surae'), Latin poets had cultivated the grouping of two adjectives and two nouns around a central verb. The young Vergil liked the shape (e.g. *Ecl.* 6.17), and Claudian in the fourth century still favoured it (e.g. *de Rapt.Pros.*1.116). When Gildas writes, for instance, 'exceptis diversorum prolixioribus promontoriorum .tractibus' (3.1) or 'stridulo cavum lapsu aerem valide secantem' (34.2), he probably has this pattern in mind. If he did, his experiment is all of a piece with his pillaging of Vergil.

Later echoes of this mannerism raise unanswerable questions as to the influence of Gildas. The Golden Line dictates the shape of the quasi-verse 'lines' of the *Hisperica Famina,* strange product of a later Ireland; and adjectives cluster in prose in the Irish-educated Aldhelm, not to speak of the much later Aethelweard[15]. It may be that Gildas set the fashion: and that, more generally, a good deal of the typical Irish bombast is due to his influence. We cannot be sure; and in any case, later stylists, including Aldhelm, were able, thanks to direct or indirect continental influence, to attain a grasp of sentence structure that Gildas either could not or would not master. In this sense, Gildas stands alone; he has no predecessors and no successors. With much to say, he found a style that was his own.

Worcester College
Oxford

MICHAEL WINTERBOTTOM

Notes

1. First by Bede (*Hist. Eccl.* 1.22).

2. Note especially *Hist. Eccl.* 8.1.7, where the evils of the church - 'feigning in the face, deceit in the heart' and the rest - are made to lead up to the persecution of Diocletian.

3. The title given in the early editions (see Mommsen, pp.10-11) brings out the point: 'de excidio et conquestu Britanniae' ('on the downfall and conquest of Britain') corresponds to one aspect of the author, 'de flebili castigatione in reges, principes et sacerdotes' ('on the mournful invective against kings, princes and priests') to the other. I have preferred to give the snappier and perhaps correct title employed by Giraldus Cambrensis in the twelfth century, 'de excidio Britonum' (see Giraldus' *Descriptio Cambriae* 2.2 = Rolls Series 21.vi.207).

4. Williams is quite wrong to make a sharp break at the start of 108.

5. See Williams, pp. 88-99.

6. The fragments of the letters, written much later in life, are recognisably by the author of the *de Excidio*. The repetition of *non* with the biblical examples in fragment 1, the word play ('by the measure...beyond measure'), the elaborate antitheses and the treatment of the Beatitudes in fragment 3, and the air of vigorous scorn here and elsewhere are distinctive. But this is the Gildas of e.g. *Exc.* 27 rather than the Gildas of *Exc.* 8: the master of antithetical invective rather than the master of conceit and experiment.

7. 'As if a heavenly light, some ray of the sun had burst forth and were lighting up the whole world with the brilliance of its high radiance'.

8. 'He cites Virgil incorrectly several times' (M.L.W.Laistner, *Thought and Letters in Western Europe* A.D. 500-900, p.137). This is unfair. Gildas does not quote Vergil, but adapts him to his own purposes. To the passages remarked by Mommsen (6.2 = *Aen.* 2.120, 17.2 = *Aen.*2.497 and 25.2 = *Aen.*9.24), add 5.2 'presso in altum cordis dolore' (*Aen.*1.209); 7 'ensem...lateri eius accommodaturos' (*Aen.* 2.393); 9.2 'agmine denso' (*Aen.*2.450);13.1 'magna comitante...caterva' (*Aen.*2.40); 16 'lupi...fame rabidi siccis faucibus' etc. (*Aen.*2.355 seq., 9.59 seq.); 17.2 'montanus torrens' and the context (*Aen.*2.305-6). The cluster in the first two books of the *Aeneid* is significant. The narrow scope of Gildas' reading may be judged from the Index of References.

9. e.g. 19.1 'trans *Tithicam* vallem [cf. *Hisperica Famina* A 107 etc.] ... in alto *Titane* incalescenteque *caumate*'.

10. e.g. 19.1 'furciferos magis vultus pilis quam corporum pudenda pudendisque proxima vestibus tegentes'.

11. J. Morris, 'Pelagian Literature', *J.Th.Stud.* 16 (1965), 26-60. Gildas certainly refers at 38.2 to a sentence from one of these tracts as the work of 'one of us'.

12. Preliminary note, vii-viii. The following translation is my own: 'What sort of delay is this? Such calmness, and the swift ships not yet sent! Yet the stars, still high and brilliant in the sky, invite a prompt hauling up of the canvas, and the serene and dependable weather cannot bring disquiet to the prayers of men prepared to hurry. Perhaps, though the south wind presses and the oars lend their aid, the bite of sea-urchins amid the liquid waves has tied down the passage of the vessels? Perhaps the shells of the Indian ocean have attached their lips no less firmly to the ships' keels? - for, it is said, their silent touch can do more to hold back than the disturbed elements to impel'. This is part of an official government reprimand to a high officer whose department was late in delivering a cargo.

13. As shown above. For Cicero's system, see the lucid summary by R.G.M. Nisbet in his edition of the *In Pisonem* (Oxford, 1961), xvii-xx.

14. It may (or may not) be relevant that Gildas speaks of his book as an *epistola* (1.1).

15. For Aethelweard, see *Medium Aevum* 36 (1967), 114. For Gildas' patterning of adjectives and nouns see F. Kerlouégan, *Etudes Celtiques* 13 fasc. 1 (1972), 275-97, and my reply in *The Bulletin of the Board of Celtic Studies* 27.2 (1977). My views on Gildas are expanded, and to some extent modified, in other articles in *Vigiliae Christianae* ('Columbanus and Gildas') and in *Cymmrodorion Transactions* 1974-5, 277-87 ('The preface of Gildas' *de Excidio*'). Some of my textual decisions are defended, and the text of the fragments modified, in 'Notes on the text of Gildas', *Journal of Theological Studies* 27 (1976), 132-40. For Aldhelm, see my forthcoming article in *Anglo-Saxon England*.

11

Note on Text and Translation

New light may well be thrown on the text of Gildas by the current researches of Mr. D.N. Dumville. But meanwhile it has seemed best to offer a text which is basically that established by Theodor Mommsen (MGH AA xiii = Chronica minora iii, pp.25-88). A list of variants from Mommsen's text is given below. His page numbers are printed in the margin of the text. The numbering of chapters is traditional, but I have added a division into sub-sections that will, I hope, prove useful.

The eleventh-century Cotton manuscript Vitellius A vi was treated by Mommsen as primary: but it was badly damaged in the disastrous fire that ravaged the Cotton collection in the eighteenth century, and has to be supplemented from two early editions (Polydore Virgil 1525, Josselin 1568), whose compilers made use of the undamaged book.

I offer (with proper misgivings) my own translation of Gildas' numerous Biblical extracts, partly because I feel that the stark Latin of his Bible rang differently in the ears of his countrymen from the stately splendour of the Authorised Version, partly because Gildas used, over large stretches of the Bible, versions older than Jerome's Vulgate and nearer to the Greek: thus removing himself one stage further from the texts translated by King James' committee or any later rivals. For details of Gildas' Bible, see F.C. Burkitt, *Revue Bénédictine* 46(1934), 206-15.

Basic account and bibliography in M. Manitius, *Gesch.der lat.Lit. des Mittelalters* i.208-10; less reliable but more recent, W.F. Bolton, *A History of Anglo-Latin literature* (Princeton U.P., 1967) i.27-37, 244-8. For Gildas' style and vocabulary see F. Kerlouégan in *Christianity in Britain, 300-700*, ed. M.W. Barley and R.P.C. Hanson (Leicester U.P., 1968), 151-76.

Previous translation by Hugh Williams, *Cymmrodorion Record Series 3* (two parts only, 1899, 1901). This includes, besides the *De Excidio* and the fragments, the 'Penitential of Gildas', the hymn called the *Lorica*, two lives of Gildas, and a helpful list of references to Gildas in later literature.

The translation owes a great deal to the taste as well as the expert knowledge of John Morris. I am indebted to Barbara Mitchell, James Campbell and Andrew Louth for their generosity with books and advice. My especial thanks are due to Professor Ludwig Bieler and the Governing Board of the School of Celtic Studies, Dublin Institute for Advanced Studies, for permission to reprint here the text and translation of the so-called Penitential of Gildas from the collection of Irish Penitentials in *Scriptores Latini Hibernae* 5.60-65.

M.W.

THE RUIN OF BRITAIN

PREFACE

1   In this letter I shall deplore rather than denounce; my style may be worthless, but my intentions are kindly. What I have to deplore with mournful complaint is a general loss of good, a heaping up of bad. But no one should think that anything I say is said out of scorn for humanity or from a conviction that I am superior to all men. No, I sympathise with my country's difficulties and troubles, and rejoice in remedies to relieve them.

2   I had decided to speak of the dangers run not by brave soldiers in the stress of war but by the lazy. And it was, I confess, with unmeasured grief at heart that I kept silent (the Lord, scanner of consciences, is my witness) as the space of ten years or more passed by. Then, as now, my inexperience and my worthlessness restrained me from writing any warning, however modest.

3   But I could not help reading how a revered law-giver was prevented by a single word's doubt from entering the land he longed for; how the sons of a priest died a swift death because they brought strange fire to the altar; how a people that transgressed the word of God, six hundred thousand of them, all but two truthful men, fell scattered about the Arabian deserts, a prey to beasts, the sword and fire (though they had been very dear to God: their smooth-spread way was the gravel in the depths of the Red Sea, their food bread from heaven, their drink a new traveller from within the rock, their unconquered battle-line the

4 mere raising of hands). I read how, after they entered, as it were, the unknown gate of Jordan, and after the walls of the city that faced them were uprooted by the mere clangour of trumpets at God's order, a cloak and a little money stolen from a cursed offering were the undoing of many. I read how the breaking of the treaty with the Gibeonites (though it had been wrung from them by a trick) brought destruction on not a few. I read how, because of the sins of men, the voice of the holy prophets rose in complaint, especially Jeremiah's, as he bewailed the ruin of his city in four alphabetic songs.

5   And I could see that in our time too, just as Jeremiah had lamented,'the city' (that is, the church) 'sat solitary, bereaved;

formerly it had been full of peoples, mistress of races, ruler of provinces: now it had become tributary'. I saw that 'gold' (that is, the lustre of the word of God) 'had been dimmed and the best colour changed'. I saw that 'the sons of Sion' (that is, of the holy mother church), 'once glorious and clad in fine gold, had embraced

6 dung'. And I saw how - in a manner as intolerable to him in his greatness as to me for all my humbleness - things in one way or another came to a pitch of suffering where he so grieved for the nobles, once so prosperous, that he said: 'Her Nazarites were whiter than snow, redder than antique ivory, more beautiful than the sapphire'.

7 I gazed on these things and many others in the Old Testament as though on a mirror reflecting our own life; then I turned to the New Testament also, and read there more clearly what had previously, perhaps, been dark to me: the shadow passed away,

8 and the truth shone forth more boldly. I read, I say, that the Lord said:'I have not come except to the lost sheep of the house of Israel'. And on the other hand: 'But the sons of this kingdom shall be cast forth into outer darkness, and there will. be wailing there, and gnashing of teeth'. And again: 'It is not good to take one's son's bread and throw it to the dogs'. And also: 'Woe

9 on you,scribes and Pharisees, hypocrites!' I heard: 'Many shall come from east and west, and lie with Abraham and Isaac and Jacob in the kingdom of heaven'. And on the other hand: 'And then I shall say to them: Depart from me, workers of iniquity'. I read: 'Blessed are the barren women and the breasts that give no milk'. And against that: 'Those who were ready came in with him to the wedding. Later the other girls arrived too, saying: Lord, Lord, open the door for us. The reply was: I do not know you'.

10 I heard indeed: 'He who believes and is baptised shall be safe, but he who does not believe shall be condemned'. I read in the words of the apostle that a branch of wild olive was grafted on a good olive: but if it had high thoughts and did not fear, it was to be cut off from sharing the root of the fatness of the olive.

11 I knew the Lord was merciful, but I feared his judgement too. I praised his graciousness, but I was afraid of the reward of every man according to his deeds. I saw that in the same fold there are different sheep, and I used to say that it was right that Peter was most blessed because he wholly confessed Christ, Judas most wretched because he loved greed: Stephen glorious because of his martyr's palm, Nicolas unhappy because of the stain of his foul

12 heresy. True, I read: 'They held everything in common'; but

I read too the saying: 'Why are you agreed on trying out the spirit of God?' I saw clearly how men of our day have increasingly put care aside, as though there were nothing to fear.

13   This, and much more besides that I have decided to leave out in the interests of brevity, I frequently pondered, my mind bewildered, my heart remorseful. For (I said to myself) when they strayed from the right track the Lord did not spare a people that was peculiarly his own among all nations, a royal stock, a holy race, to whom he had said: 'Israel is my first-born son', or its priests, prophets and kings, over so many centuries the apostle, minister and members of that primitive church. What then will he do with this great black blot on *our* generation? It has heinous and appalling sins in common with all the wicked ones of the world; but over and above that, it has as though inborn in it a load of ignorance and folly that cannot be erased or avoided.

14   What, you wretch (I say to myself), have you, like some important and eminent teacher, been given the task of standing up against the blows of so violent a torrent, against the rope of congenital sins that has been stretched far and wide for so many years together? Look after what is committed to your trust, and keep silent. Otherwise it is like saying to the foot: Keep watch, and to the hand: Speak. Britain has her governors, she has her watchmen. Why should *you* stutter out your ineptitudes? Yes, she has them, I answer: if not more than she needs, at least not fewer. But they are bowed under the pressure of their great burdens, and have no time to take breath.

15   This was how my thoughts, like joint debtors, kept checkmating each other with opposed objections like this or even more stinging. They wrestled, as I said, for no short time when I read: 'There is a time for speech and a time for silence', as though they were in a narrow corridor of fear. Finally the victory went to the creditor. 'Perhaps', he said, 'you are not bold enough to be numbered among the truth-telling rational creatures of descent second only to the angels, and fear to be branded with the glorious mark of golden liberty. But at least you should not shun the attitude of the intelligent ass, hitherto tongueless, that was inspired with the spirit of God. She refused to carry the crowned magician who proposed to curse the people of God, and in a narrow place between vineyard walls she lamed and crushed his foot: though she received unkind blows for it. He was ungrateful and angry, and struck at her innocent sides quite unjustly; yet she pointed out to him, as with a finger, an angel from heaven, drawn sword in hand, on the path, whom he, in his

blind stupidity, had failed to see'.

16 Therefore, in zeal for the sacred law of the house of the Lord,
spurred on by my own thoughts and the devout prayers of my
brethren, I now pay the debt so long ago incurred: a poor payment,
doubtless, but, as I think, true to the faith and well-intentioned towards every noble soldier of Christ, though burdensome and in-
supportable for foolish rebels. The former will receive it, if I am not
mistaken, with the tears that flow from the charity of God, but the
others with sadness - the sadness that is wrung from the indignation and
faintheartedness attending a pricked conscience.

THE HISTORY OF BRITAIN

2 But before I make good my promise, I shall try, God willing, to
say a little about the situation of Britain; about her obstinacy,
subjection, and rebellion, her second subjection and harsh servitude;
about religion, persecution, the holy martyrs, diverse heresies, tyrants,
two plundering races; about defence and a further devastation,
about a second vengeance and a third devastation; about hunger,
about the letter to Aëtius, about victory, crimes, enemies suddenly
announced, a memorable plague, a council, an enemy much more
savage than the first, the destruction of cities; about those who
survived, and about the final victory of our country that has been
granted to our times by the will of God.

The Land of Britain

3 The island of Britain lies virtually at the end of the world,
towards the west and north-west. Poised in the divine scales that
(we are told) weigh the whole earth, it stretches from the south-
west towards the northern pole. It has a length of eight hundred miles,
a width of two hundred: leaving out of account the various large
headlands that jut out between the curving ocean bays. It is
fortified on all sides by a vast and more or less uncrossable ring of sea,
apart from the straits on the south where one can cross to
Belgic Gaul; but it has the benefit of the estuaries of a number of
streams, and especially two splendid rivers, the Thames and the
Severn, arms of the sea along which luxuries from overseas used to
2 be brought by ship. It is ornamented with twenty eight cities and a
number of castles, and well equipped with fortifications - walls,
castellated towers, gates and houses, whose sturdily built roofs
3 reared menacingly skyward. Like a chosen bride arrayed in a variety

of jewellery, the island is decorated with wide plains and agreeably
set hills, excellent for vigorous agriculture, and mountains especially
suited to varying the pasture for animals. Flowers of different hues
4 underfoot made them a delightful picture. To water it, the island has
clear fountains, whose constant flow drives before it pebbles white
as snow, and brilliant rivers that glide with gentle murmur,
guaranteeing sweet sleep for those who lie on their banks, and lakes
flowing over with a cold rush of living water.

Roman Britain

4 Ever since it was first inhabited, Britain has been ungratefully
rebelling, stiff-necked and haughty, now against God, now against
its own countrymen, sometimes even against kings from abroad and
their subjects. What daring of man can, now or in future, be more
foul and wicked than to deny fear to God, charity to good fellow-
countrymen, honour to those placed in higher authority (for that is
their due, granted, of course, that there is no harm to the faith) : to
break faith with man and God: to cast away fear of heaven and earth,
and to be ruled each man by his own contrivances and lusts?
2 I shall not speak of the ancient errors, common to all races,
that bound the whole of humanity fast before the coming of Christ in
the flesh . I shall not enumerate the devilish monstrosities of my land,
numerous almost as those that plagued Egypt, some of which we can
see today, stark as ever, inside or outside deserted city walls:
3 outlines still ugly, faces still grim. I shall not name the mountains
and hills and rivers, once so pernicious, now useful for human needs,
on which, in those days, a blind people heaped divine honours. I shall
be silent on the long past years when dreadful tyrants reigned, tyrants
who were spoken of in other distant parts: in fact Porphyry, the 'mad
dog' of the east who vents his fury on the church, has this to add to
his crazy and meaningless writings: 'Britain is a province fertile of
4 tyrants'. I shall simply try to bring to light the ills she suffered
in the time of the Roman emperors and inflicted on other men,
even those far away. I shall do this as well as I can, using not so much
literary remains from this country (which, such as they were, are not
now available, having been burnt by enemies or removed by our
countrymen when they went into exile) as foreign tradition: and *that*
has frequent gaps to blur it.
5 The Roman kings, having won the rule of the world and
subjugated all the neighbouring regions and islands towards the
east, were able, thanks to their superior prestige, to impose peace

for the first time on the Parthians, who border on India:
whereupon wars ceased almost everywhere. But the keen edge
of flame, holding its unbending course westward, could not be
restrained or extinguished by the blue torrent of the ocean.

2 Crossing the strait, and meeting no resistance, it brought the
laws of obedience to the island. The people, unwarlike but
untrustworthy, were not subdued, like other races, by the sword,
fire and engines of war, so much as by mere threats and legal
penalties. Their obedience to the edicts of Rome was superficial:
their resentment they kept repressed, deep in their hearts.

6 The conquerors soon went back to Rome - allegedly for want of
land - and had no suspicion of rebellion. A treacherous lioness
butchered the governors who had been left to give fuller voice

2 and strength to the endeavours of Roman rule. On this, the news
was reported to the senate, which hastened to send an army with
all speed to seek revenge on what were pictured as tricky foxes. But
there was no warlike fleet at sea, ready to put up a brave fight
for its country; no orderly square, no right wing or other apparatus
of war drawn up on the beach. The British offered their backs
instead of shields to their pursuers, their necks to the sword. A
cold shudder ran through their bones; like women they stretched
out their hands for the fetters. In fact, it became a mocking
proverb far and wide that the British are cowardly in war and
faithless in peace.

7 So the Romans slaughtered many of the treasonable, keeping a few
as slaves so that the land should not be completely deserted. The
country now being empty of wine and oil, they made for Italy,
leaving some of their own people in charge, as whips for the backs
of the inhabitants and a yoke for their necks. They were to make
the name of Roman servitude cling to the soil, and torment
a cunning people with scourges rather than military force. If
necessary they were to apply the sword, as one says, clear of its
sheath, to their sides: so that the island should be rated not as
Britannia but as Romania, and all its bronze, silver and gold should
be stamped with the image of Caesar.

8 Meanwhile, to an island numb with chill ice and far removed,
as in a remote nook of the world, from the visible sun, Christ
made a present of his rays (that is, his precepts), Christ the true
sun, which shows its dazzling brilliance to the entire earth, not
from the temporal firmament merely, but from the highest citadel
of heaven, that goes beyond all time. This happened first, as
we know, in the last years of the emperor Tiberius, at a time when
Christ's religion was being propagated without hindrance: for,

against the wishes of the senate, the emperor threatened the death penalty for informers against soldiers of God.

9 Christ's precepts were received by the inhabitants without enthusiasm; but they remained, more or less pure, right up till the nine year persecution by the tyrant Diocletian, when churches were razed throughout the world, the holy scriptures, wherever they could be found, were burned in the squares, and the chosen priests of the Lord's flock , together with their harmless sheep, were slaughtered - so that there should, if possible, be no trace

2 of the Christian religion remaining in some provinces. Church history tells what flights then took place, what killings, what varieties of death penalty, what falls of apostates, what crowns for the glorious martyrs: what mad rage afflicted the persecutors, what matching endurance was displayed by the saints. Indeed, the whole church, in close array, competed to turn its back on the shadows of this world and hastened to the pleasant kingdom of heaven, as to its proper abode.

10 God therefore increased his pity for us; for he wishes all men to be saved, and calls sinners no less than those who think themselves just. As a free gift to us, in the time (as I conjecture) of this same persecution, he acted to save Britain being plunged deep in the thick darkness of black night; for he lit for us the brilliant

2 lamps of holy martyrs. Their graves and the places where they suffered would now have the greatest effect in instilling the blaze of divine charity in the minds of beholders, were it not that our citizens, thanks to our sins, have been deprived of many of them by the unhappy partition with the barbarians. I refer to St. Alban of Verulam, Aaron and Julius, citizens of Caerleon, and the others of both sexes who, in different places, displayed the highest spirit in the battle-line of Christ.

11 Alban, for charity's sake, and in imitation even here of Christ, who laid down his life for his sheep, protected a confessor from his persecutors when he was on the point of arrest. Hiding him in his house and then changing clothes with him, he gladly exposed himself to danger and pursuit in the other's habit. Between the time of his holy confession and the taking of his blood, and in the presence of wicked men who displayed the Roman standards to the most horrid effect, the pleasure that God took in him showed itself: by a miracle he was marked out by wonderful signs. Thanks to his fervent prayer, he opened up an unknown route across the channel of the great river Thames - a route resembling the untrodden way made dry for the Israelites,

when the ark of the testament stood for a while on gravel in the midstream of Jordan. Accompanied by a thousand men, he crossed dry-shod, while the river eddies stayed themselves on either side like precipitous mountains. In this way he changed from wolf to lamb his first executioner, when he saw such a wonder, and made him too thirst strongly for the triumphal palm of martyrdom and bravely receive it.

2   As for the others, they were so racked with different torments, so torn with unheard of rending of limbs, that there was no delay in their fixing the trophies of their glorious martyrdom on the splendid gates of Jerusalem. The survivors hid in woods, desert places and secret caves, looking to God, the just ruler of all, for severe judgements, one day, on their tormentors, and for protection for their own lives.

12   Before ten years of this whirlwind had wholly passed, the wicked edicts were beginning to wither away as their authors were killed. Glad-eyed, all the champions of Christ welcomed, as though after a long winter's night, the calm and the serene light

2 of the breeze of heaven. They rebuilt churches that had been razed to the ground; they founded, built and completed chapels to the holy martyrs, displaying them everywhere like victorious banners. They celebrated feast days. With pure heart and mouth they carried out the holy ceremonies. And all her sons exulted, as though warmed in the bosom of the mother church.

3   This pleasant agreement between the head and limbs of Christ endured until the Arian treason, like a savage snake, vomited its foreign poison upon us, and caused the fatal separation of brothers who had lived as one. And as though there were a set route across the ocean there came every kind of wild beast, brandishing in their horrid mouths the death-dealing venom of every heresy, and planting lethal bites in a country that always longed to hear some novelty - and never took firm hold of anything.

13   At length the tyrant thickets increased and were all but bursting into a savage forest. The island was still Roman in name, but not by law and custom. Rather, it cast forth a sprig of its own bitter planting, and sent Maximus to Gaul with a great retinue of hangers-on and even the imperial insignia, which he was never fit to bear: he had no legal claim to the title, but was raised to

2 it like a tyrant by rebellious soldiery. Applying cunning rather than virtue, Maximus turned the neighbouring lands and provinces against Rome, and attached them to his kingdom of wickedness with the nets of his perjury and lying. One of his wings he stretched

to Spain, one to Italy; the throne of his wicked empire he
placed at Trier, where he raged so madly against his masters
that of the two legitimate emperors he drove one from Rome,
the other from his life - which was a very holy one. Soon,
though entrenched in these appalling acts of daring, he had
his evil head cut off at Aquileia - he who had, in a sense, cast
down the crowned heads that ruled the whole world.

Independent Britain

14   After that Britain was despoiled of her whole army, her
military resources, her governors, brutal as they were, and her
sturdy youth, who had followed in the tyrant's footsteps, never
to return home. Quite ignorant of the ways of war, she groaned
aghast for many years, trodden under foot first by two ex-
ceedingly savage overseas nations, the Scots from the north-west
and the Picts from the north.

15   As a result of their dreadful and devastating onslaughts,
Britain sent envoys with a letter to Rome, plaintively requesting
a military force to protect them and vowing whole-hearted and
uninterrupted loyalty to the Roman empire so long as their
2 enemies were kept at a distance. A legion was soon despatched
that had forgotten the troubles of the past. Soundly equipped,
it crossed to our country by ship, came to grips with the dreadful
enemy, laid low a great number of them, drove them all from
the country, and freed from imminent slavery a people that had
3 been subjected to such grievous mangling. The British were told
to construct across the island a wall linking the two seas;
properly manned, this would scare away the enemy and act as
protection for the people. But it was the work of a leaderless
and irrational mob, and made of turf rather than stone: so
it did no good.

16   The legion returned home triumphant and joyful. Meanwhile
the old enemies re-appeared, like greedy wolves, rabid with
extreme hunger, who, dry-mouthed, leap over into the sheepfold
when the shepherd is away. They came relying on their oars
as wings, on the arms of their oarsmen, and on the winds swelling
their sails. They broke through the frontiers, spreading destruction
everywhere. They went trampling over everything that stood in
their path, cutting it down like ripe corn.

17   And so a second time envoys set out with their complaints,

21

their clothes (it is said) torn, their heads covered in dust, to beg
help from the Romans. Like frightened chicks huddling under
the wings of their faithful parents, they prayed that their
wretched country should not be utterly wiped out, that the name
of Rome, which echoed in their ears as a mere word, should not be
2 cheapened by the gnawing of foreign insult. The Romans were as
upset as is humanly possible by the narration of such a tragedy.
They hurried the flight of their horsemen like eagles on the
land and the course of their sailors on the sea, and planted in
their enemies' necks the claws of their sword-points - claws
at first unexpected, finally terrifying; and they caused among them
a slaughter like the fall of leaves at the due time of the year.
They were like a mountain torrent increased by tributaries
tempest-swollen, that, thundering as it goes, wells out beyond its
channel, back furrowed, forehead fierce, waves - as they say -
cloud-high (because of them the pupils of the eyes are darkened,
despite their constant refreshment from the flickering of the eye-
lids, when they encounter the lines of the whirling clefts); it
foams wonderfully, and with a single surge it overcomes the
3 obstacles in its path. This was the way our worthy allies instantly
put to flight across the sea the columns of their rivals - such
as could get away: year after year they had greedily taken heaps
of plunder overseas with none to resist them.
18   The Romans therefore informed our country that they could
not go on being bothered with such troublesome expeditions;
the Roman standards, that great and splendid army, could not be
✗ worn out by land and sea for the sake of wandering thieves who
had no taste for war. Rather, the British should stand alone,
get used to arms, fight bravely, and defend with all their powers
their land, property, wives, children, and, more important, their life
and liberty. Their enemies were no stronger than they, unless
Britain chose to relax in laziness and torpor; they should not
hold out to them for the chaining hands that held no arms, but
hands equipped with shields, swords and lances, ready for the kill.
2 This was the Romans' advice; and, in the belief that this would
be a further boon to the people whom they proposed to abandon,
they built a wall quite different from the first. This one ran
straight from sea to sea, linking towns that happened to have been
sited there out of fear of the enemy. They employed the normal
method of construction, drew on private and public funds, and made
the wretched inhabitants help them in the work. They gave the
frightened people stirring advice, and left them manuals on weapon training.

3 They also placed towers overlooking the sea at intervals on the
south coast, where they kept their ships: for they were afraid
of the wild barbarian beasts attacking on that front too. Then
they said goodbye, meaning never to return.

19 As the Romans went back home, there eagerly emerged from
the coracles that had carried them across the sea-valleys the foul X
hordes of Scots and Picts, like dark throngs of worms who
wriggle out of narrow fisssures in the rock when the sun is
high and the weather grows warm. They were to some extent
different in their customs, but they were in perfect accord in
their greed for bloodshed: and they were readier to cover their
villainous faces with hair than their private parts and neighbouring
regions with clothes. They were more confident than usual now
that they had learnt of the departure of our fellow-debtors and
the denial of any prospect of their return. So they seized the whole
of the extreme north of the island from its inhabitants, right up
2 to the wall. A force was stationed on the high towers to oppose
them, but it was too lazy to fight, and too unwieldy to flee;
the men were foolish and frightened, and they sat about day
and night, rotting away in their folly. Meanwhile there was no
respite from the barbed spears flung by their naked opponents,
which tore our wretched countrymen from the walls and dashed
them to the ground. Premature death was in fact an advantage
to those who were thus snatched away; for their quick end
saved them from the miserable fate that awaited their brothers
and children.
3 I need say no more. Our citizens abandoned the towns and
the high wall. Once again they had to flee; once again they were
scattered, more irretrievably than usual; once again there were
enemy assaults and massacres more cruel. The pitiable citizens
were torn apart by their foe like lambs by the butcher; their
4 life became like that of beasts of the field. For they resorted to
looting each other, there being only a tiny amount of food to
give brief sustenance to the wretched people; and the disasters
from abroad were increased by internal disorders, for as a result
of constant devastations of this kind the whole region came to lack
the staff of any food, apart from such comfort as the art of the
huntsman could procure them.

20 So the miserable remnants sent off a letter again, this
time to the Roman commander Aëtius, in the following terms:
'To Aëtius, thrice consul: the groans of the British'. Further on
came this complaint: 'The barbarians push us back to the sea,

23

the sea pushes us back to the barbarians; between these two kinds of death, we are either drowned or slaughtered'. But they got no help in return.

2   Meanwhile, as the British feebly wandered, a dreadful and notorious famine gripped them, forcing many of them to give in without delay to their bloody plunderers, merely to get a scrap of food to revive them. Not so others: they kept fighting back, basing themselves on the mountains, caves, heaths and

3   thorny thickets. Their enemies had been plundering their land for many years; now for the first time they inflicted a massacre on *them*, trusting not in man but in God - for, as Philo says, 'when human help finishes, we need the help of God'. For a little while their enemies' audacity ceased - but not our people's wickedness. The enemy retreated from the people, but the people did not retreat from their own sins.

21   It was always true of this people' (as it is now) that it was weak in beating off the weapons of the enemy but strong in putting up with civil war and the burden of sin: weak, I repeat, in following the banners of peace and truth but strong for crime and falsehood. So the impudent Irish pirates returned home (though they were shortly to return); and for the first time the Picts in the far end of the island kept quiet from now on, though they

2   occasionally carried out devastating raids of plunder. So in this period of truce the desolate people found their cruel scars healing over. But a new and more virulent famine was quietly sprouting. In the respite from devastation, the island was so flooded with abundance of goods that no previous age had known the like of it. Alongside there grew luxury. It grew with a vigorous growth, so that to that time were fitly applied the words: 'There are actually reports of such fornication as is not known even among the Gentiles'.

3   And it was not only this vice that flourished, but all those that generally befall human nature - and especially the one that is the downfall of every good condition nowadays too, the hatred of truth and its champions and the love of falsehood and its contrivers: the taking up of evil instead of good, the adoration of wickedness instead of kindness, the desire for darkness instead of sun, the welcoming of Satan as an angel of light.

4   Kings were anointed not in God's name, but as being crueller than the rest; before long, they would be killed, with no enquiry into the truth, by those who had anointed them, and others still crueller chosen to replace them. Any king who seemed gentler

and rather more inclined to the truth was regarded as the downfall of Britain: everyone directed their hatred and their weapons at him, with no respect.

5   Things pleasing and displeasing to God weighed the same in the balance - unless indeed things displeasing were regarded with more favour. In fact, the old saying of the prophet denouncing his people could have been aptly applied to our country: 'Lawless sons, you have abandoned God, and provoked to anger the holy one of Israel. Why go on being beaten for adding to your wickedness? Every head is sick, every heart is sorrowful; from the sole of the foot to the crown of the head there is no health

6   in it'. Everything they did went against their salvation, just as though the true doctor of us all granted the world no medicine. And this was true not merely of worldly men; the flock of the Lord and his shepherds, who should have been an example to the whole people, lay about, most of them, in drunken stupor, as though sodden in wine. They were a prey to swelling hatreds, contentious quarrels, the greedy talons of envy, judgement that made no distinction between good and evil: it looked very much as though, then as now, contempt was being poured on the princes, so that they were seduced by their follies and wandered in the trackless desert.

The Coming of the Saxons

22   God, meanwhile, wished to purge his family, and to cleanse it   X
from such an infection of evil by the mere news of trouble. The feathered flight of a not unfamiliar rumour penetrated the pricked ears of the whole people - the imminent approach of the old enemy, bent on total destruction and (as was their wont) on settlement from one end of the country to the other. But they took no profit from the news. Like foolish beasts of burden, they held fast to the bit of reason with (as people say) clenched teeth. They left the path that is narrow yet leads to salvation, and went racing down the wide way that takes one steeply down through various vices to death.

2   'The stubborn servant', says Solomon, 'is not corrected with words'. The fool is flogged, but feels nothing. For a deadly plague swooped brutally on the stupid people, and in a short period laid low so many people, with no sword, that the living could not bury all the dead. But not even this taught them their lesson, so that the word of the prophet Isaiah was fulfilled

here also: 'And God has called to wailing and baldness and
girding with sackcloth: look at the killing of calves and the
slaughter of rams, the eating and drinking, and people saying:
3 Let us eat and drink, for tomorrow we must die'. The time
was indeed drawing near when their wickedness, like that of
the Amorites of old, would be complete. And they convened
a council to decide the best and soundest way to counter the
brutal and repeated invasions and plunderings by the peoples I
have mentioned.

23 Then all the members of the council, together with the
proud tyrant, were struck blind; the guard - or rather the method
of destruction - they devised for our land was that the ferocious
Saxons (name not to be spoken!), hated by man and God,
should be let into the island like wolves into the fold, to beat
2 back the peoples of the north. Nothing more destructive,
nothing more bitter has ever befallen the land. How utter the
blindness of their minds! How desperate and crass the stupidity!
Of their own free will they invited under the same roof a
people whom they feared worse than death even in their absence -
'the silly princes of Zoan', as has been said, 'giving foolish
advice to Pharaoh'.

3 Then a pack of cubs burst forth from the lair of the barbarian
lioness, coming in three *keels*, as they call warships in their
language. The winds were favourable; favourable too the omens and
auguries, which prophesied, according to a sure portent among
them, that they would live for three hundred years in the land
towards which their prows were directed, and that for half the
time, a hundred and fifty years, they would repeatedly lay it waste.

4 On the orders of the ill-fated tyrant, they first of all fixed
their dreadful claws on the east side of the island, ostensibly to
fight for our country, in fact to fight against it. The mother
lioness learnt that her first contingent had prospered, and she sent
a second and larger troop of satellite dogs. It arrived by ship,
and joined up with the false units. Hence the sprig of iniquity,
the root of bitterness, the virulent plant that our merits so well
deserved, sprouted in our soil with savage shoots and tendrils.

5 The barbarians who had been admitted to the island asked to be
given supplies, falsely representing themselves as soldiers ready to
undergo extreme dangers for their excellent hosts. The supplies were
granted, and for a long time 'shut the dog's mouth'. Then they
again complained that their monthly allowance was insufficient,
purposely giving a false colour to individual incidents, and swore

that they would break their agreement and plunder the whole island unless more lavish payment were heaped on them. There was no delay: they put their threats into immediate effect.

24   In just punishment for the crimes that had gone before, a fire heaped up and nurtured by the hand of the impious easterners spread from sea to sea. It devastated town and country round about, and, once it was alight, it did not die down until it had burned almost the whole surface of the island and was

2   licking the western ocean with its fierce red tongue. So it was that in this assault, comparable with that of the Assyrians of old on Judaea, there was fulfilled according to history for us also what the prophet said in his lament: 'They have burned with fire your sanctuary on the ground, they have polluted the dwelling-place of your name'. And again: 'God, the heathen have come into your inheritance; they have desecrated your holy temple'; and the rest.

3   All the major towns were laid low by the repeated battering of enemy rams; laid low, too, all the inhabitants - church leaders, priests and people alike, as the swords glinted all around and the flames crackled. It was a sad sight. In the middle of the squares the foundation-stones of high walls and towers that had been torn from their lofty base, holy altars, fragments of corpses, covered (as it were) with a purple crust of congealed blood, looked as though they had been mixed up in some dreadful wine-press.

4 There was no burial to be had except in the ruins of houses or the bellies of beasts and birds - saving the reverence due to their holy spirits, if indeed many were found at that time to be carried by holy angels to the heights of heaven. For by then the vineyard that had once been good had degenerated into sourness, so that (as the prophet puts it) there was rarely to be seen grape-cluster or corn-ear behind the backs of the vintagers and the reapers.

The Victory at Badon Hill

25   So a number of the wretched survivors were caught in the mountains and butchered wholesale. Others, their spirit broken by hunger, went to surrender to the enemy; they were fated to be slaves for ever, if indeed they were not killed straight away, the highest boon. Others made for lands beyond the sea; beneath the swelling sails they loudly wailed, singing a psalm that took the

place of a shanty: 'You have given us like sheep for eating and scattered us among the heathen'. Others held out, though not without fear, in their own land, trusting their lives with constant foreboding to the high hills, steep, menacing and fortified, to the densest forests, and to the cliffs of the sea coast.

2   After a time, when the cruel plunderers had gone home, God gave strength to the survivors. Wretched people fled to them from all directions, as eagerly as bees to the beehive when a storm threatens, and begged whole-heartedly, 'burdening heaven with unnumbered prayers', that they should not be altogether

3   destroyed. Their leader was Ambrosius Aurelianus, a gentleman who, perhaps alone of the Romans, had survived the shock of this notable storm: certainly his parents, who had worn the purple, were slain in it. His descendants in our day have become greatly inferior to their grandfather's excellence. Under him our people regained their strength, and challenged the victors to battle. The Lord assented, and the battle went their way.

26   From then on victory went now to our countrymen, now to their enemies: so that in this people the Lord could make trial (as he tends to) of his latter-day Israel to see whether it loves him or not. This lasted right up till the year of the siege of Badon Hill, pretty well the last defeat of the villains, and certainly not the least. That was the year of my birth; as I know, one month of the forty-fourth year since then has already passed.

2   But the cities of our land are not populated even now as they once were; right to the present they are deserted, in ruins and unkempt. External wars may have stopped, but not civil ones. For the remembrance of so desperate a blow to the island and of such unlooked for recovery stuck in the minds of those who witnessed both wonders. That was why kings, public and private persons, priests

3   and churchmen, kept to their own stations. But they died; and an age succeeded them that is ignorant of that storm and has experience only of the calm of the present. All the controls of truth and justice have been shaken and overthrown, leaving no trace, not even a memory, among the orders I have mentioned: with the exception of a few, a very few. A great multitude has been lost, as people daily rush headlong to hell; and the rest are counted so small a number that, as they lie in her lap, the holy mother church in a sense does not

4 see them, though they are the only true sons she has left. By their holy prayers they support my weakness from total collapse, like posts and columns of salvation; and no one should suppose that I am carping at their worthy lives, which all men admire and which God loves, if I speak freely, even sorrowfully, of those who are slaves of

the belly, slaves, too, not of Christ, who is God, blessed for ever,
but of the devil: if, forced to it by an accumulation of evil, I employ
lament rather than analysis. Indeed, why should their own countrymen conceal what surrounding nations are aware of and reprove?

THE COMPLAINT : KINGS

27   Britain has kings, but they are tyrants; she has judges, but they
are wicked. They often plunder and terrorize - the innocent; they
defend and protect - the guilty and thieving; they have many wives -
whores and adulteresses; they constantly swear - false oaths; they
make vows - but almost at once tell lies; they wage wars - civil
and unjust; they chase thieves energetically all over the country - but
love and even reward the thieves who sit with them at table; they
distribute alms profusely - but pile up an immense mountain of
crime for all to see; they take their seats as judges - but rarely seek
out the rules of right judgement; they despise the harmless and humble,
but exalt to the stars, so far as they can, their military companions,
bloody, proud and murderous men, adulterers and enemies of God -
if chance, as they say, so allows: men who should have been rooted
out vigorously, name and all; they keep many prisoners in their jails,
who are more often loaded with chafing chains because of intrigue
than because they deserve punishment. They hang around the altars
swearing oaths - then shortly afterwards scorn them as though they
were dirty stones.

The Five Tyrants

28   This unspeakable sin is not unknown to Constantine, tyrant
whelp of the filthy lioness of Dumnonia. This very year he bound
himself by a dreadful oath not to work his wiles on our countrymen
(who trusted first of all in God and the oath, then in their companions
the choirs of holy men and the mother); then, in the bosom of two
mothers he should have respected - the church, and their mother in
the flesh - and in the habit of a holy abbot, he most cruelly tore
at the tender sides and vitals of two royal youths and their two
2 guardians. Their arms were stretched out not to weapons - though
almost no man handled them more bravely than they at this time -
but to God and the altar; and those same arms shall, in the day of
judgement, hang at the gates of Christ's city, the honourable
standards of their suffering and their faith. He tore them, I say, at
the holy altar, using as teeth his wicked sword and spear, so that
the place of divine sacrifice was touched by the purple cloaks (as

it were) of their drying blood.

3   Nor did this deed follow upon any commendable actions. For many years before, overcome by the stench of frequent and successive adulteries, he put away his lawful wife against the ban of Christ and the Teacher of the Gentiles, who say: 'What God has joined, let not man separate' and 'Husbands, love your wives'.

4   For, from the bitter vine of the men of Sodom, he had planted a slip of unbelieving folly in the soil of his heart - soil that bore no fruit to good seed. He watered the slip with public and domestic wickedness, as though with poisoned showers of rain. Growing eagerly to the offence of God, it brought forth the crime of parricide and sacrilege. But it is as one not yet freed from the nets of his former sins that he is adding new evils to old.

29   I know full well you are still alive, and I charge you as though you were present; come, executioner of your own soul, why are you stupified? Why do you of your own free will light for yourself flames of hell that will not die down? Why do you take the place of your enemies, and voluntarily stab yourself with your own swords and spears? Could not even the virulent draughts of your

2   sins satisfy your heart? Look back, I pray you, and come to Christ, for you are in trouble, and bent under an immense burden, and he - as he has said - will make you rest. Come to him who does not want the death of a sinner, but rather his conversion and life. Break, as the prophet says, the chains on your neck, son of Sion; come back, I beg you, though from the far-off haunts of sin, to your loving father, who is used, when his son rejects the filthy food given to pigs and fears death by dread famine, and returns to him, to kill the fatted calf gladly for him, to bring out the best

3   robe for the wanderer, and a royal ring. *Then* you will have a foretaste of the savour of the heavenly hope, and feel how sweet the Lord is. For if you turn your back on this, know that you must soon be whirled and burnt by dark torrents of hell-fire that you can never escape.

30   What are *you* doing, Aurelius Caninus, lion-whelp (as the prophet says)? Are you not being engulfed by the same slime as the man I have just talked of, if not a more deadly one, made up of parricides, fornications, adulteries: a slime like sea-waves rushing fatally upon you? Do you not hate peace in our country as though it were some noxious snake? In your unjust thirst for civil war and constant plunder, are you not shutting the gates of

2   heavenly peace and consolation to your soul? You are left like

a solitary tree, withering in the middle of the field. Remember, I pray you, the empty outward show of your fathers and brothers, their youthful and untimely deaths. Will *you*, for services to religion, live to be a hundred or as old as Methuselah, surviving almost all your offspring? Of course not!

3   But unless, as the psalmist says, you soon turn to the Lord, the king will shortly brandish his sword at you - that king who through his prophet says: 'I shall kill, and I shall make to live; I shall strike, and I shall heal; and there is no one who may deliver from my hand'. Therefore, shake yourself free of your stinking dust, and turn with all your heart to your creator, so that 'when his anger shortly blazes forth you may be blessed, hoping in him': but otherwise eternal punishments await you; the fierce jaws of hell will wear you continually away, without consuming you.

31   Why are *you* senseless and stiff, like a leopard in your behaviour, and spotted with wickedness? Your head is already whitening, as you sit upon a throne that is full of guiles and stained from top to bottom with diverse murders and adulteries, bad son of a good king (like Manasseh son of Hezekiah): Vortipor, tyrant of the Demetae. The end of your life is gradually drawing near; why can you not be satisfied by such violent surges of sin, which you suck down like vintage wine - or rather allow yourself to be engulfed by them? Why, to crown your crimes, do you weigh down your wretched soul with a burden you cannot shrug off, the rape of a shameless daughter after the removal and honourable death of your own wife?

2   Do not, I pray you, use up the remainder of your days to the offence of God, for now is the acceptable time, the day of salvation shines on the faces of the penitent, the day on which you can make sure that your flight is not on the sabbath or in winter-time. Turn aside (to adapt the psalmist) from evil and do good, search out good peace and follow it, for the eyes of the Lord will be on you as you do good things and his ears will go out to your prayers, and he will not destroy your memory from the land of the living. You will shout - and he will hear you and pluck you from all your tribulations. The contrite heart that humbles itself in fear of him is never rejected by Christ. Otherwise, the worm of your torture will not die, and the fire of your burning will not be extinguished.

32   Why have *you* been rolling in the filth of your past wickedness ever since your youth, you bear, rider of many and driver of the chariot of the Bear's Stronghold, despiser of God and oppressor of his lot, Cuneglasus, in Latin 'red butcher'? Why do you wage such a war against men and God? - against men, that is our countrymen, with

2   arms special to yourself, against God with infinite sins. Why, aside from countless other lapses, have you rejected your own wife and now, against the ban of the apostle, who says that adulterers cannot be citizens of the kingdom of heaven, do you cast your eyes, with all the reverence (or rather dullness) of your mind, on her villainous sister, although she has promised to God perpetually chaste widowhood, like, as the poet says, the supreme tenderness of the dwellers in heaven? Why do you provoke with continual injuries the groans and sighs of the holy men who are present in the flesh by your side; they are the teeth of an appalling lioness that will one day break your bones.

3   Cease, I pray you (in the words of the prophet) from anger, and abandon the rage that brings destruction and that will some day waste you also, the rage that you breathe against heaven and earth, that is, against God and his flock. Change your ways, and make them rather pray for you - those who have the power of binding above the world when they have bound the guilty in the world, and of

4   loosing when they have loosed the penitent. Do not, as the apostle says, be haughty; do not trust in the uncertainty of riches, but in God, who gives you much in abundance, so that by reforming your character you may lay up a good foundation for the future

5   and have a true life - eternal, not mortal. Otherwise you will see and know even in this life, how bad and bitter it is that you have left the Lord your God and that you have no fear of him, and that, without ever dying, you will eventually burn in the filthy mass of the eternal fires. For the souls of the wicked have as long an eternity in perpetual fire as the souls of the saints in joy.

33   What of you, dragon of the island, you who have removed many of these tyrants from their country and even their life? You are last in my list, but first in evil, mightier than many both in power and malice, more profuse in giving, more extravagant in sin, strong in arms but stronger still in what destroys a soul, Maglocunus. Why wallow like a fool in the ancient ink of your crimes, like a man drunk on wine pressed from the vine of the Sodomites?

2   Why choose to attach to your royal neck such inescapable masses of sin, like high mountains? The King of all kings has made you higher than almost all the generals of Britain, in your kingdom as in your physique: why do you not show yourself to him better

3   than the others in character, instead of worse? Listen quietly for a while to the assertion of these undisputed complaints; putting on one side slight domestic matters, if indeed any of them are slight, they will bear witness only to those of your crimes that

have been published on the wind far and wide.

4　Did you not, in the first years of your youth, use sword and spear and flame in the cruel despatch of the king your uncle and nearly his bravest soldiers, whose faces in battle were not very different from those of lions' whelps? Little did you heed the words of the prophet: 'Men of blood and craft will not live out

5　half their days'. What retribution would you expect for this alone from the just judge, even if it had not been followed by the sort of thing that did follow: for again he said through his prophet: 'Woe to you who plunder - will you not yourself be plundered? and to you who kill - will you not be killed? And when you have ceased to plunder, then will you fall'.

34　After your dream of rule by force had gone according to plan, were you not seized by the desire to return to the right road? Perhaps remorseful in the knowledge of your sins, you first pondered a great deal at that time, day and night, on the godly life and the Rule of the monks; then, publishing it to the knowledge of the public breeze, you vowed to be a monk for ever, with (as you said) no thought of going back on your promise, before

2　almighty God and in the sight of men and angels. You seemed to have broken through the vast nets that normally entangle fat bulls of your kind in an instant. You broke through the chains of all royal power, gold, silver, and, what is more than these, your own will. Where you had been a raven, you became a dove: as though you were stoutly cleaving the hollow air with your whirring glide and avoiding with sinuous twists the savage talons of the swift hawk, you came swiftly and in safety to the caves and consolations of the saints that you can trust so well.

3　What would be the joy of the church our mother if the enemy of all mankind had not somehow stolen you, to her grief, from her very bosom! If you had stayed on the good path, how generous a tinder of hope in heaven would blaze up in the hearts of men despaired of! How great and how glorious would be the prizes that awaited your soul from the kingdom of Christ on the day of judgement had not that cunning wolf snatched you (not much against your will) from the Lord's fold - a lamb now where you had been a wolf; but

4　he was to make you a wolf like himself instead of a lamb. What exultation would your salvation cause in the heart of God, the Holy Father of all the saints, had not the evil spirit, ill-omened father of all the damned, whisked you, with no respect for what is right and just, into the unhappy company of his sons, pouncing on you like an eagle vast in wing and talon!

5   In fact, your conversion to good fruit brought as much joy and
sweetness in heaven and earth then as your wicked return (like some
sick hound) to your disgusting vomit has brought grief and weeping
now. And after that return your limbs are presented to sin and the
devil as instruments of wickedness when they should properly

6   have been presented eagerly to God as instruments of justice. Your
excited ears hear not the praises of God from the sweet voices of
the tuneful recruits of Christ, not the melodious music of the church,
but empty praises of yourself from the mouths of criminals who
grate on the hearing like raving hucksters - mouths stuffed with lies
and liable to bedew bystanders with their foaming phlegm. Hence
a vessel that was once being prepared for the service of God is turned
into an instrument of the devil, and what was once thought worthy
of heavenly honours is rightly cast into the pit of Hell.

35   Your mind is dulled by a heap of folly: yet it finds such stumbling-
blocks of evil no obstacle. Like a lively foal to whom everything
unknown seems attractive, it is whirled by an uncontrollable fury

2   over wide plains of crime, piling new sins on old. Your presumptive
first marriage, after your vow to be a monk had come to nothing,
was illegal - but at least it was to your own wife. You spurned it,
and sought another, not with some widow, but with the beloved
wife of a living man, no stranger either, but your brother's son. So
that hard neck of yours, already laden with many burdens of sin,
is bent from the lowest depths to still lower; for to crown your
sacrilege, you ventured on two murders, the killing of this man and

3   of your wife, after you had enjoyed her for some little time. Next you
married the woman with whose collusion and encouragement you
lately entered on such masses of sin. The wedding was public, and
as the lying tongues of your parasites cry (but from their lips only,
not from the depths of their hearts), legitimate: for she was a widow.
But I call it most scandalous.

4   Any saint whose bowels were wrung by such a story would
burst at once into tears and sobs. Any priest whose rightness of
heart lies open to God would wail aloud on hearing these things, and
say, with the prophet: 'Who will give water for my head, a fountain
of tears for my eyes? Night and day will I lament the slain among

5   my people'. Alas, how little have you heeded the rebuke of the
prophet: 'Woe to you, impious men, who have abandoned the
law of the highest God. If you are to be born, you will be born to
cursing, and if you have yet to die, your lot will be a curse. All
things which are of earth shall go to earth: so the impious shall
go from cursing to damnation'. The implication is: if they do not

6 return to God, at least on hearing this warning: 'Son, you have
sinned. Do not add to your sins, but beg forgiveness for your former
ones'. And again: 'Do not be slow to turn to the Lord, and do not
put it off from day to day. For sudden is the coming of his wrath',
because, as the scripture says, if a ruler listens to unjust words, all
his subjects are wicked'. Indeed, as the prophet said, 'the just king
establishes the land'.

36   Yet surely you have no lack of warnings: for you have had as
your teacher the refined master of almost all Britain. Therefore beware
lest what is noted by Solomon befall you: 'Like one who wakes a
sleeper from deep slumber is he who tells a fool wisdom. For at
the end of the story, he will say: What was it you said first?'
'Wash your heart clean of wickedness, Jerusalem', as it is said, 'and
2 be saved'. Do not reject, I beseech you, the unspeakable mercy of
God, who by his prophet thus calls the wicked to leave their sins:
'I shall speak suddenly to the people and to the kingdom, to uproot
and scatter and destroy and ruin'. This is how he vehemently
encourages the sinner to repent: 'And if that people repents its
sin, *I* shall repent of doing the evil thing I said I should do to them'.
And again: 'Who will give them the heart to hear me and keep my
3 commands, and prosper all the days of their life?' And again, in
the Song of Deuteronomy: 'A people without plan or prudence:
would that they would be wise and understand and have regard for
what comes last of all! How can one man pursue a thousand, and
two put ten thousand to flight?' And again the Lord in the
gospels: 'Come to me, all of you who are burdened and in trouble,
and I will make you rest. Lay my yoke on you, and learn from me,
for I am gentle and humble of heart, and you will find rest for
your souls'.

4   You may hear this with deaf ears, spurning the prophets,
despising Christ, regarding me, worthless as I am, as of no
importance; though it is with sincere piety of mind that I obey
the pronouncement of the prophet: 'I shall surely fill my courage
with the spirit and virtue of the Lord, to announce to the house of
Jacob its sins, and its crimes to the house of Israel', to avoid being
one of the 'dogs that are dumb and cannot bark': and the words of
Solomon: 'He who says the wicked man is just will be cursed by
peoples and hated by nations; but those who condemn shall have
5 hope of better', and again: 'Do not be respectful of your neighbour if
it should cause his fall, and do not keep back a word when it would
do good', and also: 'Save those who are being led to die, and do not

35

hesitate to ransom those who are being killed': because, as the same prophet says, 'riches will be of no avail on the day of wrath: it is justice that frees from death'; 'if the just can scarce be saved,

6   where will the wicked and the sinner appear?' But if so you will surely be caught up in the dreadful eddying and the fiercest surges of the dark torrent of Hell. It will always torment you, yet never consume you. Useless and too late then will be the clear sight of your punishment and your repentance from sin; for at this favoured time and on the day of salvation you are delaying your conversion to the true path of life.

The Words of the Prophets

37   Here, or even earlier, I should have finished this tearful history, this complaint on the evils of the age, so that my lips should not any longer have to speak of the actions of men. But in case people should think me afraid or tired of constantly heeding the warning of Isaiah: 'Woe to those who say good is bad and bad good, putting darkness for light and light for darkness, bitter for sweet and sweet for bitter', who 'seeing do not see and hearing do not hear', whose

2   heart is veiled in a thick cloud of vices, I want to give a summary of the threats uttered by the oracles of the prophets against these five mad and debauched horses from the retinue of Pharaoh which actively lure his army to its ruin in the Red Sea, and against those like them. These oracles will form a reliable and beautiful covering for the endeavour of my little work, to protect it from the rain-showers of the hostile that will compete to beat upon it.

3   Now, as before, therefore, let the holy prophets reply in my stead. So it was in the past. Favouring the good and forbidding men the bad, they were in a sense the mouth of God and the instrument of the holy spirit. Let them reply to the proud and stubborn princes of this age, in case they say that it is by my own fabrication and merely from a rash loquacity that I hurl such warnings and such

4   terrors at them. In fact, no wise man is in doubt how much more serious are the sins of today than those of the early days. As the apostle says, 'anyone breaking the law dies, on the evidence of two or three witnesses present: how much greater, do you think, is the punishment deserved by one who has trampled on the son of God?'

38   We are met first by Samuel, who, at the orders of God, established a lawful kingship, and was dedicated to God before his birth; from Dan to Beersheba he was a truthful prophet to all the people of Israel, and one known by tokens that were truly wonderful.

From his mouth the holy spirit spoke in thunder to all the powers of the world, denouncing Saul, first king of the Hebrews, for infringements in obeying the orders of the Lord. He said: 'You have been foolish. You have not kept the commands given you by the Lord your God. If you had not done this, God would even now be establishing your rule over Israel for ever. As it is, your kingdom

2 shall rise no higher'. But what had Saul done that resembled the crimes of the present time? Did he commit adultery or parricide? By no means. He merely changed a command, in part. As one of us well says, it is not a question of the nature of the offence, but of the breaking of an order.

3 Saul (as he supposed) cleared himself of the charges, and cleverly strung together excuses, as men do, along these lines: 'But I listened to the voice of the Lord and walked along the way he sent me'. But Samuel reproved him again. 'Does the Lord want burnt offerings and victims', he said, 'and not rather obedience to the voice of the Lord? Obedience is better than victims. To listen is better than to offer the fat of rams, for rebellion is like the sin of witchcraft and recalcitrance like idolatry. Because you rejected the word of the Lord, he has rejected you, so that you should not be

4 king'. And a little later: 'God has torn the kingdom of Israel from you today, and given it to a neighbour of yours, who is better than you. The victor over Israel will not hold back, he will not be turned by remorse, for he is not a man, that he should repent' - that is, as to the hard hearts of the wicked.

5 We should note, then, that he said it is the sin of idolatry to be recalcitrant towards God. These wicked men, therefore, should not be proud of themselves for abstaining from conspicuous sacrifice to the gods of the heathen: for they are idolators when, like pigs, they trample underfoot the most costly pearls of Christ.

39 This one example, like an irrefutable witness, would be quite sufficient to correct the wicked. But that all the evil of Britain may be proved from the mouth of many witnesses, let us pass to the rest.

2 What happened to David when he numbered his people? The prophet Gad said to him: 'The Lord says this: You have a choice between three things. Choose which you want me to do to you. Either famine will come upon you for seven years, or you will flee from your enemies for three months and they will pursue you, or there will be pestilence in your land for three days'.

3 Under the constraint of these choices, and wishing to fall into the hands of a merciful God rather than of men, David was laid low by the death of seventy thousand of his people; and, if he had not, thanks to his apostolic charity, prayed to die for his countrymen,

so that the plague should not touch them, saying: 'It is I who sinned, I was the shepherd and I did wrong. What was the sin of the sheep? I beseech you, let your hand be turned against me and against my father's house', he would have paid for his presumptuous self-confidence with his own death.

4   Indeed, what is it that the scriptures tell afterwards of his son? 'Solomon acted in a way that displeased the Lord, and did not succeed in following the Lord, as his father did'. 'The Lord said to him: Because you were like this and did not keep my ordinance and the orders I gave you, I shall rend and tear your kingdom and give it to your slave'.

40   Hear what happened to two kings of Israel as sacrilegious as the kings of today, Jeroboam and Baasha. They received the judgement of the Lord through these words of the prophet: 'Because I exalted you and made you prince over Israel, and because they have annoyed me by their follies, I hereby uproot the posterity of Baasha and his house, and I shall make his house like the house of Jeroboam, son of Nebat. His descendants who die in the city shall be eaten by dogs, and their dead bodies shall be eaten on the plains by the birds of the sky'.

2   Hear too the threat uttered by the sacred lips of Elijah, lips briefed by the voice of the Lord issuing from the fire. This was his warning to that wicked king of Israel - companion-in-arms to these kings of ours - by whose collusion in a plot of his wife's the innocent Naboth was eliminated for the sake of his ancestral vineyard: 'Further, you have killed and taken possession. And you shall say to him also: The Lord says: In the place where the dogs licked up the blood of Naboth, they shall lick up yours too'. And well we know that it turned out just like that.

3   But, in case you are deceived (as was that same Ahab) by 'a lying spirit speaking false things through the mouth of your prophets', please listen to the words of the prophet Micaiah: 'Behold, God allowed a spirit of deception to speak through the mouths of all your prophets here present, and the Lord spoke evil against you'.

4   For today also it is certain that there are some teachers filled with a spirit of perversity, affirming evil pleasures in preference to the truth. 'Their words are softer than oil - yet they are sharp weapons'. These men say: Peace, peace, but there will be no peace for those who remain in sin. As the prophet says in another place:'There is no joy for the wicked, says the Lord'.

41   Further, Azariah, son of Oded, said to Asa on his return from killing a thousand thousand of the Ethiopian army: 'The Lord is with you so long as you are with him, and if you look for him you will find him. But if you desert him, he will desert you'.

2   When Jehoshaphat brought help to a wicked king, he was reprimanded by the prophet Jehu, son of Hanani: 'If you help a sinner or love one whom the Lord hates, then the wrath of God is upon you'. What, then, will become of those who are pinioned by the cords of their *own* sins? If we wish to fight on the side of the Lord, we must hate the sins of such men, though not their souls. As the psalmist says: 'You who love the Lord must hate evil'.

3   What was it that the prophet Elijah, chariot and charioteer of Israel, said to the same Jehoshaphat's son, the murderer Jehoram, who killed his distinguished brothers so that he, a bastard, could reign in their stead? 'These are the words of the Lord God of your father David: Because you have not walked in the way of your father Jehoshaphat and in the ways of Asa, king of Judah, but have walked in the ways of the kings of Israel, and behaved lustfully like the house of Ahab, and killed your brothers, the sons of Jehoshaphat, who were better than you, behold, the Lord will strike you and your

4   sons with a great plague': and a little further on: 'Your stomach will be sick in a great illness, and finally it will drop out as your illness continues, day by day'.

5   Take heed, too, of the warnings given to Joash, king of Israel, when he abandoned the Lord as you are doing; the son of the prophet Jehoiada, Zachariah, stood up and said to the people: 'These are the words of the Lord: Why do you neglect the commands of the Lord and fall into misfortune? You have abandoned the Lord, and he will abandon you'.

42   What of Isaiah, chief of the prophets? This is how he began the proem of his prophecy - or rather his vision: 'Hear, heavens, and earth, give ear. The Lord has spoken. I have nourished my sons and seen them grow up: but they have scorned me. An ox recognises his owner, an ass his master's stall. But Israel does not recognise me,

2   and my people has not understood'. After a little while, in the course of threats that such folly so well justified, he says: 'The daughter of Sion shall be left abandoned like a shed in a vineyard or a hut in a cucumber-patch, like a city that is being plundered'. Addressing the princes in particular, he says: 'Hear the word of the Lord, you princes of Sodom. Hear the law of the Lord, people of Gomorrah'.

3   It should be observed that these wicked kings are called 'princes of Sodom'. The Lord forbids such men to offer him sacrifices and gifts (though we in our greed receive things that are an abomination to God, and, to our own undoing, refuse to have them distributed

to the needy and indigent), saying to those who are burdened with
widespread riches and intent on squalid sins: 'Bring me no more
vain sacrifices; incense is hateful to me'.

4   And so his denunciation goes on: 'And when you hold out your
hands, I shall turn away my eyes from you; and when you re-double
your prayers, I shall pay no heed'. He shows why he does this: 'Your
hands are full of blood'. But at the same time he shows how he
might be placated: 'Wash, get yourselves clean. Remove the evil of
your thoughts from my sight. Cease your wicked deeds, learn to
do good. Seek judgement, succour the oppressed, give judgement

5 to the fatherless'. He appends (as it were) the change to satisfaction:
'If your sins are like scarlet dye, they shall become white as snow.
If they are red like vermillion, they shall be white as wool. If you
are willing and hear me, you shall eat the good things of the earth.
But if you are unwilling and provoke me to anger, the sword will
devour you'.

43   Here is a truthful witness, speaking for all to hear, testifying
with no colour of flattery to the rewards that will attend your
goodness and your sin. No room here for the poisons that your
respectful parasites hiss into your ear.

2   He turns his attention also to greedy judges: 'Your princes are
disloyal, they are thieves' accomplices. They all love bribes, pursue
profit. They let the orphan's case go unheard, and the widow
cannot plead before them. That is why the Lord of hosts, the
strong one of Israel, says: I will find comfort as to my enemies, and
be revenged on my foes'. 'The wicked and the sinners shall be
crushed in the same moment, and all those who have deserted the

3 Lord shall be consumed'. And below: 'The eyes of the lofty man
shall be cast down, and the haughtiness of men shall be bowed'.
And again: 'Woe to the wicked - for the reward of what his hands
have done will come upon him'. And a little later: 'Woe to those
of you who get up in the morning to go in search of drunkenness, to
drink through till evening, so that you sweat with wine. At
your parties are lute and lyre, drum and flute and wine. You
have no regard for the work of the Lord, and you neglect the works
of his hands. That is why my people has been led captive: they
had no knowledge; their nobles have perished of hunger, and
their multitude has dried up with thirst. Hell·has enlarged her soul,
opened her mouth without end: and into it shall go down their

4 strong men, their people, their lofty men and their famous'. And
below: 'Woe to you who are powerful at wine-bibbing, strong at
mixing drunkenness: who give judgement for the wicked in return

for bribes, and deprive the just man of his justice. Therefore, as
the tongue of fire devours the stubble and the heat of the flame
burns it up, so shall their root be turned to cinders, and their
shoot rise up like dust. For they have rejected the law of the Lord
of hosts, and made mock of the words of the holy one of Israel.
For all that, the Lord's anger is not turned away, but his hand is
stretched out still'.

44   After a while, he discusses the day of judgement and the unspeakable
fear of sinners: 'Howl! The day of the Lord is near' (and if it
was near then, what we are we to suppose today?) 'for destruction
is on its way from the Lord. Because of this every hand shall
lose its grip, every man's heart shall melt and be crushed; tortures
and torments shall take hold, and they shall have pain like a woman
in labour. Each man shall be astonished as he looks at his neighbour,
their faces aflame. Behold, the day of the Lord shall come, cruel
and full of wrath and anger and indignation, to make a wilderness
of the land, to wipe its sinners off its face; the brilliant stars in the
sky shall cease to spread their light, and the sun shall be shadowed
at its rising, and the moon shall not be bright at its due time. I
shall punish the evils of the world, visit their wickedness on the
wicked; I shall silence the pride of the rebellious, and lay low the
2   arrogance of the strong'. And again: 'Behold, the Lord will scatter
the land, and lay it bare, scar its face, disperse its inhabitants.
People and priest, master and slave, mistress and maid, buyer and
seller, borrower and lender, creditor and debtor, shall be on the
same footing. The land will be scattered and laid waste by plunder.
For the Lord has spoken this. The land has grieved and ebbed
away, the world has ebbed away; the haughtiness of the people
of the land has been weakened, and the land defiled by its inhabitants: because they have broken the laws, changed the right,
broken the eternal compact. Because of this a curse shall devour
45   the earth'. And below: 'All who rejoice at heart shall wail. The joy
of the drums shall cease, the sound of the glad grow still, the
sweetness of the lute fall silent. They will drink no wine with a
song, and drink shall be bitter in the mouths of the drinkers. The
city of Folly is broken down; every house is shut, and none
enters. There will be cries for wine in the squares; all pleasure
is abandoned, the joy is passed from the land, and desolation is
left in the city. Disaster shall overwhelm its gates, for these things
shall be amid the land and its peoples'.
2   A little later: 'The sinners have sinned and they have sinned with
the sin of transgressors. Upon you, the inhabitant of the earth,

is fear, the pit, the noose. So shall it be: the man who flees from
the voice of fear shall fall into the pit; and the man who ex-
tricates himself from the pit shall be held fast by the noose: for
the floodgates from on high shall be open, and the foundations
of the earth shall be shaken. There will be a breaking to break
the earth, and quakes to move it: it will reel like a drunkard, and
disappear like a tent pitched for a single night. Its wickedness
will weigh heavy on it; it will fall, never to rise again. So shall it
be: on that day the Lord will punish the soldiery of heaven on
high and the kings of the earth on the earth; they will be crowded
in one bundle into a vault, and imprisoned there, and be visited only
after many days. The moon will grow red, the sun will be confounded,
when the Lord of hosts reigns on Mount Sion and in Jerusalem, and
is glorified in the sight of his elders'.

46   After a while, giving the reason for such threats, Isaiah says:
'Behold, the hand of the Lord is not too short to save, nor his ears
too heavy to hear. But your sins have made a division between you
and your God, and your wrongdoings have hidden his face from you,
so that he does not hear you. For your hands are stained with blood,
your fingers with iniquity; your lips have spoken lies, your tongue
speaks wickedness. There is no one to summon justice or to judge
according to the truth; they trust in nothing and speak empty words;
2   they have conceived pain and brought forth wickedness'. And
below: 'Their works are without use, and their hands are turned to
deeds of mischief. Their feet run on evil errands and hurry to shed
innocent blood. Their thoughts are profitless thoughts; on their ways
are destruction and ruin, they do not know the way of peace, and
there is no judgement in their goings. They have made their paths
crooked, and all who walk on them have no knowledge of peace.
Therefore has judgement been removed from you, and justice does
not take hold of you'.

3   And a little way on: 'And judgement has been turned back in its
tracks, and justice stands far away: for truth has fallen in the street,
and fairness could find no entry. Truth has been forgotten, and
the man who avoids evil has laid himself open to plunder. And the
Lord saw, and he was displeased that there is no judgement'.

47   Let this short extract from the many words of the prophet
Isaiah suffice. But now pay heed for a little to the words of one
who was known before his conception and made a holy prophet
to all nations before his birth: I mean Jeremiah. Listen to his
2   pronouncements on a foolish people and stiff-necked kings. He
starts off in a gentle tone: 'The Lord said to me: Go and shout in
the ears of Jerusalem': 'Hear the word of the Lord, you house of

Jacob and you relations of the house of Israel. The Lord says:
What wickedness did your fathers find in me, that they left me
and walked in search of folly and became foolish and would not
say: Where is he who made us come up out of the land of Egypt?'
3   And a little way on: 'Of old you broke my yoke, burst my bonds
and said: I shall not be a slave. I planted you as my chosen vine,
a true seed through and through. How then have you gone to the
bad, and become another's vine? You may wash yourself with
nitre and lay in great store of soap, but you are stained with wicked⸱
4   ness in my eyes, says the Lord'. And below: 'Why do you want to
dispute with me? You have all abandoned me, says the Lord. It was
in vain that I struck your sons: they would not learn their lesson.
Hear the word of the Lord: Have I been a desert to Israel or a land
of evening? Why then has my people said: We have gone, we
shall not come to you again? Does the girl forget her jewellery,
or the bride her wedding girdle? Yet my people has forgotten me
for many days'. 'For my people is foolish, it does not know me.
They are foolish sons, and crazy. They are wise - to do evil; they do
not know how to do good'.

48   Then the prophet says, in his own person: 'Lord, your eyes
have regard for honesty. You have struck them, but they felt no
pain; you crushed them, and they refused to learn their lesson;
they made their faces harder than stone, and would not come back'.
2   Again, the Lord says: 'Announce this to the house of Jacob, and
make yourself heard in Judah, saying: Listen, foolish people, you
who have no sense, who have eyes but do not see, ears but do not
hear. Will you then not fear me, says the Lord, and will you not feel
pain at my face? I placed the sand as a boundary to the sea; by my
eternal ordinance it shall go no further. The waves may toss, but
they shall be powerless; they may swell, but they shall not pass. But
this people has become faithless and rebellious. They have departed
and gone, and have not said to themselves: Let us fear the Lord our
3   God'. And again: 'For there are found among my people wicked men,
laying traps like fowlers, placing nets and snares to take men. As a
cage is full of birds, so are their houses full of guile. So they have grown
great and rich, fat and gross; they have most grievously neglected
my words; they have not pleaded the orphan's case, or judged the
cause of the poor. Am I not to punish them?, says the Lord. Shall
my soul not have its vengeance on such a nation?'

49   Let us hope you escape what follows: 'You will speak all
these words to them, and they will not hear you. You will call
them and they will not reply. You will say to them: This is the race
which did not listen to the Lord's voice or learn his lesson. Faith is
dead and removed from their mouths'. And a little way on: 'Shall

the fallen not rise again, the estranged not return? Why has this
people in Jerusalem turned away in quarrelsome estrangement?
They have taken hold of falsehood, and refused to return. I have
paid heed and listened: no one speaks what is good. No one is
penitent for his sins or says: What have I done? They all keep
turned the way they are going, like a horse going into battle at a
gallop. The kite in the sky knows when its time comes; the dove,
the swallow, the stork keep to the time for their arrival. Yet
my people does not recognise the judgement of God'.

2   The prophet is frightened out of his wits by this blind onrush of
sacrilege, this unspeakable drunkenness; he weeps for those who would
not weep for themselves (like the wretched tyrants of today), and
asks the Lord to give him fresh store of tears: 'I am hurt because
the daughter of my people is hurt. I am gripped by amazement.
Is there no balm in Gilead, no doctor there? Why then has the scar
of the daughter of my people not healed over? Who will give water
for my head, a fountain of tears for my eyes? Night and day will I
lament the slain among my people. Who will give me a travellers'
resthouse in the desert? I will leave my people and go from them: for
they are all adulterers, gatherings of sinners. They have stretched
their tongues like bows, in the service of lies, not truth. They have
grown strong in the land, for they have gone from evil to evil, and

3   they do not know me, says the Lord'. And again: 'And the Lord said:
Because they have broken the law I gave them, and refused to listen
to my voice and walk in its paths, and gone away at the dictates of
their evil minds, this is the word of the God of Israel, Lord of hosts:
Behold, I will feed this people on wormwood, and give them gall for

4   their drink'. And after a little (something that the prophet frequently
added to his writings) he says in the person of God: 'Do not, then,
pray for this people, and raise no praise or prayer for them: for I
shall not listen when they cry to me in their affliction'.

50   What will our ill-starred commanders do now, then? The few
who have found the narrow path and left the broad behind are
prevented by God from pouring forth prayers on your behalf as
you persevere in evil and so grievously provoke him. On the other
hand, if you had gone back to God genuinely (for God does not
want the soul of a man to perish, and pulls a man back when he
is cast out in case he is utterly destroyed), they could not have brought
punishment upon you: after all the prophet Jonah himself could
not on the Ninevites, for all his desire to.

2   But for the present let us lay our own words aside and hear the
sound of the prophet's trumpet: 'If you say to yourself: Why have

these evils come?, the answer is: Because of the vastness of your wickedness. If the Ethiopian can change his skin or the leopard his spots, *you* will be able to do good, though you have learnt bad':

3   with the implication that you do not want to. And below: 'This is what the Lord says to this people, which loved to move its feet and would not be still and displeased the Lord: Now will he remember their wickedness and punish their sins. And the Lord said to me: Do not pray for the good of this people. When they fast, I shall not listen to their prayers, and if they offer holocausts and sacrificial victims, I shall reject them'. And again: 'And the Lord said to me: If Moses and Samuel stood before me, I should not feel for this people: remove them from my sight and let them depart'.

4   And after a while: 'Who will pity you, Jerusalem? Who will feel sorrow for you, or go to beg for your peace? You left me, says the Lord, and went away from me. I shall stretch out my hand on you,

5   and kill you'. And later: 'This is what the Lord says: Look, I am plotting against you. Let each return from his evil path; set straight your paths and your intentions. They said: We have no hope; we will go our own ways, and each do what his wicked heart recommends. So the Lord says this: Ask the world: Who ever heard tell of such terrible things as the virgin of Israel has done beyond measure? Shall the snow of Lebanon ever fail from the rock of the field? Can the cold waters that burst forth and flow down ever be plucked out? For my

6   people has forgotten me'. After a while he puts forward a choice, and says: 'The Lord says: Make judgements and pronounce justice; free the man who is oppressed by force from the hand of his accuser; bring no sorrow to the stranger, the orphan and the widow. Cause no unjust oppression. Shed no innocent blood. For if you do as I say, there shall enter through the doors of this house kings who are of the race of David and who sit on his throne. But if you do not heed these words, I have sworn, says the Lord, that this house

7   shall become a wilderness'. And again (on the subject of a wicked king): 'As I live, says the Lord, if Coniah is the ring on my right hand, I shall pluck him off and give him up to those who seek his life'.

51   Moreover, the holy Habakkuk has a cry to raise: 'Woe to those who build a city in blood, and found a city on wickedness, saying: Is not this the doing of the almighty Lord? And many peoples have fainted in the fire, and many nations have been diminished'. And so he uses a complaint to launch his prophecy: 'How long shall I have to shout before you listen? I shall cry to you, why have you given me toils and pains, misery and impiety to look upon? In my sight judgement is passed and the judge has received (a bribe).

For this reason has the law been scattered, and the judgement is not brought to its full end, because an impious man uses his power to oppress the just. And so the judgement has ended as crooked'.

52   Listen also to what the blessed prophet Hosea has to say of princes: 'They have broken my ordinance and gone against my law, and cried: We know that you are the enemy of Israel. They have persecuted the good man as though he were wicked, and have ruled for their own sakes and not according to my way. They have held on to their high places, and do not know me'.

53   Hear too the threat of the holy prophet Amos: 'After three wickednesses by the sons of Judah and after four I shall not turn them away, for they have rejected the law of the Lord and failed to keep his orders. They have been seduced by their follies. I shall cast fire on Judah, and it will consume the foundations of Jerusalem. The Lord says: After three wickednesses by Israel and after four, I shall not turn them away, for they have bartered the just man for money and the poor man for a pair of shoes, which they tread on the dust of the earth, and they beat the heads of the poor, and turned

2   aside the way of the humble'. And after a little: 'Seek the Lord, and you shall live, so that the house of Joseph does not blaze up like a flame and be consumed, with none to put it out'. 'The house of Israel hated the critic at the gate, and loathed the word of justice'.

3   This Amos was forbidden to prophesy in Israel; without tempering his reply with flattery, he answered: 'I was not a prophet, nor the son of a prophet, but a goatherd who plucked the fruit of the mulberry. The Lord took me from my sheep, and said to me: Go and prophesy to my people Israel. Now listen to the word of the Lord' (for he was addressing the king): 'You say, Do not prophesy in Israel, and do not assemble crowds to threaten the house of Jacob. Therefore the Lord says: Your wife shall be a whore in the city; your sons and daughters shall fall by the sword; your land shall be measured out with a cord, and you shall die on unclean soil. And

4   Israel shall be led captive from its land'. And below: 'Hear this, you who bring dreadful tribulations to the poor and tyrannise over the needy of the land, and who say: When will the month be past, so that we can make money, and the Sabbath, so that we can open up our treasures? ' And after a little: 'The Lord swears against the pride of Jacob that he will not forget or belittle what you have done; the earth will quake for this, and all its dwellers shall mourn, and the

5   end shall rise like a river'. 'And I shall turn your festal days to days of grief. I shall find a hairshirt for every back, and baldness for every head. I shall make it like the mourning for the death of one beloved, and those with it as a day of sorrow'. And again: 'By the sword

shall die all the sinners of my people, who say: Evil will not approach us or come upon us.'

54 Hear too the words of the holy seer Micah: 'Hear, O people. What shall ornament the city? Shall fire, and the house of the wicked piling up wicked treasures and injustice with injury? Shall the wicked man be justified on the balance, and the deceitful weights in the sack - from which they piled up their riches in wickedness?'

55 The famous prophet Zephaniah, too, has his warnings to heap up. Listen to him. 'The great day of the Lord is at hand; it is near, and coming quickly nearer. The voice of the day of the Lord is made bitter and powerful. That day is a day of wrath, a day of tribulation and distress, a day of cloud and fog, a day of trumpets and shouting, a day of misery and destruction, a day of shadows and darkness over strong cities and high corner towers. I shall bring distress to men, and they will go like blind men, because they have sinned in the eyes of the Lord; and I shall shed their blood like dust, and their flesh like the dung of oxen, and their gold and silver will not be able to save them on the day of the wrath of the Lord. And in the fire of his displeasure will be consumed the whole land, and the Lord will bring ruin and devastation to all the dwellers in the land. Gather together and assemble, unruly nation, before you are made as the passing flower, before the wrath of the Lord comes upon you'.

56 Hear also what the holy prophet Haggai says: 'The Lord says: In one moment I shall move heaven and earth, sea and dry land, and overturn the kingdom and destroy the strength of the kings of the heathen, and overturn their chariots and charioteers'.

57 Have regard next to the words of the chosen prophet Zechariah, son of Iddo. This is how he starts his prophecy: 'Return to me, and I will return to you, says the Lord. And do not be as your fathers were, whom the earlier prophets blamed, saying: The almighty Lord says:

2 Turn from your ways; but they did not heed me or obey me'. And below: 'And the angel said to me: What do you see? I replied: I see a flying sickle, twenty cubits long. It is a curse that goes over the face of the whole land; for every thief in the land shall be punished from it, even with death, and I shall cast it forth, says the almighty Lord, and it shall enter the house of the thief and the house of the man who swears to a lie in my name'.

58 Further, the holy prophet Malachi says: 'Behold, the day of the Lord shall come, blazing like an oven. All the proud and all the wicked shall be as stubble, and the day that approaches shall burn them up, says the Lord of hosts, and leave of them neither root nor

shoot'.

59 But pay heed too to what the holy Job said about the beginning
and end of the wicked: 'Why do the wicked live? They grow
old in their dishonest ways; their descendants are according to
their desire; their sons are in their sight, their houses are fruitful.
They never feel fear, and the Lord's scourge is not laid upon them.
Their cows do not abort, their pregnant animals carry their young
through to birth without mishap. They live on like everlasting
sheep, and their children are glad as they pick up the psaltery and
the lute. They finish their lives amid prosperity, and they sleep the
2 sleep of the world below'. Does God then have no regard for the
deeds of the impious? 'Surely; the lamp of the impious shall be
extinguished, and there will come upon them destruction; they
will be gripped with pains like the pangs of childbirth, because of
(God's) anger. They will be as chaff in the wind, as dust snatched
up by the whirlwind. Let his property fail his sons. May he see his
destruction with his own eyes, and not be saved by the Lord'.

3 And about the same people a little further on: 'They have seized
the flock with its shepherd, driven away the orphans' pack-animal,
taken the widow's ox as a pledge. They have turned the powerless
aside from the path of necessity. They have reaped the field of
another before due time. The poor have laboured in the vineyards
of the powerful with no pay and no food. They have caused many
to sleep naked without coverings, and removed the protection that
kept them alive'.

4 And after a while, knowing their deeds, he handed them over to
the shades: 'Let his portion be cursed on the land, let his plants
appear withered'. 'Let him be rewarded according to his actions,
let every wicked man be crushed like a rotten tree. For rising high
in his anger, he has overthrown the powerless. Therefore he shall
have no confidence in his life; when he falls ill, let him have no
hope of health; but he shall fall into feebleness. For his pride has done
harm to many; he has become faint like a mallow in the heat, like a
5 corn ear when it is fallen from its stalk'. And below: 'But be his sons
never so many, they shall be for the slaughter': 'but if he collects
silver like earth, and gathers gold like mud, all these things the just
men gain'.

60 Hear, besides, the threats of the blessed prophet Esdras, library
of the law. 'My Lord says: My right hand shall not spare sinners,
nor my sword cease its work on those who shed innocent blood on
the earth. From my wrath shall go fire to devour the foundations
of the earth, and the sinners like straw that is set alight. Woe to those

who sin and do not observe my decrees, says the Lord, I shall
not spare them. Go, rebellious children, and do not pollute my
holiness. God knows those who sin against him, and he will hand
them over to death and slaughter. For now are many evils come
2 upon the whole earth'. 'A sword of fire is sent against you, and
who is there to parry them? Shall anyone drive off the lion that
ravens in the jungle? Shall anyone put out the fire when the
straw is ablaze? The Lord God shall send evils: and who is there
to turn them away? Fire shall issue from his wrath - and who is
there to extinguish it? He shall send lightning, and who shall not
fear it? He shall thunder, and who shall not shudder? God shall
threaten, and who shall not shrink terrified from his face? The
earth shall tremble, and the foundations of the sea are agitated to
their depths'.

61 Heed too what was said of the wicked by the excellent prophet
Ezekiel, whom we admire for his vision of the four beasts of the
gospels. When he bewailed in pitiable language the scourge laid on
Israel, the Lord said first: 'The wickedness of the house of Israel
and Judah has grown apace: the earth is filled with many peoples,
and the city is full of wickedness and uncleanness'. 'Behold, it is I'.
'My eye will not spare you, nor shall I feel pity'. And below: 'Since
the earth is full of peoples and the city is full of wickedness, I shall
destroy the onrush of their valour, and their holy places shall be
polluted. They will come to beg and to seek peace, but there will
2 be none'. And further on: 'The Lord said to me: Son of man, if a
land has sinned, so as to do a wrong deed, I shall stretch out my
hand against it and break its staff of bread; I shall send famine on it,
and destroy the men and beasts that inhabit it. Were there three
such men as Noah, Daniel and Job in it, they should not free it,
though they themselves would be saved, because of their justice,
says the Lord. If I bring evil beasts into the land and punish it and
it falls into destruction and there is no one able to journey across
it in face of the beasts, and those three men are in the midst of it,
as I live, says the Lord, its sons and daughters shall not go free,
but they only shall be safe, while the land goes to rack and ruin'.
3 And again: 'The son will not bear the injustice of the father,
nor the father that of the son. The justice of the just shall be upon
him. As for the wicked man, if he turns from all the wicked things
he has done and keeps all my ordinances and acts justly and
compassionately, then he will live his life and not die. All the crimes
he has committed shall be wiped out. He shall live, for the justice
that he has done. Do I, says the Lord, prefer the death of the

unjust man, rather than that he turn from his evil ways and live? But when the just man turns from his justice and commits injustices like all those of the wicked man, all the just acts he has done will be forgotten. He will die for the crime into which he fell, and for

4 the sins he committed'. And further on: 'And all the nations will know that it was because of their sins that the house of Israel were led captive, because they forsook me. I turned my face from them, and handed them over to their enemies and they all fell by the sword. According to their uncleanness and their wickedness did I deal with them, and I turned my face away from them'.

62 That is enough of the holy prophets' threats. I have thought it necessary to insert in my small book just a little of the Wisdom of Solomon, containing, as well as threats to the kings, exhortation and warning for them. For people might say I was glad to load heavy and unbearable burdens of words on the shoulders of men, without being ready to move them with my finger - that is, with addresses of consolation. So let us hear what the prophet said.

2 'Love justice, you who judge the earth'. If this one piece of witness were kept whole-heartedly, it would be quite enough to put the commanders of our country right. For if they loved justice, they would love, surely, him who is in a sense the fount and origin of the whole of justice, God.

3 'Serve the Lord in goodness, and in simplicity of heart seek him'. Alas, who will live (as one of my predecessors says) to see that carried out by our countrymen? - if indeed it can be carried out anywhere.

4 'For he is found by those who do not put him to the test, and he appears to those who have faith in him'. These men have no conscience in putting God to the test: for they scorn his precepts with an obstinate mockery, and do not keep faith with him: on his kind or rather severe oracles they turn their backs instead of their faces.

5 'For perverse thoughts separate from God'. This too can be clearly seen in the tyrants of our day.

6 But the sense is so clear - why mix my poor abilities with it? Let there speak for me, as I have said, one who alone is truthful, the holy spirit: of whom we now find it said: 'The holy spirit of discipline will flee from deceit', and again: 'Since the spirit of God

7 has filled the world'. And below, putting forward the ends awaiting the good and bad with acute judgement, he says: 'The hope of the impious is like down that the wind tosses, like smoke that the wind scatters, like a thin spray that the storm disperses, like the memory of a guest who stays for a single day and travels on. But the just will live

50

for ever. Their reward is with God, and the most high keeps his thoughts on them. So they shall receive the kingdom of beauty, a glorious diadem from the hand of the Lord. For with his right hand shall he protect them, and with his holy arm shall he defend

8   them'. For very different in character are the just and the wicked. Indeed, as the Lord says, 'I will honour those who honour me, and those who spurn me shall be without glory'.

63   But let us go on to what remains: 'Hear, all you kings, and understand, learn, you judges of the ends of the earth; give ear, you who control multitudes, and have your way among the thronging nations. God gave you your power; your virtue is from the most high. He will inquire into what you do, and scrutinise your thoughts. You were servants of his kingdom, yet you did not judge aright, or keep the law of justice, or walk according to his will; swiftly and dreadfully shall he come upon you, for those who rule will receive the harshest judgement. Pity is granted to the small; but the powerful shall suffer powerful torments. The ruler of all will have no respect of persons, nor will he stand in awe of anyone's greatness; it was he who made great and small, and his care goes out equally to all. But the stronger will receive stronger torture. These, then, are my words to you, kings: that you may learn wisdom and not fall. Those who have kept to just ways will be found just; and those who have learnt the ways of holiness will be made holy'.

64   So far I have addressed the kings of my country both in my own words and in the oracles of the prophets, wishing them to know (as the prophet said): 'Flee from sins as from the face of a serpent; if you draw near them, they will get you. Their teeth are lion's teeth, that slay the souls of men', and again: 'How great is the pity of the

2   Lord, how ready he is to forgive those who turn to him'. And if I do not have in me that apostolic virtue that would allow me to say: 'I could wish to be cast out from Christ for my brothers', yet I can say with all my heart what the prophet said: 'Alas, a soul perishes', and again: 'Let us scrutinise our ways and examine them, and return to the Lord; let us raise our hearts and hands to God in heaven', and the saying of the apostle also: 'We wish each one of you to be in the bowels of Christ'.

65   How glad I should be to let modesty step in and to rest here, like one long tossed on the sea-waves and at last carried by his oars to the longed-for haven: if I did not see such great mountains of wickedness raised against God by bishops and other priests and clerics of my order also. These persons must be stoned with hard word-rocks - for I do not wish to be accused of making exceptions of persons - first by me, as the law enjoined on the witnesses, then by

the people, if indeed they cleave to the decrees: stoned with all
our might, not that they may be killed in the body, but that they
2 may die in their sins, and live in God. But, as I have said earlier,
I beg to be forgiven by those whose life I praise and indeed
prefer to all the riches of the world. If it may be so, I desire and
thirst to be a participant in that life for a time before I die. Now
my two sides are protected by the victorious shields of the saints;
my back is safe at the walls of truth; my head as its helmet has
the help of the Lord for its sure covering. So let the rocks of
my truthful vituperations fly their constant flights.

THE COMPLAINT : CLERGY

66   Britain has priests, but they are fools; very many ministers, but
they are shameless; clerics, but they are treacherous grabbers. They
are called shepherds, but they are wolves all ready to slaughter
souls. They do not look to the good of their people, but to the
filling of their own bellies. They have church buildings, but go to
them for the sake of base profit. They teach the people - but by
giving them the worst of examples, vice and bad character. Rarely
do they sacrifice and never do they stand with pure heart amid
2 the altars. They do not reprimand the people for their sins; indeed
they do the same things themselves. They make mock of the precepts
of Christ, and all their prayers are directed to the fulfilment of their
lustful desires. They usurp with unclean feet the seat of the apostle
Peter, yet thanks to their greed they fall into the pestilential chair of
the traitor Judas. They hate truth as an enemy, and love lies like
favourite brothers. They look askance at the just poor as though
they were dreadful snakes; and, showing no regard for shame, they
respect the wicked rich as though they were angels from heaven.
3   They preach, lip-deep, that the poor should be given alms, but
themselves contribute not a groat. They keep quiet about terrible
public crimes, but make much of injuries done to themselves as if
it were Christ who suffered them. They may drive a religious mother
or sisters from their house, but they indecently make light of
strange women, as being suited for a more intimate service: or
rather - to tell a truth that brings disgrace not so much on me as
4 on those responsible - they degrade them. After that, they canvass
posts in the church more vigorously than the kingdom of heaven;
they get them and keep them like tyrants, and bring to them no
lustre of lawful behaviour. They yawn stupidly at the precepts of

holy men - if they ever do hear them: though they should constantly; while they show alert interest in sports and the foolish stories of worldly men, as though they were the means to life and not death.

5   So fat are they that they are hoarse like bulls; and they are unhappily prompt to grasp at what is forbidden. They arrogantly keep their heads in the air - but their minds are kept down, amid the pangs of their consciences, to the lowest depths of Hell. If they lose a single penny, they grieve; if they gain one, they cheer up. They are dull and dumb in passing on the decrees of the apostles, because of their ignorance and the weight of their sins, and they shut the mouths even of those who do have knowledge of them. Yet in the treacherous twists and turns of worldly business they are highly skilled.

6   Fresh from their wicked dealings with these matters, many, rather than being drawn into the priesthood, rush into it or spend almost any price on attaining it. There, they remain in the same old unhappy slime of intolerable sin even after they have obtained the priestly seat of bishop or presbyter (they never sit in it, but wallow there disgracefully, like pigs). They have grabbed merely the name of priest - not the priestly way of life. They have received the apostolic dignity,

7   without yet being suitable for entire faith and penitence for evil. How can they be fitting and apt for any church rank, let alone the top one? For such a rank only the holy and perfect man, the imitator of the apostles, and (to use the word of the Teacher of the Gentiles) the irreproachable can undertake lawfully and without falling under the great sin of sacrilege.

67   For what is so impious and so wicked - even supposing that diverse other charges do not come up meanwhile - for anyone to want to purchase, like Simon Magus, the office of bishop or presbyter for a worldly price, when such office is more fittingly acquired through

2   holiness and right behaviour? But the error they are most prone to - and the error that leaves least hope for them - is that they buy priesthoods, which are tainted and cannot avail them, not from the apostles or their successors, but from the tyrants and their father the devil. In fact, they are crowning the whole wicked structure of their lives with a kind of roof that can protect all their evils: the effect of which is that no one can easily reproach them with their crimes old and new, and that, being set in charge of many, they can the more easily grab

3   at what their greed and their avarice desire. For if these impudent men had suggested the same bargain, I do not say to the apostle Peter but to any holy priest or pious king, they would have got the same reply as Simon Magus, their original, received from the apostle Peter: 'To hell with you and your money!'

4   But (alas!) it may well be that those who ordain these candidates

for priesthood (or rather degrade them and curse them for a blessing, making of sinners not, as would be better, repenters, but sacrilegious and desperate men, and, in a sense, placing Judas, betrayer of the Lord, in the seat of Peter, and that contriver of a filthy heresy, Nicolas, in the place of the martyr Stephen) were themselves called to the priesthood in just the same way: and so do not greatly detest (and even respect) in their sons something which certainly happened in their own case and that of their fathers too.

5   If they cannot find a pearl of this kind in their own district, because their boon companions stand in their way and sternly refuse them so valuable an acquisition, they send urgent messages ahead, and take a positive pleasure in sailing across seas and traversing wide lands in order to attain at last such a glory, so unequalled a beauty, or (I should rather say) an illusion sent by the devil, even if it means

6   selling all their goods. Then, with great pomp and great show, or rather madness, they return home, making their gait, which had been erect before, erecter still. Long had they fixed their gaze on the tops of the mountains; now they raise their half-awake eyes straight up to the sky and the topmost fleeces of the brilliant clouds: and burst on their country as though they were new creations (in fact they are instruments of the devil), as once did Novatus at Rome, that despoiler of the Lord's pearl, the black swine. Placed in the position they are, they will be stretching out in violence to the holy sacrifices of Christ hands that are worthy not of the sacred altars but of the avenging flames of hell.

68   What do you expect, unhappy people, from such beasts of the belly (as the apostle said)? Will you find correction at the hands of men who not only do not turn to good deeds but even (in the words of a reproachful prophet) labour to do ill? Will you find light from such eyes, which look with greed only on things that lead steeply down to

2   vice - that is, to the doors of hell? Indeed, in the words of our saviour, if you do not swiftly flee these rapacious wolves of Arabia, like Lot fleeing to the hills from the fiery rain that fell on Sodom, then, the blind led by the blind, you will fall together into the pit of hell.

A Pattern for the Better Priest

69   But it may be said: not all bishops and presbyters as categorised above are bad, for they are not all stained with the disgrace of schism, pride and uncleanness. I agree entirely. But though we know them to be chaste and good, I shall make a brief reply.

What availed it for the priest Eli that he alone did not break the precepts of the Lord in snatching flesh up out of the pot on hooks before the fat was offered to the Lord? For he was punished with the same fatal anger as his sons.

2   Which of these men, I ask you, was killed like Abel because of the envy felt for a better sacrificial victim - one that went up to heaven in heavenly fire? For they scorn the reproach even of a moderate word.

Which hated the counsel of the ill-wishers and refused to sit with the impious, so that it might truly be said of him as of Enoch: 'Enoch walked with God, and was not found', found, that is, to have left God and to be limping downhill after idols at that time amid the folly of the whole foolish world?

3   Which of them refused to admit into the ark of salvation (now, the church) anyone who was God's adversary, as did Noah in the time of the flood, so as to make it quite clear that only the innocent and most worthy repenters should be present in the house of the Lord?

Which like Melchizedek offered sacrifice and gave blessing to the victors only when they had, to the number of three hundred (that is, the mystery of the trinity) freed a just man and defeated the dire armies of five kings and their conquering squadrons, and had no desire for what belonged to others?

4   Which on the orders of God freely offered his own son to be slaughtered on the altar as did Abraham, so as to fulfil a command similar to that of Christ, who said that when one's right eye offends it should be plucked out, and so as to avoid the curse of the prophet on one preventing the sword and the shedding of blood?

Which, like Joseph, plucked the memory of an injury from his heart by the roots?

5   Which like Moses spoke on the mountain with the Lord, and felt no fear when the trumpets blared, and (to use a figure) brought two tablets to show the unbelievers and a face that was horned, displeasing and dreadful to look at?

Which of them, like that same Moses, when begging for the sins of his people, cried from the bottom of his heart: 'Lord, this people has committed a great sin: but if you forgive them, forgive them; otherwise, blot me out of your book'?

70   Which was inspired with a wonderful zeal for God, and rose energetically like the priest Phinehas to punish fornication with no delay, healing the emotion of lust with the medicine of penitence, so that anger should not blaze against the people: so that this might be counted to him as justice for ever?

Which of them imitated Joshua either in the utter uprooting (in a moral significance) of seven races from the promised land or in the establishment of spiritual Israel in their place?

2   Which of them showed to the people of God the boundary lines
beyond Jordan, so that it should be known what properly belonged to
each tribe, in the manner of the wise division made by the same
Phinehas and Joshua?

Which, in order to lay low the innumerable thousands of the Gentiles,
enemies to the people of God, sacrificed his only daughter (by which
is understood his own pleasure) because she came to meet the victorious
army with drum and dancing (that is, carnal desires), in payment of a
vow? In doing this, Jephthah was acting in accordance with the words
of the apostle: 'Not seeking what is expedient to me, but what is
expedient to many, that they may be saved'.

3   Which of them went forth full of faith like Gideon to confound, put
to flight and lay low the camps of proud Gentiles with men symbolising
(as above) the mystery of the trinity, fine pitchers and resonant
trumpets in their hands (that is, the sentiments of the prophets and
apostles: as the Lord said to the prophet: 'Raise your voice like a
trumpet', and as the psalmist said of the apostles: 'Their sound went
out into every land')? The pitchers gleamed in the darkness with the
brilliant light of fire (to be understood as the bodies of the saints
attached to good works and blazing with the fire of the holy spirit:
compare what the apostle says: 'Having this treasure in pottery vases'),
after the felling of the trees in the grove of idolatry (which morally
interpreted is that of dark and dense desire) and the clear signs of the
Jewish fleece that was untouched by the rain of heaven and the
heathen fleece that was wetted by the dew of the holy spirit.

71   Which of them, being ready to die to the world and live in Christ,
laid low, as did Sampson, so many debauched heathen banqueters,
praisers of their own gods - the senses, that is, which glorify riches
(as the apostle says: 'And avarice, which is slavery to images'): for
he used the strength of his arms to shake two columns (understood as
the corrupt pleasures of soul and flesh), columns on which the house
of every human wickedness is in a sense fixed and supported.

2   Which, like Samuel, dispelled by prayers and by the burning of
a sucking lamb the fear inspired by the Philistines, aroused unexpected
voices of thunder and showers from the clouds, appointed a king
without flattering him, rejected the same man when he displeased God,
and anointed a better in his royal place? And which, like Samuel, when
he has to say farewell to his people, will stand up and say: 'Behold,
I am here; speak in the presence of the Lord and his anointed, say
whether I have taken any man's ox or ass, if I have slandered any man,
oppressed any man, received a bribe from any man's hand?' The
people's reply was: 'You have not slandered us, or oppressed us, or
taken anything from the hand of any man'.

3   Which of them, like the excellent seer Elijah, burned up a
hundred proud men with fire from heaven, preserving fifty humble
men, and with no colour of flattery announced his coming death to
a wicked king, who consulted not God through his prophets but the
idol Ekron; all prophets of the idol Baal (which interpreted means
the human emotions, which, as I have said, are always directed towards envy and avarice) did he lay low with his glittering sword (that
is, the word of God); moved by zeal for God he took away from the
land of the wicked the showers from heaven, which he locked up for
three years and six months as if in a strong prison of need. Dying of
hunger and thirst in the desert he made a complaint: 'Lord, they have
killed your prophets and dug up your altars, and I am left alone and
they are seeking my life'.

72   Which of them punished his dearest follower - if not with incurable
leprosy, like Elisha, at least with dismissal - when he found him
weighed down beyond due measure with worldly burdens that he
himself had earlier rejected, despite urgent entreaty to accept them?

2   Which of them among us, like that same Elisha, has by fervent
prayer to God opened the eyes of a boy sweating in despair of his
life and suddenly terrified at the warlike preparations of the enemy
besieging the city they were in, so that he could see the mountain full
of allies from the heavenly army, armed chariots and horsemen flashing
with fiery countenances, and believe that he was stronger to save than
his enemies to fight?

And which of them by the touch of his body, dead doubtless to
the world but alive in God, shall bring help as did Elisha to another
dying a different death, dead, no doubt, before God but alive in his
vices, so that he suddenly starts up and gives thanks to Christ for the
health that the lips of almost all mortals had despaired of?

3   Which of them, like Isaiah, had his lips cleansed, so that his sins
might be blotted out in the humility of confession, by a burning
coal carried from the altar by the tongs of the cherubs? Which, like
the same Isaiah, tripped up and overthrew, with the help of the
effective prayers of the pious king Hezekiah, a hundred and eighty
five thousand of the army of the Assyrians by the hand of an angel,
no wound appearing?

4   Which of them, like the blessed Jeremiah, endured the squalors
and stenches of prison, like small deaths, because he passed on the
commands of God, threats from heaven and the truth even to those
who did not want to hear him?

And, to be brief, which of them (in the words of the Teacher of the
Gentiles) endured, like the holy prophets, wandering in the mountains

and caves and caverns of the earth, suffered stoning, cutting, and every manner of death, in the name of the Lord?

73   But why do I linger over Old (Testament) instances as if there were none in the New? Let those who think they are entering on this narrow path of the Christian religion at the cost of no labour merely by flaunting the name of priest listen to me as I pluck a few flowers - the top ones, as it were - from the wide and lovely meadow of the holy soldiery of the New Testament.

2   Which of you, who slouch rather than sit lawfully in the priestly seat, was cast out of the council of the wicked like the holy apostles and beaten with diverse rods, and then thanked the trinity with whole heart for being judged worthy to suffer insult for Christ, the true God?

Which died in the body after being brained with a fuller's club like James, first bishop of the New Testament, for bearing true witness to God?

3   Which of you was executed by the sword of a wicked ruler, like James, brother of John?

Which, like the first deacon and martyr of the gospels, was stoned by wicked hands for the mere crime of having seen God when the faithless had been unable to see him?

Which was fixed feet upwards to the gibbet of a cross for his reverence to Christ, and there breathed his last, honouring Christ in death as in life, like the fit keeper of the keys of the kingdom of heaven?

4   Which of you was executed by a sword blow for confessing the truth-teller Christ after enduring the bonds of prison, shipwreck on the sea, the blow of rods, continual danger from rivers, brigands, heathen, Jews and false apostles, after agonies of fasting, hunger and lack of sleep, after continual anxiety for all churches, after worry about those who gave scandal, after sickness on behalf of the sick, after a remarkable circuit of almost the whole earth preaching the gospel of Christ, like the chosen vessel and the elect Teacher of the Gentiles?

74   Which of you, like the holy martyr Ignatius, bishop of the city of Antioch, after remarkable deeds in the name of Christ, paid for his witness by being crunched in the molars of lions at Rome? When you hear his words as he was led to his martyrdom, supposing that you ever blush, you will think yourselves by comparison not even middling

2 Christians, let alone priests. For in the letter that he sent to the Roman church he says: 'From Syria to Rome, I have been fighting with beasts on land and sea: night and day I am bound to ten leopards, by which I mean the soldiers set to guard me, who are the more savage because of what I do for them. Rather, I am being educated by their wickedness. Yet I am not justified by this. When, when will there come forth the

beasts that are being made ready for my salvation? When will they be let loose? When will they be allowed to enjoy my flesh? I pray that they may be the fiercer for their preparation. I shall encourage them to devour me, beg them not to be afraid, as they have been in some cases, of touching my

3 body. In fact, if they hold back *I* shall attack, I shall rush at *them*. Forgive me, I beg of you: I know where my profit lies. It is now that I am beginning to be the disciple of Christ. An end to envy, whether of human feeling or spiritual wickedness, so that I may attain to Jesus Christ. Let there be fulfilled fires, crucifixions, beasts, scattering of bones and tearing of limbs, punishments for my whole body, every kind of torment invented for me alone by the devil's art: so long as I deserve to attain to Jesus Christ.'

4 Why look on these things with the eyes of your souls asleep? Why listen to such things with the ears of your senses dulled? Scatter, I beg you, the black shadowy fog of the faintness of your hearts, that you may see the radiant light of truth and humility. A Christian not middling but perfect, a priest not worthless but outstanding, a martyr not lazy but pre-eminent, says: 'It is now that I am beginning to be the disciple of Christ'.

5 As for you, like that Lucifer who was cast out of heaven, you thrive on verbiage, not on power. You ponder on what your pattern conceived, using it as an excuse for your doings: 'I shall ascend into heaven', said Lucifer, 'and be like the most high', and again: 'I dug and I drank water and I dried with

6 my footprints all the rivers of the banks'. Far better would it have been for you to imitate and listen to him who is truly the unconquered exemplar of all goodness and humility, who said through his prophet: 'But I am a worm and not a man, the reproach of men and cast out by the people'. How extraordinary that *he* should be called the reproach of men, when he blotted out the reproaches of all the world - so too in the gospel: 'I can do nothing by myself', though he, as old as the Father and the Holy Spirit, and of the same joint substance as they, made heaven and earth with all their unimaginable ornamentation, using his own power and no other's - while *you* are arrogant and puff up your words: as the prophet said: 'Why do earth and ash feel pride?'

*7*5 But I must return to my theme. Which of you, I say, like the excellent Polycarp, shepherd of the church of Smyrna and Christ's witness, thoughtfully provided a meal for his guests when they were eager to start dragging him off to the flames, and when cast on the fire for the love of Christ said: 'He who granted that I should bear the punishment of the fire will grant that I should bear the flames to the end unmoving, without being nailed down.'

2 My words must fly past a great abundance of saints: but I shall put forward one by way of example, Basil, bishop of Caesarea. He was threatened with certain death by an unjust emperor if he did not, like the rest, stain himself by the next day with the filth of

59

the Arians. But he is said to have replied: 'Tomorrow I shall be what I am today; let us hope *you* do not change'. And again: 'If only I had a proper present to offer the man who would free Basil more quickly from the knot of these bellows'.

3   Which of you under the shock of the tyrants kept rigidly to the rule given by the words of the apostle, a rule that has always been kept in every age by all the holy priests who reject the proposals of men that try to hasten them down the slope to wickedness: 'One must obey God rather than men'?

Denunciation of Corrupt Priests

76   Therefore let us take refuge, as usual, in the pity of the Lord and in the words of his holy prophets; let them instead of us direct the shafts of their oracles at imperfect shepherds, as they did before at the tyrants, so that they can sting and so heal them. Let us see what threats the Lord sends through his prophets to idle and dishonest priests who give evil instruction to the people by word and example alike.

2   Eli the priest in Shiloh was reprimanded because he had not punished his sons severely and with a zeal worthy of God when they made mock of God, but had warned them gently and compassionately, with a fatherly feeling; the prophet said to him: 'The Lord says: I showed myself clearly to the house of your father when they were in Egypt as slaves of Pharaoh, and I chose the house of your father, out of all

3 the tribes of Israel, to take on my priesthood'; and after a little: 'Why have you looked with wicked eyes at my incense and my sacrifice, and honoured your sons more than me, so as to give them the first blessing in all sacrifices made before me?' 'And now the Lord says: I will honour those who honour me; and those who count me as naught shall be reduced to naught. Behold the day will come when I shall destroy

4 your name and the seed of your father's house'. 'And the sign shall be that your two sons, Hophni and Phinehas, shall die in a single day by the sword of men'. If such is the fate of those who correct those beneath them with words rather than condign punishment, what will become of those who encourage and lure others to evil by their own sins?

77   It is well-known, too, what happened to a true seer after the fulfilment of the sign that he had foretold himself and the restoring of the dried up arm for the impious king: he was sent from Judaea to prophesy in Bethel, and forbidden to taste any food there; but he was deceived by another, false prophet into taking a little bread and

2 water. His host said to him: 'The Lord God says: You have been disobedient to what the Lord said and have not kept the command given

you by the Lord your God, but have returned and eaten bread
and drunk water in the place where I forbade you to eat bread and
drink water. Therefore your body shall not be placed in the tomb
of your fathers'. 'And' (so the story goes on) 'it happened that
after he had eaten the bread and drunk the water, he saddled himself
his ass and went away; and a lion found him on the road and
killed him'.

78   Hear too what the holy prophet Isaiah has to say about priests:
'Woe to the wicked for evil, for he shall be punished for his deeds.
His extortioners have plundered my people, and women have lorded
it over them. My people, those who call you happy are deceiving you,
and destroying the steps of your way. The Lord stands to judge,
stands to judge peoples. The Lord shall come to judgement with the
elders of his people and its princes. You have eaten up my vineyard,
and your house contains the spoil of the poor. Why do you crush
my people and grind the faces of the poor?, says the Lord of hosts'.

2   And again: 'Woe to those who found unfair laws and when they
write have written wickedness, that they should oppress the poor in
court and do violence to the causes of the humble among my people,
that widows should be their prey and orphans the victims of their
plunder. What will you do in the day of punishment and calamity
that comes from afar? ' And below: 'But these too have been
ignorant because of wine and erred because of drunkenness, the
priests have been ignorant because of drunkenness, they have been
engulfed in wine, they have erred in drunkenness, they have failed
to know him who sees, they have been ignorant of judgement. For
all the tables were filled with the filth of the vomit, so that there

79   was no room left'. 'Therefore hear the word of the Lord, you
scoffers, you who lord it over my people in Jerusalem. For you said:
We have struck a bargain with death, and made a pact with hell. When
the overflowing scourge passes over, it will not come upon us, because
we put our hope in lies and lies are our protection'. And after a little:
'And hail will sweep away the hopes placed in lying and the waters
will flood the defending walls; your bargain with death will be
destroyed, and your pact with hell will not stand. When the overflowing scourge passes over, you will be trampled under. Whenever

2   it passes by, it will destroy you'. And again: 'And the Lord said:
This people comes near with its mouth and glorifies me with its lips;
but its heart is far away from me. Therefore, behold, I shall cause
wonder in this people, with a great and staggering miracle. Wisdom
shall perish from their wise men, and the understanding of the
prudent among them shall be obscured. Woe to you who dive deep in
your hearts so as to hide your plans from the Lord: whose works are

in darkness, and who say: Who can see us? Who knows of us? For
3 this plan of yours is topsy-turvy'. And after a little: 'The Lord says:
The heavens are my seat and the earth the footstool for my feet. What
is this house that you propose to build me? What will be the place
for me to rest? My hands made all these things, and all these things
have been made, says the Lord. But to whom am I to look except
the poor man who is contrite in spirit and trembles at my words?
He who sacrifices an ox is like one who kills a man; he who slaughters
a sheep is like one who brains a dog; he who offers an oblation is
like one who offers the blood of a pig; he who bethinks himself of
incense is like one who blesses an idol. All these things have they
chosen in their ways, and their souls have delighted in their
abominations'.

80 Hear too what the celibate prophet Jeremiah says to foolish
shepherds: 'The Lord says: What wickedness did your fathers find
in me that they left me and walked in search of folly and became
foolish?' And a little later: 'And when you entered my land, you
defiled it and made an abomination of my heritage. The priests did
not say: Where is the Lord? And those who deal with the law did not
know me, and the shepherds did me wrong. Therefore I shall continue
to contend with you, says the Lord, and I shall dispute with your sons'.
2 Again after a while: 'Astonishing miracles have taken place in the land;
the prophets preached a falsehood and the priests applauded with
their hands and my people loved such things. What will happen at the
end of it all?' 'To whom shall I speak and proclaim so that he hears
me? Behold, their ears are uncircumcised, and they cannot hear.
Behold, the word of the Lord has become a reproach to them, and
they do not receive it'. 'For I will stretch out my hand over the
dwellers in the land, says the Lord. From the lowest to the highest
everyone is given to avarice; and from prophet to priest all are
guileful. And they treated the hurt done to the daughter of my people
shamefully, saying: Peace, peace, and there shall be no peace. Those who
have done abominable things are confounded. Or rather they are not
confounded in confusion, for they do not know how to blush. Therefore they shall fall when all fall, and fall down at the time of their
3 punishment, says the Lord'. And again: 'All these are princes of a
people that turns aside; they walk in treachery; they are bronze and
iron, all corrupt. The bellows failed in the fire, the smelter blew in
vain: their wickedness is not consumed. You may call them false silver,
4 for the Lord has rejected them'. And after a little while: 'I am, I am,
I saw, says the Lord. Go to my place in Shiloh, where my name has
dwelt from the first, and see what I did to it because of the wickedness

of my people Israel. And now, because you have done all these things, says the Lord, and I have spoken to you, rising in the morning to address you, yet you have not heard: because I have called you and you have not replied, I shall deal with this house, in which my name has been invoked and in which you place your confidence, and with this place, which I gave to you and your fathers, just as I dealt with

81 Shiloh: and I shall cast you from my sight'. And again: 'My sons have departed from me and are not here: there is no one to raise my tent any longer and put up my hides, for the shepherds have been foolish and not sought the Lord. Therefore they have had no under-

2 standing, and their flock has been scattered'. And after a while: 'Why is it that my loved one does many crimes in my house? Shall holy flesh remove from you the wickedness in which you gloried? The Lord called your name the olive, rich, beautiful, full of fruit and fair to look at. At the sound of speech a great fire blazed up in it,

3 and its groves are burned'. And again: 'Come, gather, all the beasts of the land, hasten to devour. Many shepherds have destroyed my vineyard, trampled on my portion, made of my lovely portion a desert wilderness'. And again he says: 'This is what the Lord says to this people, which loved to move its feet and would not be still and displeased the Lord: Now will he remember their wickedness and

4 punish their sins'. 'The prophets say to them: You will not see the sword, and you will not have hunger, but the Lord will give you true peace in this place. And the Lord said to me: Prophets are prophesying falsely in my name; I did not send them or give them instructions; they are prophesying to you a vision that is false, a divination, a fraud, a deceit of their heart. And so the Lord says: By sword and famine shall those prophets be consumed, and the peoples to whom they prophesied shall be cast forth into the streets of Jerusalem, victims of

82 famine and the sword, with no one to bury them'. And again: 'Woe to the shepherds who destroy and tear apart the flock in my pasture, says the Lord. So the Lord God of Israel says to the shepherds who pasture my people: You have dispersed my flock, and cast them out,

2 and failed to visit them. Behold, *I* shall visit on you the wickedness of your ways, says the Lord'. 'For prophet and priest are polluted, and in my house have I found their evil, says the Lord. Therefore their way shall be like a slippery path in the darkness. They will be driven on, and will fall on the way; for I shall bring ills upon them, the year of their punishment, says the Lord. And in the prophets of Samaria I have seen folly, and they prophesied in the name of Baal, and

3 misled my people Israel. And in the prophets of Jerusalem I have seen the likeness of adulterers and the way of lies. They have

strengthened the hands of the worst of men, so that they would not
return each from his wickedness. They have all become as Sodom to
me, and their dwellers as Gomorrah. Therefore, says the Lord to the
prophets: Behold, I shall feed them on wormwood and make gall
their drink. For from the prophets of Jerusalem pollution has gone
out over all the earth. This is what the Lord of hosts says: Do not
listen to the words of the prophets who prophesy to you and
deceive you. They speak the vision of their heart, and not with the
4 voice of the Lord. To those who curse me they say: The Lord said:
Peace will be with you; and to all those who walk in the wickedness
of their hearts, they have said: Evil will not come upon them. For
who has stood in the council of the Lord, and seen and heard his
5 words? Who has considered his word and heard it? Behold, the
whirlwind of the wrath of the Lord is going forth, and the tempest
shall come to burst on the heads of the wicked. And the fury of the
Lord shall not turn back till he acts, till he completes what his heart
intends. In the last day you will understand what he intended'.

83   For you too little heed and do what the holy Joel too proclaimed
when he warned idle priests and bewailed the losses of the people
because of their wickedness: 'Awake, you who are drunk with
your wine; wail and lament all you who drink wine until you are
drunk, for pleasantness and joy are removed from your mouths.
Wail, priests who serve at the altar, for the fields are become sad.
Let the earth lament, for the corn is become sad, and the wine is
dried up, the oil is diminished and the farmers are grown dry. Wail,
estates, for the wheat and the barley, because the vintage has perished
from the field, the vine is withered, the figs are diminished; the pome-
granates and palms and apples and all the trees of the field are dried up:
for the sons of men have brought confusion to joy'.

2   You will have to understand all this in the spiritual sense, as a
warning that your souls may wither because of such a pestilential
famine for the word of God.

3   And again: 'Weep, priests who serve the Lord, saying: Spare your
people, Lord, and do not hand your heritage over to disgrace or
allow the heathen to rule over them and say: Where is their God?'
Yet you do not listen to these things, but commit every offence that
could make the wrath and rage of heaven blaze the more readily.

84   Heed with care the words of the holy prophet Hosea to priests
of your type: 'Hear this, priests, and let the house of Israel attend
and the house of the king mark it carefully, for judgment is upon
you, because you have been a snare for spying, and as it were a net
spread over Tabor which the followers of the hunt fashioned'.

85   May your estrangement from the Lord be such as he threatened through the prophet Amos: 'I hated and rejected your feast days, and I shall not accept the scent of sacrifice in your solemn assemblies. Although you offer your holocausts and victims, I shall not take them. I shall not look at the peace offering of your profession. Take from me the sound of your songs; I shall not listen to the melody of your organs'.

2   Hunger for the food of the gospels stalks among you, eating out the vitals of your souls in the very kitchen. This is what the same prophet foretold: 'Behold, the day is coming when I shall send famine into your land, says the Lord, not hunger for bread or thirst for water, but hunger to hear the word of God; and the waters shall be moved from sea to sea, and from north to east they shall run looking for the word of the Lord, and they shall not find it'.

86   Listen too to the blessed Micah, as he brays like some heavenly trumpet in brief fulmination against the guileful chiefs of the people: 'Listen now, princes of the house of Jacob: Is it not for you to know judgement, you who hate the good and seek for the bad, snatching their skins from them and their flesh from their bones? So it is that they have eaten the flesh of my people and stripped the skins from their backs, broken their bones and torn them apart like flesh for

2   the pot. They will cry aloud to God and he will not hear them, and he will turn away his face from them at that time, because they have acted wickedly in their contrivances against themselves. This is what the Lord says about the prophets who seduce my people, who bite with their teeth while preaching peace to them. But peace was not given to their mouths; I have raised up a war against the people. Therefore night shall come upon you instead of your vision, and you shall have darkness instead of foreknowledge, and the sun will set over the prophets, and the day will darken over them, and those who see dreams will be confounded, and the diviners will be scorned, and everyone will rail at them, for there will be no one to hear them. I shall surely fill my courage with the spirit of the Lord, with judgement and power, to announce to the house of Jacob its sins, and its

3   crimes to Israel. Hear these things, then, you leaders of the house of Jacob, and you who remain from the house of Israel, who hate judgement and pervert all that is right, who build Sion in blood and Jerusalem in wickedness; its leaders judged for bribes, and its priests gave their replies for profit, and its prophets foretold for money, and they rested in the Lord, saying: Is not the Lord among us? No trouble will come our way. Therefore, because of you, Sion will be ploughed up like a field, and Jerusalem will be like the watch-tower of an orchard, and the mountain of the house like a woodland spot'.

4   And after a while: 'Woe is me, for I have become like one who collects straw in the harvest, like a grape-cluster in the vintage when there is no grape for the eating of the first fruit. Alas, my soul has perished in the works of the world; reverence for sin always arises from the land, and there is no one among men to correct it. All contend at law for blood, and each man has troubled his neighbour, preparing his hands for mischief'.

87   Hear also what the excellent prophet Zephaniah said once about your fellows: for he was talking about Jerusalem, which spiritually may be understood as the church or the soul. 'O what a splendid and ransomed city she was, a confiding dove; she did not hear the voice or learn her lesson; she did not trust in the Lord, and she did not go to

2   her God'. And he shows why: 'Her princes were like roaring lions, her judges like the wolves of Arabia did not leave till the morning, her prophets bore within them the spirit of a despiser, her priests profaned holy things and acted impiously in the law. But the Lord is just in her midst, and he will do no injustice; morning by morning will he give his judgement'.

88   But hear too the blessed Zechariah, the prophet, warning you with the word of God: 'The almighty Lord says: Give just judgement, and be merciful and compassionate each to his brother, and do not by your power harm the widow and orphan, the stranger and pauper; and let no one remember his brother's wickedness in his heart. And they were stubborn, so that they did not listen, and gave their backs to folly, and burdened their ears so as not to hear, and they made their hearts immoveable, so as not to hear my law and the words which the almighty Lord sent in his spirit and in the hands of former prophets;

2   and great anger was roused in the almighty Lord'. And again: 'Those who spoke said displeasing things, and the seers spoke false visions and false dreams, and their consolation was foolish. Hence they have become dry as sheep, and they have been afflicted, because there was no health. My wrath is piled up on the shepherds, and I shall punish the lambs'.

3   And after a little: 'The voice of lamenting shepherds, because their greatness has become wretched. The voice of roaring lions, because the downrush of Jordan has become wretched. The almighty Lord says: Those who possessed killed and were not penitent. And those who sold them said: Blessed is the Lord, we have become rich, and their shepherds felt no sorrow for them. Therefore I shall no longer spare the dwellers in the land, says the Lord'.

89   Hear besides the denunciations launched at you by the holy prophet Malachi: 'It is you priests who despise my name, but you have said: How do we despise your name? In offering at my altar bread that is tainted. And you have said: How do we taint it? In

saying: The table of the Lord counts for nothing. And you have despised what is laid upon it; for if you bring a blind creature as victim, is not that an evil? If you bring a lame or sick animal, is not that an evil? Try offering that to your ruler, see if *he* will accept it, or receive your person, says the almighty Lord. And now beg the face of your God and try to win him over; these things have been

2   done at your hands: shall I receive your persons from you?' And again: 'And you have brought the lame and the sick to offer from the plunder, and you have brought a present. Am I to take *that* from your hand? says the Lord. Cursed is the trickster who has a male in his flock, yet when he makes a vow, sacrifices a feeble creature to the Lord! For I am a great king, says the Lord of hosts, and my name causes shudders among the heathen. And now this command is upon you, priests. If you refuse to hear it, and take it to heart, to give glory to my name, says the Lord of hosts, I shall despatch need among you, and I shall curse your blessings, because you have not taken it to heart. Behold, I shall launch my arm against you, and scatter over your faces the dung of your solemn feasts'.

3   But now, so that you can the more eagerly prepare your organs of wickedness for the good, hear what he says of the holy priest, if you still have any remnant of internal hearing in you: 'My covenant was with him' (he was talking, as far as the historical sense was concerned, of Levi or Moses) 'for life and peace; I gave him fear, and he feared me, and shrank from the face of my name. The law of truth was in his mouth, and wickedness was not found on his lips. He walked with me in peace and uprightness, and turned many away from wickedness. For the lips of the priest shall guard knowledge, and people shall look for the law from his mouth, because he is a messenger of the Lord of hosts'.

4   Now he changed his sense, while continuing to criticise evil men: 'You have strayed from the way and caused many to stumble in the law and invalidated the covenant with Levi, says the Lord of hosts. Therefore I have disgraced and humiliated you among all peoples, for you have not kept my ways and have been partial in the law.

5 Have we not all the same father? Did not one God create us? Why then does each man despise his brother?'And again: 'Behold, the Lord of hosts will come. And who will be able to contemplate the day of his coming? And who will stand to see him? For he will come forth like blazing fire, like the washers' lye. He will sit smelting and refining silver, and he will cleanse the sons of Levi, and he will strain them

6 like gold and silver'. And after a little: 'Your words have been strong against me, says the Lord, and you have said: Vain is he who serves

God: and what reward do we have for keeping his commands and walking a melancholy path in the sight of the Lord of hosts? Therefore we shall now call the arrogant blessed: for those who do wickedness are built up; they have made trial of God, and come to no harm'.

90 But hear what the prophet Ezekiel said: 'Woe upon woe shall come, and there shall be message after message; and a vision shall be sought from the prophet, and law shall perish from the priest and counsel from the elders'. And again: 'The Lord says: Because your words are lying and your prophecies false, behold, says the Lord, I am against you; I shall stretch out my hand against the prophets who see lying visions and speak untruths. They shall not come under the teaching of my people, and they shall not be written in the book of the house of Israel, and they shall not enter the land of Israel, and you shall know that I am the Lord. For they led my people astray, saying: The peace of the Lord - and there is no peace of the Lord. One man builds a wall, and they plaster it, and it will

2 fall'. And after a little: 'Woe to those who set bolsters under every elbow and make veils for the heads of people of all ages to corrupt souls. And the souls of my people are corrupted, and they took possession of their souls, and tainted me with my people for a handful of barley and a bite of bread, to destroy souls which ought not to have died, and to free souls which ought not to have lived, while

3 you speak to the people and they hear false words'. And below: 'Say, son of man: you are a land that is not rained upon, nor has rain fallen upon you in the day of wrath. The princes in the midst of it are as roaring lions ravening for plunder, devouring souls in their power and receiving bribes, and your widows are multiplied in your midst, and its priests have despised my law and polluted my holy places. They made no distinction between holy and profane, no division between clean and unclean; they veiled their eyes from my

91 sabbaths, and caused pollution in their midst'. And again: 'And I looked among them for a man of upright behaviour who would stand up to me altogether at the crisis of the land, lest in the end I should destroy it; and I could not find one. And I poured out my heart on the land in the fire of my wrath, to consume them; I have made their ways turn on their

2 heads, says the Lord'. And a little later: 'And the Lord said to me: Son of man, speak to the sons of my people, and say to them: Suppose I draw my sword against a land, and the people of the land take one of their number and use him as their watchman, and he sees the sword coming over the land, and he blows the trumpet as a sign to the people: and suppose a man who hears does hear the voice of the trumpet but takes

no heed, and the sword comes and gets him: then his blood will be on his own head, for though he heard the voice of the trumpet he took no notice, and his blood will be on himself. But the other man, because he

3 kept guard, managed to get away with his life. But if the watchman sees the sword coming and does not give the signal with the trumpet and the people does not take heed, and the sword comes and takes a life from them, that life is taken because of its wickedness, and I shall demand blood from the hand of the watchman. So, son of man, I have set you as watchman for the house of Israel. You will hear the word from my mouth when I say to the sinner: You will die the death. If you do not speak, so that the wicked man can turn from his way, the wicked man will die for his wickedness: but I shall demand recompense from your hand for his blood. But if you tell the wicked man of his ways in good time, so that he can turn from his way, but he fails to turn, he will die for his wickedness: but you will have got away with your life'.

92   These few testimonies out of many from the prophets, which serve to restrain the pride and laziness of stubborn priests, may suffice to prevent them supposing that it is by my own fabrication rather than on the authority of law and the saints that I bring such denunciations against them.

2   Let us see, then, what the trumpet of the gospels, that echoes through the world, says to irregular priests. I have to speak (as I have said) not of those who are in lawful possession of the apostolic seat and know well how to grant spiritual food in due season to their fellow servants - supposing there are many such at the present day - but of the unskilled shepherds, who abandon their sheep and pasture them on folly and do not have the words that the skilled shepherd has.

3 It is a clear sign that a man is no lawful shepherd or even middling Christian if he denies or rejects pronouncements that originate not so much from me (and I am very worthless) as from the Old and New Testaments. One of us is right to say: 'We greatly desire that the enemies of the church be our enemies also, with no kind of alliance, and that her friends and protectors be not only our allies but our fathers and masters too'.

4   Let all examine their consciences in a true balance; only thus will they be able to determine if it is right for them to sit in the chair of priest. Let us see, I repeat, what the saviour and maker of the world says.

5   'You are the salt of the earth: but if the salt vanishes, what will there be to salt it? It has no further value, except to be thrown out of

93 doors and trampled underfoot'. This one testimony might be abundantly sufficient to confute all the impudent. But so that the words of Christ may prove with yet clearer evidence what intolerable burdens

of crime these false priests heap on themselves, I must add further
2   details. For there follows: 'You are the light of the world. A city
placed on a mountain top cannot be hidden: nor does one light a
lamp and place it under a bushel, but on a candlestick, so that it can
give light to all in the house'. Who then among the priests of today,
plunged as they are in the blindness of ignorance, could shine like
the light of the clearest lamp to all those in a house by night, with
the glow of knowledge and good works? Who is there who is looked
upon as a safe and obvious common refuge for all the sons of the
church, as is a strong city, placed on the peak of a high mountain,
for its citizens?

3   But look at what follows: 'Let your light so shine in the presence
of men that they see your good works and glorify your father in
heaven'. Which of them can fulfil this even for a single day? Rather
does a dense cloud and black night of their sin so loom over the
whole island that it diverts almost all men from the straight way and
makes them stray along the trackless and entangled paths of crime;
and by their works the heavenly father is intolerably blasphemed
rather than praised.

4   I should certainly like, so far as my feeble talents allow, to
interpret, in the historical and moral sense, all these testimonies
from the holy scripture that I have so far inserted or have yet to insert
94 in this letter. But I do not want this little work to seem interminable
in the eyes of those who despise, loathe and abominate words that
are God's rather than mine; so those testimonies have been and will
be gathered together simply and without any periphrastic verbiage.

2   And after a little: 'For whoever breaks one of these least commands,
and teaches men to follow his example, will be called the least in the
kingdom of heaven'. And again: 'Do not judge, in case you are yourself
judged; for with whatever judgement you judge, you shall be judged'.

3   I ask you, which of you will take heed of what follows? 'Why do
you see a speck in your brother's eye and yet take no note of a plank
in your own? Why do you say to your brother: Let me get rid of the
speck in your eye, when lo and behold you have a plank in your
own eye?' Or what follows: 'Do not give a holy thing to the dogs, or
throw your pearls before swine, in case they trample them underfoot
and turn to rend you apart' (something that frequently happens to
you)?

4   And warning the people not to be led astray by treacherous
teachers (such as you are), he said: 'Beware of false prophets, who
come to you dressed as sheep, though within they are ravening wolves.
You will know them by their fruits. Do men collect grapes from

thorns or figs from thistles? Thus every good tree bears good fruit and bad bad'. And below: 'Not everyone who says to me: Lord, Lord, shall enter the kingdom of heaven; but it is he who does the will of my father in heaven who shall enter the kingdom of heaven'.

95   What will happen to you who (as the prophet said) cleave to God with your lips only and not with your heart? How do you comply with what follows: 'Behold, I send you like sheep in the midst of wolves'? For - quite the opposite - you go forth like wolves into a

2   flock of sheep. Or: 'Be prudent as serpents and simple as doves'. Certainly you are prudent - in biting a man in your fatal mouths: not in defending your head (that is, Christ) by putting your body in the way; for Christ you trample underfoot with all the endeavours of your wicked deeds. Nor do you have the simplicity of doves: rather you are black like crows, and once you have flown out from the ark (that is, the church) and discovered the stink of carnal pleasures, you never return to it with a pure heart.

3   But let us look at the rest: 'Do not fear those who kill the body without being able to kill the soul: fear him who can destroy both body and soul in hell'. Go over in your minds which of these things you have done.

4   But which of you would not be wounded in the secret recesses of his heart by the testimony that follows, spoken by the saviour to the apostles about evil bishops: 'Let them be: they are blind leading the blind. But if a blind man shows the way for another blind man, both will fall into a pit'.

96   The peoples whom you rule (or rather whom you have deceived) need to hear. Listen to the words of the Lord addressing the apostles and multitudes - words which, as I hear, even you are not ashamed to use often in public. 'In the seat of Moses have sat down scribes and Pharisees. Observe and do whatever they tell you. But do not act as

2   they act. For they talk - but do not themselves act'. Dangerous and useless to priests is teaching darkened by bad deeds. 'Woe to you, hypocrites. You shut the kingdom of heaven in the faces of men, yet you do not enter it yourselves or allow those going in to enter'. For you will in the future be punished not only for all the evil deeds you do, but because of the men who perish every day as a result of your example. Their blood shall be required of your hands at the day of judgement.

3   But consider the evil pointed out in the parable of the slave who said to himself: 'My master is in no hurry to come', and so doubtless began to beat his fellow-slaves and eat and drink with drunkards. 'The lord of that servant will come on a day when he does not expect

71

him, at an hour when he does not know, and separate him' (that
is, from the holy priests) 'and place his portion with the hypocrites'
(that is, no doubt, with those who hide a deal of wickedness under
the cloak of priesthood), 'and there will be wailing there and gnashing
of teeth' for those to whom that rarely happens in this life despite
the daily calamities suffered by the sons of the mother church and the
losses incurred by the kingdom of heaven.

97 But let us see what the true disciple of Christ, Teacher of the
Gentiles, Paul (one to be imitated by every teacher in the church, as
he himself suggests: 'Imitate me, just as I imitate Christ') says on such
a subject in his first epistle: 'When they came to know God, they did
not magnify him as God, or give him thanks, but they became foolish
in their thoughts, and their silly hearts were blinded. They said they
were wise, but they became stupid'. This may appear to be addressed
to the heathen; but observe how readily it may be applied to the
2 priests and peoples of this age. And after a little: 'They changed the
truth of God into lies, and worshipped and served creature rather than
creator - the creator who is blessed for ever. Therefore God handed them
3 over to base passions'. And again: 'And as they did not see fit to show
knowledge of God, he handed them over to a reprobate instinct, so as to
do what is unfitting. He filled them with all wickedness, malice, unchastity, fornication, avarice, iniquity. They are full of envy, murder'
(that is, of the souls of the people) 'contentiousness, guile, malignity;
they are whisperers, detractors, hated by God; stubborn, proud,
puffed up; contrivers of evil, disobedient to their parents; senseless,
faithless, without pity, without affection; though they had learned of the
justice of God, they did not understand that those who do such
things are worthy of death'.

98 Which of those I have named was free from all these evils in very
truth? Indeed, if there were such a one, he would perhaps come under
the following sentence: 'Not only those who do these things, but
those who consent to their doing' - for none of them is immune from
this evil. And below: 'But as a result of the hardness of your im-
penitent heart, you are laying up anger for yourself at the day of
wrath and the revelation of the just judgement of God, who will
2 reward everyone according to what he does'. And again: 'There is
no respect of persons in the presence of God. Whoever sinned outside
the law shall perish outside the law; while those who have sinned in
the law shall be judged at the law. It is not those who hear the law
that count as just with God: it is those who do the law that shall be
3 found just'. What harsh fate then is rushing upon these men, who
not only fail to do what they ought to do, and do not turn aside from
what is forbidden, but even shun, as though it were a savage snake,

72

the reading of the word of God when it is in the slightest degree brought to their attention.

99 But let us pass to what follows: 'What shall we say? Shall we continue in sin, that grace may abound? By no means. We are dead to our sin: how shall we live again in it?' And after a while: 'Who will separate us from the love of Christ? Shall tribulation, or hardship, or persecution, or hunger, or nakedness, or danger, or the sword?' Which of you, I ask, will find that emotion occupying his inmost heart? You do not labour for piety, indeed you suffer a great deal to act wickedly

2 and give offence to Christ. Or what follows: 'The night is far gone, the day approaches. Let us therefore throw away the works of darkness and put on the armour of light. Let us walk honourably, as in the daylight: not in fasting and drunkenness, not in lust and unchastity, not in contention and rivalry. But put on the Lord Jesus Christ, and take no thought for the flesh and its desires'.

100 And again in the first epistle to the Corinthians: 'Like a wise master-builder, I have laid the foundation for another man to build upon. Let each see to it how he builds. No man can lay any foundation except the foundation that is Jesus Christ. Now if any one builds on this foundation gold and silver, precious stones, wood, hay, straw, each work will be obvious: the day of the Lord will make it plain, for it will be revealed in the fire, and the fire will show what each man's work is like. But if any man's work lasts that he builds upon it, he will receive his reward. If any man's work goes up in flames, he will be the loser. Do you not know that you are the temple of God and that the spirit of God dwells within you? But if any man violate

2 the temple of God, God will destroy him'. And again: 'If any man is thought among you to be wise in this life, let him become stupid, that he may be wise. The wisdom of this world is foolishness before God'. And further on: 'Your boasting is not good. Do you not know that a little leaven taints the whole lump? So get rid of the old leaven, so that you can be a new dough'. How will the old leaven (that is, sin,

3 that is piled up daily in all your doings) be purged away? And again: 'I wrote to you in my letter not to mix with fornicators - not meaning literally the fornicators of this world, or greedy and rapacious and idolatrous men: otherwise you would have to leave this world. No, I meant you not to mix with anyone who is called brother but is in fact a fornicator or greedy or idolatrous or blasphemous or drunken or rapacious, and not even to take bread with them'. But a robber does not condemn another thief for theft or robbery; rather, he cherishes, protects and loves him as a partner in his crime.

101 Again, in the second epistle to the Corinthians: 'As we have this ministry, and seeing that we have received mercy, let us not fail; but let us cast away hidden infamies, and not walk in the ways of guile or taint the word of God' (that is, by setting a bad example, or

2 by flattery). But in what follows he speaks thus of evil teachers: 'For such men are false apostles, workers of deceit disguised as apostles of Christ. And no wonder: for Satan himself disguises himself as an angel of light. It is no great thing, then, if his attendants disguise themselves as angels of justice: and their end will be in accord with what they do'.

102 Listen too to what he says to the Ephesians. Do you not realise that you are held guilty here too? 'This I say and witness in the Lord, so that henceforth you do not walk as the heathen walk in the folly of their minds, their understanding obscured by shadows, estranged by their ignorance from the way of God - ignorance that is in them because of the blindness of their hearts. In their despair they have turned themselves over to unchastity, to do all that is unclean and

2 avaricious'. And which of you would of his own accord comply with what follows: 'Therefore do not be foolish, but understanding of the will of God, and do not make yourselves drunk with wine, in which lies debauchery, but be filled with the holy spirit'?

103 There is also what he says to the Thessalonians: 'We never used flattery with you, as you know, nor did we seize the opportunity to be avaricious. We did not seek honour from men, either you or others, when we can be a burden, like the other apostles of Christ. But we have been like little children in your midst, or like a nurse cherishing her little ones. Such was our love of you that we urgently desired to pass over to you not only the gospel, but our own souls too'. If you preserve this feeling of the apostle in all that you do, then you may know how to sit in his seat lawfully.

2 Or even what follows: 'You know my commands to you. This is the will of God and the means to your holiness, that you should abstain from fornication, that each of you should know how to possess his vessel in honour and holiness, not in the passion of desire, like the heathen who are ignorant of God. Let no one trick or deceive his brother in this matter, for the Lord punishes all these things. God called us not to uncleanness but to holiness. And so he who spurns these things is spurning not man but God'.

3 Which of you has cautiously and carefully kept to what follows: 'Therefore mortify your limbs that are upon the earth, fornication, uncleanness, lust and evil desire, for which the wrath of God comes upon the disobedient'? For you can see what sins especially arouse the anger of God.

104   And so listen to what the same holy apostle predicted in a spirit
of prophecy about you and your like, when he wrote openly to
Timothy: 'Know that in the last days dangerous times will threaten.
There will be men who love themselves, greedy, puffed up, proud,
blasphemous, disobedient to their parents, ungrateful, wicked, without
affection, uncontrolled, cruel, without kindness, traitors, provocative,
swollen, lovers of pleasure rather than of God, with a semblance of
piety but deniers of its virtue. Avoid these': as the prophet says: 'I
hated the assembly of the malignant and I shall not sit with the impious'.

2   Later on, he mentions something we see spreading in our time:
'Always learning and never coming to knowledge of the truth: they
resist truth as Jamnes and Jambres resisted Moses; men corrupt in mind,
traitors to the faith. But they shall not profit. Their folly will be
obvious to all, just as those men's was'.

105   Indeed, he makes it very clear in his letter to Titus how priests
should conduct themselves in office: 'Show yourself as an example of
good works, in learning, uprightness and seriousness: your word should
be sound and not to be reproached, so that he who is against you respects

2   you and has no evil to speak of us'. And again to Timothy: 'Labour
like a good soldier of Christ Jesus. No soldier of God involves himself
in affairs of this world, so that he may please him to whom he has
proved himself. For the contender in a wrestling bout, too, will not
get the crown unless he competes according to the rules'.

3   This is his exhortation to good men. But he also includes denunciation of bad men (which is what you appear to all thinking men):
'If any man teaches otherwise, and does not acquiesce in the sound
words of our Lord Jesus Christ and the teaching according to piety,
he is proud, ignorant, a doter on problems and disputes concerning
words: from which arise envy, contention, blasphemy, evil suspicion,
disputes between men who are corrupt at heart, men devoid of truth
who regard piety as profit'.

106   But why do I go on using scattered testimonies, and risk the
despised skiff of my intellect foundering (as it were) amid the waves of
different pronouncements? I think it necessary to have recourse
finally to the readings that have very properly been extracted from
almost the whole corpus of the sacred scriptures not only to be read
out, but also to add their support to the blessing by which the hands
of priests and ministers receive their initiation, and to teach them
perpetually not to degenerate in the dignity of priest or retreat from
the commands which are faithfully contained in them. By this means
it will become clearer to all men that those who do not fulfil the

teaching and instruction contained in these readings in practice, so far as they are able, are no priests or ministers of God, but have eternal punishments to look forward to.

2   Let us then hear what the chief of the apostles, Peter, made clear on such a matter: 'Blessed be God, father of our Lord Jesus Christ, who in his great mercy enabled us to be born again in the hope of eternal life by means of the resurrection from the dead of our Lord Jesus Christ, to a heritage incorruptible, never decaying, unstained, which is preserved in heaven for you who are guarded by the power of God'. Why do you foolishly violate such a heritage, which is not, like an earthly heritage, corruptible, but imperishable and eternal?

3   And further on: 'So gird up the loins of your mind, being sober and having perfect hope in the grace that is offered you in the revelation of Jesus Christ'. Search out the depths of your heart. Are you sober? Do you keep perfectly to the priestly grace that must be weighed in the balance when the Lord is revealed? And again he says: 'As sons of blessing, not shaping yourselves according to the former desires of your ignorance, but in the manner of him who called you to be holy, so be saint-like in all your dealings with men. For it is written: Be holy, because I am holy'. Which of you, may I ask, has pursued holiness so whole-heartedly that he is in a burning hurry to comply with this so far as lies in him?

4   But let us see what is contained in the second reading from the same apostle: 'Dearest ones, make your hearts pure to obey the faith, through the spirit, in charity and brotherhood, loving each other without cease from the heart, as if reborn, not from corruptible seed but from incorruptible, by the word of God, who lives and endures

107 for ever'. These things were prescribed by the apostle and read on the day of your ordination so that you should keep them unbroken. But you have not fulfilled them in judgement, nor have you pondered or understood them much. And below: 'Therefore laying aside all malice and all guile and pretence and envy and carping, be like newborn children, and desire the guileless milk of reason, that you may increase to salvation, for the Lord is sweet'. Consider whether, in this case too, it was with deaf ears that you heard these things, so that you con-

2 tinually trample them under foot. And again: 'You are a chosen stock: a royal priesthood, a holy race, a people adopted to announce the virtues of him who called you from the darkness into that wonderful light of his'. Not only do you fail to announce the virtues of God: those virtues are despised by every unbeliever because of the evil example you set.

3 Perhaps you did hear what was read on the same day from the Acts

of the Apostles: Peter got up in the midst of the disciples and said:
'Brothers, the writing must be fulfilled that was foretold by the
holy spirit through the mouth of David, concerning Judas': and a little

4 later: 'and so he purchased a field with the price of wickedness'. It was
with a careless or rather a dulled heart that you heard this, as though
the reading had no application to you. Which of you, I ask, does not
seek to purchase a field with the price of wickedness? Judas rifled purses:
you plunder the offerings made to the church and the souls of her sons.
He approached the Jews in order to sell God; you approach tyrants and
your father the devil in order to despise Christ. He thought the price
for the saviour of all men was thirty silver pieces; your price is but a
single groat.

108   What further? I bring before you to confound you the example of
Matthias [and the holy apostles]; he drew his lot not at his own will,
but by the choice and judgement of Christ. Yet you are blind to this
instance, and do not see how far removed you are from his merits: for
you have rushed headlong and of your own volition into the greed
and disposition of the traitor Judas.

2   It is quite clear, then, that anyone who calls you priests knowingly
and from his heart is no excellent Christian. I will tell you what I feel.
My reproach might be gentler; but what is the point of merely stroking
a wound or smearing it with ointment when it already festers with
swelling and stink, and requires cautery and the public remedy of fire?
- if indeed it can be cured at all when the sick man is not looking for
a cure and shrinks right away from this doctor.

3   O you are enemies of God and not priests, veterans in evil and not
bishops, traitors and not successors to the holy apostles or ministers of
Christ: you have heard the sound of the words in the second reading
from the apostle Paul, but you have in no way retained their warnings
or virtue. That day you stood at the altar like images that neither see
nor hear. Yet that day and every day Paul thunders at you: 'Brothers,
this saying is to be trusted' and is worthy of every respect. He spoke
of it as to be trusted and worthy, you have despised it as not to be
trusted and unworthy. 'If anyone desires a bishopric, he desires a
good work'. You desire a bishopric greatly, because of your avarice
and not on the pretext of the spiritual advancement it offers, and

4 you do not at all regard good work as suitable to it. 'Such a man must
therefore be beyond reproach'. Indeed in this saying there is cause for
tears rather than words, as if the apostle had said he ought to be further
beyond reproach than everyone else. 'The husband of one wife'. That too
is despised among us, as though it were not heard, or meant the same as
'husband of more than one wife'. 'Sober, prudent'. Which of you ever

even prayed that this should eventually be part of his character?

5 'Hospitable'. If that is by some chance complied with, it is because of the desire to be popular, not because of the command, and it is of no avail: for the Lord our saviour says: 'Indeed I say to you, they have received their reward'. 'Distinguished, not bibulous, not aggressive, but decent, not litigious, not greedy'. What a dire change! What a dreadful trampling underfoot of the precepts of heaven! You never tire, do you, of snatching up every weapon of word or deed to attack or rather overthrow these commands, when you ought to be ready, if need be, to offer yourself for punishment and even lay down your life to preserve and strengthen them?

109 But let us have a look at what follows: 'One who rules his house well, keeping his sons subject to him in all chastity'. So the chastity of fathers is incomplete unless it is crowned by that of his sons too. But what of a case where both the father and the son corrupted by his evil father's example are notoriously unchaste? 'But if a man does not know how to govern his own house, how can he give due attention to the church of God?' These are words proved by results that leave no room for doubt.

2 'Deacons similarly should be chaste, not deceitful, not much devoted to wine, not pursuers of base gain, possessing the mystery of the faith in a pure conscience. Let them be approved first, and so take up their ministry if they are free of all crime'. I do not care to dwell long on this appalling topic: but one thing I can say with truth, that all these things are in practice turned upside down, so that clerics (and I do not confess this without pain at heart) are unchaste, deceitful, drunken, greedy for base gain, possessing their faith - or rather their lack of it - in an impure conscience. They take up their ministry not approved in good works but known in advance for bad; and it is with innumerable crimes charged against them that they are called to the holy office.

3 You heard also on that day - a day on which it would have been more proper and correct for you to be dragged to prison or the scaffold for punishment rather than to the priesthood - that when the Lord asked who the disciples thought he was, Peter replied: 'You are Christ, son of the living God', and that the Lord said to him in reply to this confession: 'You are blessed, Simon Bar-Jona, because it is not flesh and blood that has given you this revelation but my father in heaven'. So Peter, taught by God the father, rightly confesses Christ; you, advised by your father the devil, wrongly deny the saviour

4 by your evil acts. To the true priest is said: 'You are Peter, and on this rock I shall build my church': while you are like 'the foolish man who built his house upon sand'. It should be observed that the Lord does

not assist the foolish in building their house on the doubtful shifting
of the sands, according to the saying: 'They have made kings for themselves and not through me'. And what follows has the same ring: 'And
the gates of hell shall not prevail' [and his sins are understood]. What
is the pronouncement on your doomed structure? 'The rivers came and
the winds blew and they beat on that house: and it fell, and great
was its ruin'.

5   To Peter and his successors the Lord says: 'And I shall give you the
keys of the kingdom of heaven': but to you: 'I do not know you,
depart from me, workers of iniquity', 'that you may go separately with
the goats on the left-hand side into eternal fire'. And again every holy
priest is promised: 'And whatever you loose on earth shall be loosed in
heaven too: and whatever you bind on earth will be bound in heaven
too'. But how will *you* loose anything so that it is loosed in heaven
too, seeing that you are removed from heaven because of your
crimes and bound with the ropes of dreadful sins, as Solomon too says:

6   'Each man is constrained by the cords of his sins'? And how will you
bind anything on earth that will be bound above the world also, except
for yourselves, who are held bound so tight with iniquities in this
world that you cannot at all ascend to heaven, but must fall into the
dreadful dungeons of hell, if you do not turn to the Lord in this life?

A Prayer for the Good Pastors

110   Nor should any priest applaud himself solely because he is conscious
that his own body is pure: for if some of those he is in charge of die
because of his ignorance or laziness or flattery, their souls shall be required on judgement day from his hands as though he had killed them.
Death comes no sweeter from the hand of a good man than that of a bad.
Otherwise the apostle would not have said, when he left as it were a father's
heritage to his successors: 'I am clean of the blood of all men. For I have
not shirked announcing to you the whole mystery of God.'.

2   You are drunk with the practising of constant sins, and shaken by
the waves of accumulated crimes that incessantly rush upon you; seek
then, as though you had suffered shipwreck, with all the striving of your
mind, for the single plank of penitence that can carry you to the land of
the living, so that the fury of the Lord may be turned away from you.
For in his mercy he said: 'I do not desire the death of a sinner, but that
he may turn and live'.

3   May the almighty God of all consolation and pity preserve the very
few good shepherds from all harm, and, conquering the common
enemy, make them citizens of the heavenly city of Jerusalem, that is,
of the congregation of all the saints: the Father, the Son, and the
holy spirit, to whom be honour and glory for ever and ever, Amen.

FRAGMENTS OF LOST LETTERS OF GILDAS

1 On excommunication Gildas says: Noah did not wish to keep his son Ham,
teacher of the magic art, away from the ark or from sharing his table.
Abraham did not shrink from Aner and Eschcol when he was
warring with the five kings. Lot did not curse the banquets of the Sodomites.
Isaac did not forbid Abimelech and Ahuzzath and Phichol, leader of
the army, to share his table: but they swore oaths to each other after
eating and drinking. Jacob was not afraid of contact with his sons,
whom he knew to be idolaters. Joseph did not refuse to share the table
and cup of Pharaoh. Aaron did not spurn the table of the priest of the
idols of Midian. Moses, too, lodged and banqueted in peace with
Jethro. Our Lord Jesus Christ did not avoid eating with publicans,
so as to save all sinners and whores.

2 On abstinence from food Gildas says: Abstinence from bodily food
is useless without charity. Those who do not fast unduly or abstain
over much from God's creation, while being careful in the sight of
God to preserve within them a clean heart (on which, as they know,
their life ultimately depends), are better than those who do not eat
flesh or take pleasure in the food of this world, or travel in
carriages or on horseback, and so regard themselves as superior to the
rest of men: to these death has entered through the windows of their
pride.

3 On the last days Gildas says in his letters: 'The worst of times will come:
men will be conceited, avaricious, arrogant, proud, blasphemous,
disobedient to parents, ungrateful, unclean, without affection,
without peace, accusers, intemperate, cruel, haters of the good,
traitors, rash, puffed up, lovers of pleasure rather than of God:
possessing the form of piety but denying its virtue'. Many shall
perish doing evil: as the apostle says, 'having zeal for God, but not
in accordance with knowledge, ignorant of the justice of God and
seeking to set up their own, they are not subject to God's justice'.
They find fault with all their brothers who have not joined them in
their arrogant contrivances. They eat bread by the measure — but
boast about it beyond measure; they use water — but at the same
time drink the cup of hatred; they enjoy dry fare — and at the
same time enjoy backbiting. They keep their vigils long, while
criticising others plunged in sleep, saying to the feet and the rest
of the limbs: If you are not the head, as I am, I shall reckon you at
naught. They give this promise not so much out of love as out of
scorn. Meditating on their lofty principles, they prefer slaves to
masters, the common people to kings, lead to gold, iron to silver, the
elm-prop to the vine. So they prefer fasting to charity, vigils to
justice, their own contrivances to concord, the cell to the church,

severity to humility, man (finally) to God. They take notice not of
what the gospel orders but of what they want; not of what the
apostle but of what their pride advises. For they do not observe that
the position of the stars in the sky, and the duties of the angels, are
unequal. These men fast; but unless this enthusiasm is for the sake of
other virtues it is of no profit. Those set themselves to do charity,
which is the highest fullness of the law; for they are taught by God.
As the harps of the holy spirit say: 'All our righteousness is like a
filthy rag'. But these bellows of the devil say to men who may be
better than they, men whose angels see the face of the Father:
'Depart from us; you are unclean'. The Lord replies:'They will be
smoke in my rage, and a fire that burns every day'. The Lord calls
blessed not those who despise their brothers, but the poor; not the
haughty, but the meek; not the envious, but those who mourn for their
own sins and those of others; those who hunger and thirst not for
water, in order to despise others, but for righteousness; not those who
regard others as of no account, but the merciful; those of a pure, not a
proud heart; not those who are harsh to others,but the peaceable; not
men who cause war, but men who endure persecution for righteousness'
sake and will surely attain the kingdom of heaven.

4 On monks who come from a worse to a better monastery Gildas says:
Where an abbot has so far fallen away from the work of God that he
deserves to be barred from the table of holy men and even to be loaded
with the charge of fornication, not on suspicion, but as a clearly
detected evil, you should welcome his monks with no scruple as ones
taking refuge with you from hell fire, without any consultation with
their abbot. But as for those whose abbot we do not, for any ill
reputation, bar from the table of holy men, we ought not to take them
in if he does not agree. Still less should we welcome those who come
from holy abbots under suspicion only because they possess animals and
vehicles because it is the custom of their country or because of their
weakness: these are things that do less harm to their owners, if they are
possessed in humility and patience, than is done to those who drag
ploughs and plunge spades in the ground in presumption and pride. But
if any monk has a superabundance of worldly things, that should be put
down as luxury and riches; but he will not be blamed for owning anything
he is compelled to possess by need rather than choice, so as to avoid
destitution. For the foremost ornaments of the body, bestowed on the
head, should not despise what is lower, just as the hands, which have
their daily uses, should not be haughty towards what is higher. Neither
(is it not so?) can say to the other: 'We have no need of your services';
for both are concerned with the common advantage of the same body.
I have said this so that the highest priests may know that, just as
inferior clergy should not despise them, so they should not despise the
clergy, just as the head, too, should not despise the rest of the limbs.

5   Gildas says: An abbot of a stricter rule should not admit a monk from the monastery of a somewhat laxer abbot; and a laxer abbot should not hold a monk of his back if he is inclined to stricter ways. For priests and bishops have a terrible judge; it is his task, not ours, to judge them in both worlds.

6   Gildas: 'Cursed is he who removes boundary stones, particularly those of his neighbour'. 'Let each in God stay where he is called': so that the chief should not be changed except at the choice of his subjects, nor the subject obtain the place of his superior without the advice of an elder. 'Those parts of us that are honourable we surround with more lavish honour'. Therefore it is quite proper for bishops and abbots to judge those beneath them, for their blood will be required at their hands by the Lord if they do not rule them well. But those who disobey their fathers shall be as the heathen and publicans. And to all men, good and bad, besides their own subjects, in the words of the apostle: 'Count all men....' and the rest.
    The judgement about the uncertain end to life comes home to us when we read in the scriptures that an apostle was destroyed by greed and that a thief confessed and was carried to heaven.

7   Again: It is better for fellow bishops and abbots, and also fellow subjects, not to judge each other. But let them gently and patiently reprove those in bad odour for some ill report, rather than openly accuse them; as far as they can in conscience, they should avoid them as suspect (without excommunicating them like true criminals or keeping them from their table or the Communion), unless it is absolutely necessary to meet and talk to them. But they should be told of their wrongdoing (for we cannot condemn them): they do not deserve to be communicants; yet at the same time we may perhaps, thanks to evil thoughts, be in communion with devils. But as for persons we know without doubt to be fornicators, we keep them from communion and our table, unless they do penance in the legitimate manner, according to the order they legitimately belong to. So: 'If any man is called a brother and is a fornicator....' and the rest. We should keep our brothers away from the communion of our altar and table, when circumstances demand, only in well proved cases of major sins.

8   Gildas: A wise man recognises the gleam of truth whoever utters it.

9   Gildas: Miriam was condemned to leprosy because she and Aaron agreed in blaming Moses because of his Ethiopian wife. We should be afraid of this fate when we disparage good princes for trifling faults.

10   Again: When the ship is holed, let the man who can swim swim.

APPENDIX

The 'Penitential of Gildas'*

*Text and translation by Ludwig Bieler. See above,
Note on Text and Translation, p. 12

HERE BEGINS THE PREFACE OF
GILDAS ON PENANCE

1.   A presbyter or a deacon committing natural fornication or
sodomy who has previously taken the monastic vow shall do penance
for three years. He shall seek pardon every hour and keep a special
fast once every week except during the fifty days following the
Passion. He shall have bread without limitation and a titbit fattened
slightly with butter on Sunday; on the other days a ration of dry
bread and a dish enriched with a little fat, garden vegetables, a few
eggs, British cheese, a Roman half-pint of milk in consideration of
the weakness of the body in this age, also a Roman pint of whey or
buttermilk for his thirst, and some water if he is a worker. He shall
have his bed meagrely supplied with hay. For the three forty-day
periods he shall add something as far as his strength permits. He
shall at all times deplore his guilt from his inmost heart. Above all
things let him show the readiest obedience. After a year and a half
he may receive the eucharist and come for the kiss of peace and
sing the psalms with his brethren, lest his soul perish utterly from
lacking so long a time the celestial medicine.

2.   If any monk of lower rank (does this), he shall do penance for
three years, but his allowance of bread shall be increased. If he is a
worker, he shall take a Roman pint of milk and another of whey and
as much water as the intensity of his thirst requires.

3.   If, however, it is a presbyter or a deacon without monastic vow
who has sinned, he shall do the same penance as a monk not in holy
orders.

4.   But if a monk (merely) intends to commit (such) a sin, (he shall
do penance) for a year and a half. The abbot has authority, however,
to modify this if his obedience is pleasing to God and the abbot.

5.   The ancient fathers commanded twelve (years) of penance for a
presbyter and seven for a deacon.

6.   A monk who has stolen a garment or any (other) thing shall do
penance for two years as stated above, if he is a junior; if a senior,
one entire year. If, however, he is not a monk, likewise a year, and
especially the three periods of forty days.

7.   If a monk after loading his stomach vomits the host during the
day, he shall not venture to take his supper; and if it is not on account
of infirmity he shall wipe out his offence with seven special fasts; if it
is from infirmity, not from gluttony, with four special fasts.

8.   But if it is not the host, he is to be punished with a special fast of
one day and with much reproach.

9. If someone by a mishap through carelessness loses a host, leaving it for beasts and birds to devour, he shall do penance for three forty-day periods.

10. But if on account of drunkenness someone is unable to sing the psalms, being benumbed and speechless, he shall be deprived of his supper.

11. One who sins with a beast shall expiate his guilt for a year; if by himself alone, for three forty-day periods.

12. One who holds communion with one who has been excommunicated by his abbot, forty days.

13. One who unwittingly eats carrion, forty days.

14. It is to be understood, however, that as long a time as a person remains in sin so long is he to do penance.

15. If a certain task has been enjoined on one and through contempt he leaves it undone, he shall go without supper; but if through an oversight, he shall go without half his daily portion.

16. But if he undertakes another's task, he shall modestly make this known to the abbot, none else hearing it, and he shall perform it if he is commanded to do so.

18. One who has been offended by anyone ought to make this known to the abbot, not indeed in the spirit of an accuser, but of a physician; and the abbot shall decide. 17. For he that for a long time holds anger in his heart is in (a state of) death.

But if he confesses his sin, he shall fast for forty days; and if he still persists in his sin, two forty-day periods. And if he does the same thing again, he shall be cut off from the body as a rotten member, since wrath breeds murder.

19. One who has not arrived by the end of the second psalm shall sing eight psalms in order. If when he has been aroused he comes after the reading, he shall repeat in order whatever the brethren have sung. But if he comes at the second reading, he shall go without supper.

20. If in error anyone has changed any of the words where 'danger' is noted (he shall do penance) for three days or perform three special fasts.

21. If by neglect the host has fallen to the ground (the offender) shall go without supper.

22. He who willingly has been defiled in sleep, if the monastic house is abundantly supplied with beer and flesh, shall make a standing vigil for three hours of the night if his health is strong. But if it has poor fare, standing as a suppliant he shall sing twenty-eight or thirty psalms or make satisfaction with extra work.

23. For good rulers we ought to offer the sacrifice, for bad ones on no account.

24. Presbyters are indeed not forbidden to offer for their bishops.
25. One who is accused of any fault and is checked as an inconsiderate person shall go without supper.
26. One who has broken a hoe which was not broken before, shall either make amends by an extraordinary work or perform a special fast.
27. One who sees any of his brethren violate the commands of the abbot ought not to conceal the fact from the abbot, but he ought first to admonish the offender to confess alone to the abbot the wrong he is doing. Let him be found not so much an informer as one who truly practises the rule.

THUS FAR GILDAS

DE EXCIDIO BRITONUM

1   In hac epistola quicquid deflendo potius quam declamando, vili   25
licet stilo, tamen benigno, fuero prosecutus, ne quis me affectu cunctos
spernentis omnibusve melioris, quippe qui commune bonorum dispendium
malorumque cumulum lacrimosis querelis defleam, sed condolentis patriae
incommoditatibus miseriisque eius ac remediis condelectantis edicturum
putet.

2   Quia non tam fortissimorum militum enuntiare trucis belli pericula
mihi statutum est quam desidiosorum, silui, fateor, cum inmenso cordis
dolore, ut mihi renum scrutator testis est dominus, spatio bilustri temporis
vel eo amplius praetereuntis, imperitia sic ut et nunc una cum vilibus me
meritis inhibentibus ne qualemcumque admonitiunculam scriberem.

3   Legebam nihilominus admirandum legislatorem ob unius verbi
dubitationem terram desiderabilem non introiisse: filios sacerdotis alienum
admovendo altari ignem cito exitu periisse: populum verborum dei
praevaricatorem sexcentorum milium duobus exceptis veracibus et quidem
deo carissimum, quippe cui iter levissime stratum profundi glarea maris
rubri, cibus caelestis panis, potus novus ex rupe viator, acies invicta
manuum sola intensa erectio fuerit, bestiis ferro igni per Arabiae deserta

4   sparsim cecidisse: post ingressum ignotae ac si Iordanis portae urbisque
adversa moenia solis tubarum clangoribus iussu dei subruta, palliolum
aurique parum de anathemate praesumptum multos stravisse:
Gabaonitarum irritum foedus, calliditate licet extortum, nonnullis intulisse
exitium: ob peccata hominum querulas sanctorum prophetarum voces et
maxime Hieremiae ruinam civitatis suae quadruplici plangentis alphabeto.

5   Videbamque etiam nostro tempore, ut ille defleverat, 'solam sedisse
urbem viduam, antea populis plenam, gentium dominam, principem   26
provinciarum, sub tributo fuisse factam', id est ecclesiam, 'obscuratum
aurum coloremque optimum mutatum', quod est verbi dei splendorem,
'filios Sion', id est sanctae matris ecclesiae, 'inclitos et amictos auro

6   primo, amplexatos fuisse stercora'; et quod illi intolerabiliter utpote

praecipuo, mihi quoque licet abiecto, utcumque ad cumulum doloris
crescebat dum ita eosdem statu prospero viventes egregios luxerat ut
diceret: 'candidiores Nazaraei eius nive, rubicundiores ebore antiquo,
sapphiro pulchriores'.

7 Ista ego et multa alia veluti speculum quoddam vitae nostrae in
scripturis veteribus intuens, convertebar etiam ad novas, et ibi legebam
clarius quae mihi forsitan antea obscura fuerant, cessante umbra ac veritate
8 firmius inlucescente. Legebam, inquam, dominum dixisse: 'non veni nisi
ad oves perditas domus Israel'. Et e contrario: 'filii autem regni huius
eicientur in tenebras exteriores, ibi erit fletus et stridor dentium'. Et
iterum: 'non est bonum tollere panem filiorum et mittere canibus'.

9 Itemque: 'vae vobis, scribae et Pharisaei, hypocritae'. Audiebam: 'multi ab
oriente et occidente venient et recumbent cum Abraham et Isaac et Iacob
in regno caelorum'; et e diverso: 'et tunc dicam eis: discedite a me,
operarii iniquitatis'. Legebam: 'beatae steriles et ubera quae non
lactaverunt'; et e contrario: 'quae paratae erant, intraverunt cum eo ad
nuptias, postea venerunt et reliquae virgines dicentes: domine, domine,
10 aperi nobis; quibus responsum fuerat: non novi vos'. Audiebam sane:
'qui crediderit et baptizatus fuerit, salvus erit, qui autem non crediderit,
condemnabitur'. Legebam apostoli voce oleastri ramum bonae olivae
insertum fuisse, sed a societate radicis pinguedinis eiusdem, si non
timuisset, sed alta saperet, excidendum.

11 Sciebam misericordiam domini, sed et iudicium timebam; laudabam
gratiam, sed redditionem unicuique secundum opera sua verebar; oves
unius ovilis dissimiles cernens merito beatissimum dicebam Petrum ob
Christi integram confessionem, at Iudam infelicissimum propter cupiditatis
amorem, Stephanum gloriosum ob martyrii palmam, sed Nicolaum
12 miserum propter immundae haereseos notam. Legebam certe: 'erant illis
omnia communia'; sed et quod dictum est: 'quare convenit vobis
temptare spiritum dei?' Videbam e regione quantum securitatis hominibus
nostri temporis, ac si non esset quod timeretur, increverat.

13 Haec igitur et multo plura quae brevitatis causa omittenda decrevimus
cum qualicumque cordis compunctione attonita mente saepius volvens, si,
inquam, peculiari ex omnibus nationibus populo, semini regali gentique
sanctae, ad quam dixerat: 'primogenitus meus Israel', eiusque sacerdotibus,
prophetis, regibus, per tot saecula apostolo ministro membrisque illius
primitivae ecclesiae dominus non pepercit, cum a recto tramite deviarint,
quid tali huius atramento aetatis facturus est? cui praeter illa nefanda   27
immaniaque peccata quae communiter cum omnibus mundi sceleratis
agit, accedit etiam illud veluti ingenitum quid et indelebile insipientiae
pondus et levitatis ineluctabile.

14 Quid? (mihimet aio) tibine, miser, veluti conspicuo ac summo doctori
talis cura committitur ut obstes ictibus tam violenti torrentis, et contra

hunc inolitorum scelerum funem per tot annorum spatia ininterrupte lateque protractum? Serves depositum tibi creditum et taceas. Alioquin hoc est dixisse pedi: speculare et manui: fare. Habet Britannia rectores, habet speculatores. Quid tu nugando mutire disponis? Habet, inquam, habet, si non ultra, non citra numerum. Sed quia inclinati tanto pondere sunt pressi, idcirco spatium respirandi non habent.

15   Praeoccupabant igitur se mutuo talibus obiectionibus vel multo his mordacioribus veluti condebitores sensus mei. Hi non parvo, ut dixi, tempore, cum legerim 'tempus esse loquendi et tacendi', et in quadam ac si angusta timoris porticu luctabantur. Obtinuit vicitque tandem aliquando creditor, si non es, inquiens, talis audaciae ut inter veridicas rationalis secundae a nuntiis derivationis creaturas non pertimescas libertatis aureae decenti nota inuri, affectum saltem intellegibilis asinae eatenus elinguis non refugito spiritu dei afflatae, nolentis se vehiculum fore tiarati magi devoturi populum dei, quae in angusto maceriae vinearum resolutum eius attrivit pedem, ob id licet verbera hostiliter senserit, cuique angelum caelestem ensem vacuum vagina habentem atque contrarium, quem ille cruda stoliditate caecatus non viderat, digito quodammodo, quamquam ingrato ac furibundo et innoxia eius latera contra ius fasque caedenti, demonstravit.

16   In zelo igitur domus domini sacrae legis seu cogitatuum rationibus vel fratrum religiosis precibus coactus nunc persolvo debitum multo tempore antea exactum, vile quidem, sed fidele, ut puto, et amicale quibusque egregiis Christi tironibus, grave vero et importabile apostatis insipientibus. Quorum priores, ni fallor, cum lacrimis forte quae ex dei caritate profluunt, alii autem cum tristitia, sed quae de indignatione et pusillanimitate deprehensae conscientiae extorquetur, illud excipient.

2   Sed ante promissum deo volente pauca de situ, de contumacia, de subiectione, de rebellione, item de subiectione ac diro famulatu, de religione, de persecutione, de sanctis martyribus, de diversis haeresibus,   28 de tyrannis, de duabus gentibus vastatricibus, de defensione itemque vastatione, de secunda ultione tertiaque vastatione, de fame, de epistolis ad Agitium, de victoria, de sceleribus, de nuntiatis subito hostibus, de famosa peste, de consilio, de saeviore multo primis hoste, de urbium subversione, de reliquiis, de postrema patriae victoria, quae temporibus nostris dei nutu donata est, dicere conamur.

3   Brittannia insula in extremo ferme orbis limite circium occidentemque versus divina, ut dicitur, statera terrae totius ponderatrice librata ab Africo boriali propensius tensa axi, octingentorum in longo milium, ducentorum in lato spatium, exceptis diversorum prolixioribus promontoriorum tractibus, quae arcuatis oceani sinibus ambiuntur, tenens, cuius diffusiore et, ut ita dicam, intransmeabili undique circulo absque meridianae freto

plagae, quo ad Galliam Belgicam navigatur, vallata, duorum ostiis nobilium fluminum Tamesis ac Sabrinae veluti brachiis, per quae eidem olim transmarinae deliciae ratibus vehebantur, aliorumque minorum meliorata,

2 bis denis bisque quaternis civitatibus ac nonnullis castellis, murorum turrium serratarum portarum domorum, quarum culmina minaci proceritate porrecta in edito forti compage pangebantur, munitionibus

3 non improbabiliter instructis decorata; campis late pansis collibusque amoeno situ locatis, praepollenti culturae aptis, montibus alternandis animalium pastibus maxime convenientibus, quorum diversorum colorum flores humanis gressibus pulsati non indecentem ceu picturam eisdem

4 imprimebant, electa veluti sponsa monilibus diversis ornata, fontibus lucidis crebris undis niveas veluti glareas pellentibus, pernitidisque rivis leni murmure serpentibus ipsorumque in ripis accubantibus suavis soporis pignus praetendentibus, et lacubus frigidum aquae torrentem vivae exundantibus irrigua. 29

4 Haec erecta cervice et mente, ex quo inhabitata est, nunc deo, interdum civibus, nonnumquam etiam transmarinis regibus et subiectis ingrata consurgit. Quid enim deformius quidque iniquius potest humanis ausibus vel esse vel intromitti negotium quam deo timorem, bonis civibus caritatem, in altiore dignitate positis absque fidei detrimento debitum denegare honorem et frangere divino sensui humanoque fidem, et abiecto caeli terraeque metu propriis adinventionibus aliquem et libidinibus regi?

2 Igitur omittens priscos illos communesque cum omnibus gentibus errores, quibus ante adventum Christi in carne omne humanum genus obligabatur astrictum, nec enumerans patriae portenta ipsa diabolica paene numero Aegyptiaca vincentia, quorum nonnulla liniamentis adhuc deformibus intra vel extra deserta moenia solito more rigentia torvis

3 vultibus intuemur, neque nominatim inclamitans montes ipsos aut colles vel fluvios olim exitiabiles, nunc vero humanis usibus utiles, quibus divinus honor a caeco tunc populo cumulabatur, et tacens vetustos immanium tyrannorum annos, qui in aliis longe positis regionibus vulgati sunt, ita ut Pòrphyrius rabidus orientalis adversus ecclesiam canis dementiae suae ac vanitatis stilo hoc etiam adnecteret: 'Britannia',

4 inquiens, 'fertilis provincia tyrannorum', illa tantum proferre conabor in medium quae temporibus imperatorum Romanorum et passa est et aliis intulit civibus et longe positis mala: quantum tamen potuero, non tam ex scriptis patriae scriptorumve monimentis, quippe quae, vel si qua fuerint, aut ignibus hostium exusta aut civium exilii classe longius deportata non compareant, quam transmarina relatione, quae crebris inrupta intercapedinibus non satis claret.

5 Etenim reges Romanorum cum orbis imperium obtinuissent

subiugatisque finitimis quibusque regionibus vel insulis orientem versus
primam Parthorum pacem Indorum confinium, qua peracta in omni
paene terra tum cessavere bella, potioris famae viribus firmassent, non
acies flammae quodammodo rigidi tenoris ad occidentem caeruleo
2 oceani torrente potuit vel cohiberi vel extingui, sed transfretans   30
insulae parendi leges nullo obsistente advexit, imbellemque populum
sed infidelem non tam ferro igne machinis, ut alias gentes, quam solis
minis vel iudiciorum concussionibus, in superficie tantum vultus presso
in altum cordis dolore sui oboedientiam proferentem edictis subiugavit.
6   Quibus statim Romam ob inopiam, ut aiebant, cespitis repedantibus
et nihil de rebellione suspicantibus rectores sibi relictos ad enuntianda
plenius vel confirmanda Romani regni molimina leaena trucidavit
2 dolosa. Quibus ita gestis cum talia senatui nuntiarentur et propero
exercitu vulpeculas ut fingebat subdolas ulcisci festinaret, non militaris
in mari classis parata fortiter dimicare pro patria nec quadratum agmen
neque dextrum cornu aliive belli apparatus in litore conseruntur, sed
terga pro scuto fugantibus dantur et colla gladiis, gelido per ossa
tremore currente, manusque vinciendae muliebriter protenduntur, ita ut
in proverbium et derisum longe lateque efferretur quod Britanni nec in
bello fortes sint nec in pace fideles.
7   Itaque multis Romani perfidorum caesis, nonnullis ad servitutem, ne
terra penitus in solitudinem redigeretur, mancipalibus reservatis, patria
vini oleique experte Italiam petunt, suorum quosdam relinquentes
praepositos indigenarum dorsis mastigias, cervicibus iugum, solo nomen
Romanae servitutis haerere facturos ac non tam militari manu quam
flagris callidam gentem maceraturos et, si res sic postulavisset, ensem,
ut dicitur, vagina vacuum lateri eius accommodaturos, ita ut non
Britannia, sed Romania censeretur et quicquid habere potuisset aeris
argenti vel auri imagine Caesaris notaretur.
8   Interea glaciali frigore rigenti insulae et velut longiore terrarum
secessu soli visibili non proximae verus ille non de firmamento solum
temporali sed de summa etiam caelorum arce tempora cuncta
excedente universo orbi praefulgidum sui coruscum ostendens,   31
tempore, ut scimus, summo Tiberii Caesaris, quo absque ullo impedimento
eius propagabatur religio, comminata senatu nolente a principe morte
delatoribus militum eiusdem, radios suos primum indulget, id est sua
praecepta, Christus.
9   Quae, licet ab incolis tepide suscepta sunt, apud quosdam tamen
integre et alios minus usque ad persecutionem Diocletiani tyranni
novennem, in qua subversae per totum mundum sunt ecclesiae et cunctae
sacrae scripturae, quae inveniri potuerunt, in plateis exustae et electi
sacerdotes gregis domini cum innocentibus ovibus trucidati, ita ut ne

vestigium quidem, si fieri potuisset, in nonnullis provinciis Christianae
2 religionis appareret, permansere. Tunc quantae fugae, quantae strages,
quantae diversarum mortium poenae, quantae apostatarum ruinae,
quantae gloriosorum martyrum coronae, quanti persecutorum rabidi
furores, quantae e contrario sanctorum patientiae fuere, ecclesiastica
historia narrat, ita ut agmine denso certatim relictis post tergum mundia-
libus tenebris ad amoena caelorum regna quasi ad propriam sedem tota
festinaret ecclesia.

10   Magnificavit igitur misericordiam suam nobiscum deus volens omnes
homines salvos fieri et vocans non minus peccatores quam eos qui se
putant iustos. Qui gratuito munere, supra dicto ut conicimus persecutionis
tempore, ne penitus crassa atrae noctis caligine Britannia obfuscaretur,
2 clarissimos lampades sanctorum martyrum nobis accendit, quorum nunc
corporum sepulturae et passionum loca, si non lugubri divortio barbarorum
quam plurima ob scelera nostra civibus adimerentur, non minimum
intuentium mentibus ardorem divinae caritatis incuterent: sanctum
Albanum Verolamiensem, Aaron et Iulium Legionum urbis cives ceterosque
utriusque sexus diversis in locis summa magnanimitate in acie Christi
perstantes dico.

11   Quorum prior postquam caritatis gratia confessorem persecutoribus
insectatum et iam iamque comprehendendum, imitans et in hoc Christum
animam pro ovibus ponentem, domo primum ac mutatis dein mutuo
vestibus occuluit et se discrimini in fratris supra dicti vestimentis   32
libenter persequendum dedit, ita deo inter sacram confessionem
cruoremque coram impiis Romana tum stigmata cum horribili fantasia
praeferentibus placens signorum miraculis mirabiliter adornatus est, ut
oratione ferventi illi Israeliticae arenti viae minusque tritae, stante diu
arca prope glareas testamenti in medio Iordanis canali, simile iter ignotum,
trans Tamesis nobilis fluvii alveum, cum mille viris sicco ingrediens pede
suspensis utrimque modo praeruptorum fluvialibus montium gurgitibus
aperiret et priorem carnificem tanta prodigia videntem in agnum ex lupo
mutaret et una secum triumphalem martyrii palmam sitire vehementius et
excipere fortius faceret.

2   Ceteri vero sic diversis cruciatibus torti sunt et inaudita membrorum
discerptione lacerati ut absque cunctamine gloriosi in egregiis Ierusalem
veluti portis martyrii sui trophaea defigerent. Nam qui superfuerant silvis
ac desertis abditisque speluncis se occultavere, expectantes a iusto rectore
omnium deo carnificibus severa quandoque iudicia, sibi vero animarum
tutamina.

12   Igitur bilustro supra dicti turbinis necdum ad integrum expleto
emarcescentibusque nece suorum auctorum nefariis edictis, laetis
luminibus omnes Christi tirones quasi post hiemalem ac prolixam noctem

92

2 temperiem lucemque serenam aurae caelestis excipiunt. Renovant
ecclesias ad solum usque destructas; basilicas sanctorum martyrum
fundant construunt perficiunt ac velut victricia signa passim propalant.
Dies festos celebrant, sacra mundo corde oreque conficiunt. Omnes
exultant filii gremio ac si matris ecclesiae confoti.

3   Mansit namque haec Christi capitis membrorumque consonantia
suavis, donec Arriana perfidia, atrox ceu anguis, transmarina nobis
evomens venena fratres in unum habitantes exitiabiliter faceret seiungi, ac
sic quasi via facta trans oceanum omnes omnino bestiae ferae mortiferum
cuiuslibet haereseos virus horrido ore vibrantes letalia dentium vulnera
patriae novi semper aliquid audire volenti et nihil certe stabiliter optinenti
infigebant.

13   Itemque tandem tyrannorum virgultis crescentibus et in immanem
silvam iam iamque erumpentibus insula, nomen Romanum nec tamen
morem legemque tenens, quin potius abiciens germen suae plantationis
amarissimae, ad Gallias magna comitante satellitum caterva, insuper   33
etiam imperatoris insignibus, quae nec decenter usquam gessit, non
legitime, sed ritu tyrannico et tumultuante initiatum milite, Maximum

2 mittit. Qui callida primum arte potius quam virtute finitimos quosque
pagos vel provincias contra Romanum statum per retia periurii mendaciique
sui facinoroso regno adnectens, et unam alarum ad Hispaniam, alteram ad
Italiam extendens et thronum iniquissimi imperii apud Treveros statuens
tanta insania in dominos debacchatus est ut duos imperatores legitimos,
unum Roma, alium religiosissima vita pelleret. Nec mora tam feralibus
vallatus audaciis apud Aquileiam urbem capite nefando caeditur, qui
decorata totius orbis capita regni quodammodo deiecerat.

14   Exin Britannia omni armato milite, militaribus copiis, rectoribus licet
immanibus, ingenti iuventute spoliata, quae comitata vestigiis supra dicti
tyranni domum nusquam ultra rediit, et omnis belli usus ignara penitus,
duabus primum gentibus transmarinis vehementer saevis, Scotorum a
circione, Pictorum ab aquilone calcabilis, multos stupet gemitque annos.

15   Ob quarum infestationem ac dirissimam depressionem legatos Romam
cum epistolis mittit, militarem manum ad se vindicandam lacrimosis
postulationibus poscens et subiectionem sui Romano imperio continue tota

2 animi virtute, si hostis longius arceretur, vovens. Cui mox destinatur legio
praeteriti mali immemor, sufficienter armis instructa, quae ratibus trans
oceanum in patriam advecta et cominus cum gravibus hostibus congressa
magnamque ex eis multitudinem sternens et omnes e finibus depulit et
subiectos cives tam atroci dilacerationi ex imminenti captivitate liberavit.

3 Quos iussit construere inter duo maria trans insulam murum, ut esset
arcendis hostibus turba instructus terrori civibusque tutamini; qui vulgo
irrationabili absque rectore factus non tam lapidibus quam cespitibus non
profuit.

16   Illa domum cum triumpho magno et gaudio repedante illi priores
inimici ac si ambrones lupi profunda fame rabidi, siccis faucibus ovile   34
transilientes non comparente pastore, alis remorum remigumque
brachiis ac velis vento sinuatis vecti, terminos rumpunt caeduntque omnia
et quaeque obvia maturam ceu segetem metunt calcant transeunt.

17   Itemque mittuntur queruli legati, scissis, ut dicitur, vestibus,
opertisque sablone capitibus, inpetrantes a Romanis auxilia ac veluti
timidi pulli patrum fidissimis alis succumbentes, ne penitus misera patria
deleretur nomenque Romanorum, quod verbis tantum apud eos auribus
2   resultabat, vel exterarum gentium opprobrio obrosum vilesceret. At illi,
quantum humanae naturae possibile est, commoti tantae historia tragoe-
diae, volatus ceu aquilarum equitum in terra, nautarum in mari cursus
accelerantes, inopinatos primum, tandem terribiles inimicorum cervicibus
infigunt mucronum ungues, casibusque foliorum tempore certo adsimilan-
dam hisdem peragunt stragem, ac si montanus torrens crebris tempestatum
rivulis auctus sonoroque meatu alveos exundans ac sulcato dorso fronteque
acra, erectis, ut aiunt, ad nebulas undis (luminum quibus pupilli, persaepe
licet palpebrarum convolatibus innovati, adiunctis rimarum rotantium
lineis fuscantur) mirabiliter spumans, ast uno obiectas sibi evincit gurgite
3   moles. Ita aemulorum agmina auxiliares egregii, si qua tamen evadere
potuerant, praepropere trans maria fugaverunt, quia anniversarias avide
praedas nullo obsistente trans maria exaggerabant.

18   Igitur Romani, patriae denuntiantes nequaquam se tam laboriosis
expeditionibus posse frequentius vexari et ob imbelles erraticosque
latrunculos Romana stigmata, tantum talemque exercitum, terra ac mari
fatigari, sed ut potius sola consuescendo armis ac viriliter dimicando
terram substantiolam coniuges liberos et, quod his maius est, libertatem
vitamque totis viribus vindicaret, et gentibus nequaquam sibi fortioribus,
nisi segnitia et torpore dissolveretur, inermes vinculis vinciendas nullo
modo, sed instructas peltis ensibus hastis et ad caedem promptas
2   protenderet manus, suadentes, quia et hoc putabant aliquid   35
derelinquendo populo commodi adcrescere, murum non ut alterum,
sumptu publico privatoque adiunctis secum miserabilibus indigenis, solito
structurae more, tramite a mari usque ad mare inter urbes, quae ibidem
forte ob metum hostium collocatae fuerant, directo librant; fortia
formidoloso populo monita tradunt, exemplaria instituendorum
3   armorum relinquunt. In litore quoque oceani ad meridianam plagam,
quo naves eorum habebantur, quia et inde barbaricae ferae bestiae
timebantur, turres per intervalla ad prospectum maris collocant, et
valedicunt tamquam ultra non reversuri.

19   Itaque illis ad sua remeantibus emergunt certatim de curucis, quibus
sunt trans Tithicam vallem evecti, quasi in alto Titane incalescenteque
caumate de artissimis foraminum caverniculis fusci vermiculorum cunei,

tetri Scottorum Pictorumque greges, moribus ex parte dissidentes, sed
una eademque sanguinis fundendi aviditate concordes furciferosque magis
vultus pilis quam corporum pudenda pudendisque proxima vestibus
tegentes, cognitaque condebitorum reversione et reditus denegatione solito
confidentiores omnem aquilonalem extremamque terrae partem pro

2   indigenis muro tenus capessunt. Statuitur ad haec in edito arcis acies,
segnis ad pugnam, inhabilis ad fugam, trementibus praecordiis inepta,
quae diebus ac noctibus stupido sedili marcebat. Interea non cessant
uncinata nudorum tela, quibus miserrimi cives de muris tracti solo
allidebantur. Hoc scilicet eis proficiebat immaturae mortis supplicium qui
tali funere rapiebantur, quo fratrum pignorumque suorum miserandas
imminentes poenas cito exitu devitabant.

3   Quid plura? relictis civitatibus muroque celso iterum civibus fugae,
iterum dispersiones solito desperabiliores, iterum ab hoste insectationes,
iterum strages accelerantur crudeliores; et sicut agni a lanionibus, ita
deflendi cives ab inimicis discerpuntur ut commoratio eorum ferarum

4   assimilaretur agrestium. Nam et ipsos mutuo, perexigui victus brevi
sustentaculo miserrimorum civium, latrocinando temperabant: et
augebantur externae clades domesticis motibus, quod huiuscemodi tam
crebis direptionibus vacuaretur omnis regio totius cibi baculo, excepto
venatoriae artis solacio.

20   Igitur rursum miserae mittentes epistolas reliquiae ad Agitium   36
Romanae potestatis virum, hoc modo loquentes: 'Agitio ter consuli
gemitus Britannorum;' et post pauca querentes: 'repellunt barbari ad
mare, repellit mare ad barbaros; inter haec duo genera funerum aut
iugulamur aut mergimur;' nec pro eis quicquam adiutorii habent.

2   Interea famis dira ac famosissima vagis ac nutabundis haeret, quae
multos eorum cruentis compulit praedonibus sine dilatione victas dare
manus, ut pauxillum ad refocillandam animam cibi caperent, alios vero
nusquam: quin potius de ipsis montibus, speluncis ac saltibus, dumis

3   consertis continue rebellabant. Et tum primum inimicis per multos annos
praedas in terra agentibus strages dabant, non fidentes in homine, sed in
deo, secundum illud Philonis: 'necesse est adesse divinum, ubi humanum
cessat auxilium'. Quievit parumper inimicorum audacia nec tamen
nostrorum malitia; recesserunt hostes a civibus nec cives a suis sceleribus.

21   Moris namque continui erat genti, sicut et nunc est, ut infirma esset
ad retundenda hostium tela et fortis esset ad civilia bella et peccatorum
onera sustinenda, infirma, inquam, ad exequenda pacis ac veritatis insignia
et fortis ad scelera et mendacia. Revertuntur ergo impudentes grassatores
Hiberni domos, post non longum temporis reversuri. Picti in extrema
parte insulae tunc primum et deinceps requieverunt, praedas et

2   contritiones nonnumquam facientes. In talibus itaque indutiis desolato

populo saeva cicatrix obducitur, fame alia virulentiore tacitus pullulante.
Quiescente autem vastitate tantis abundantiarum copiis insula affluebat ut
nulla habere tales retro aetas meminisset, cum quibus omnimodis et luxuria
crescit. Crevit etenim germine praepollenti, ita ut competenter eodem
tempore diceretur: 'omnino talis auditur fornicatio qualis nec inter gentes'.

3   Non solum vero hoc vitium, sed et omnia quae humanae naturae
accidere solent, et praecipue, quod et nunc quoque in ea totius boni   37
evertit statum, odium veritatis cum assertoribus amorque mendacii
cum suis fabricatoribus, susceptio mali pro bono, veneratio nequitiae pro
benignitate, cupido tenebrarum pro sole, exceptio Satanae pro angelo

4 lucis. Ungebantur reges non per deum sed qui ceteris crudeliores exstarent,
et paulo post ab unctoribus non pro veri examinatione trucidabantur aliis
electis trucioribus. Si quis vero eorum mitior et veritati aliquatenus propior
videretur, in hunc quasi Britanniae subversorem omnium odia telaque

5 sine respectu contorquebantur, et omnia quae displicuerunt deo et quae
placuerunt aequali saltem lance pendebantur, si non gratiora fuissent
displicentia; ita ut merito patriae illud propheticum, quod veterno illi
populo denuntiatum est, potuerit aptari, 'filii' inquiens 'sine lege,
dereliquistis deum, et ad iracundiam provocastis sanctum Israel. Quid
adhuc percutiemini apponentes iniquitatem? Omne caput languidum et
omne cor maerens: a planta pedis usque ad verticem non est in eo sanitas.'

6 Sicque agebant cuncta quae saluti contraria fuerint, ac si nihil mundo
medicinae a vero omnium medico largiretur. Et non solum haec
saeculares viri, sed et ipse grex domini eiusque pastores, qui exemplo
esse omni plebi debuerint, ebrietate quam plurimi quasi vino madidi
torpebant resoluti et animositatum tumore, iurgiorum contentione,
invidiae rapacibus ungulis, indiscreto boni malique iudicio carpebantur,
ita ut perspicue, sicut et nunc est, effundi videretur contemptio super
principes, seduci vanis eorum et errare in invio et non in via.

22   Interea volente deo purgare familiam suam et tanta malorum labe
infectam auditu tantum tribulationis emendare, non ignoti rumoris
penniger ceu volatus arrectas omnium penetrat aures iamiamque adventus
veterum volentium penitus delere et inhabitare solito more a fine usque
ad terminum regionem. Nequaquam tamen ob hoc proficiunt, sed
comparati iumentis insipientibus strictis, ut dicitur, morsibus rationis
frenum offirmantes, per latam diversorum vitiorum morti proclive   38
ducentem, relicto salutari licet arto itinere, discurrebant viam.

2   Dum ergo, ut Salomon ait, 'servus durus non emendatur verbis',
flagellatur stultus et non sentit, pestifera namque lues feraliter insipienti
populo incumbit, quae in brevi tantam eius multitudinem remoto
mucrone sternit, quantam ne possint vivi humare. Sed ne hac quidem
emendantur, ut illud Esaiae prophetae in eo quoque impleretur dicentis:

'et vocavit deus ad planctum et ad calvitium et ad cingulum sacci: ecce
vitulos occidere et iugulare arietes, ecce manducare et bibere et dicere:
3 manducemus et bibamus, cras enim moriamur'. Appropinquabat
siquidem tempus quo eius iniquitates, ut olim Amorrhaeorum,
complerentur. Initur namque consilium quid optimum quidve saluberrim-
um ad repellendas tam ferales et tam crebras supra dictarum gentium
irruptiones praedasque decerni deberet.

23   Tum omnes consiliarii una cum superbo tyranno caecantur, adin-
venientes tale praesidium, immo excidium patriae ut ferocissimi illi nefandi
nominis Saxones deo hominibusque invisi, quasi in caulas lupi, in insulam
2 ad retundendas aquilonales gentes intromitterentur. Quo utique nihil ei
usquam perniciosius nihilque amarius factum est. O altissimam sensus
caliginem! o desperabilem crudamque mentis hebetudinem! Quos
propensius morte, cum abessent, tremebant, sponte, ut ita dicam, sub
unius tecti culmine invitabant: 'stulti principes', ut dictum est, 'Taneos
dantes Pharaoni consilium insipiens'.

3   Tum erumpens grex catulorum de cubili leaenae barbarae, tribus, ut
lingua eius exprimitur, cyulis, nostra longis navibus, secundis velis omine
auguriisque, quibus vaticinabatur, certo apud eum praesagio, quod ter
centum annis patriam, cui proras librabat, insideret, centum vero quin-
4 quaginta, hoc est dimidio temporis, saepius vastaret, evectus, primum in
orientali parte insulae iubente infausto tyranno terribiles infixit ungues,
quasi pro patria pugnaturus sed eam certius impugnaturus. Cui supradicta
genetrix, comperiens primo agmini fuisse prosperatum, item mittit   39
satellitum canumque prolixiorem catastam, quae ratibus advecta
adunatur cum manipularibus spuriis. Inde germen iniquitatis, radix
amaritudinis, virulenta plantatio nostris condigna meritis, in nostro cespite,
5 ferocibus palmitibus pampinisque pullulat. Igitur intromissi in insulam
barbari, veluti militibus et magna, ut mentiebantur, discrimina pro bonis
hospitibus subituris, impetrant sibi annonas dari: quae multo tempore
impertitae clauserunt, ut dicitur, canis faucem. Item queruntur non
affluenter sibi epimenia contribui, occasiones de industria colorantes, et
ni profusior eis munificentia cumularetur, testantur se cuncta insulae
rupto foedere depopulaturos. Nec mora, minas effectibus prosequuntur.

24   Confovebatur namque ultionis iustae praecedentium scelerum causa
de mari usque ad mare ignis orientali sacrilegorum manu exaggeratus, et
finitimas quasque civitates agrosque populans non quievit accensus donec
cunctam paene exurens insulae superficiem rubra occidentalem trucique
2 oceanum lingua delamberet. In hoc ergo impetu Assyrio olim in
Iudaeam comparando completur quoque in nobis secundum historiam
quod propheta deplorans ait: 'incenderunt igni sanctuarium tuum in
terra, polluerunt tabernaculum nominis tui', et iterum: 'deus, venerunt

gentes in hereditatem tuam; coinquinarunt templum sanctum tuum', et
3 cetera: ita ut cunctae coloniae crebris arietibus omnesque coloni cum
praepositis ecclesiae, cum sacerdotibus ac populo, mucronibus undique
micantibus ac flammis crepitantibus, simul solo sternerentur, et
miserabili visu in medio platearum ima turrium edito cardine evulsarum
murorumque celsorum saxa, sacra altaria, cadaverum frusta, crustis ac si
gelantibus purpurei cruoris tecta, velut in quodam horrendo torculari
4 mixta viderentur, et nulla esset omnimodis praeter domorum ruinas,
bestiarum volucrumque ventres in medio sepultura, salva sanctarum
animarum reverentia, si tamen multae inventae sint quae arduis caeli id
temporis a sanctis angelis veherentur. Ita enim degeneraverat tunc vinea
illa olim bona in amaritudinem uti raro, secundum prophetam, videretur
quasi post tergum vindemiatorum aut messorum racemus vel spica.

25 Itaque nonnulli miserarum reliquiarum in montibus deprehensi 40
acervatim iugulabantur: alii fame confecti accedentes manus hostibus
dabant in aevum servituri, si tamen non continuo trucidarentur, quod
altissimae gratiae stabat loco: alii transmarinas petebant regiones cum
ululatu magno ceu celeumatis vice hoc modo sub velorum sinibus
cantantes: 'dedisti nos tamquam oves escarum et in gentibus dispersisti
nos': alii montanis collibus minacibus praeruptis vallatis et densissimis
saltibus marinisque rupibus vitam suspecta semper mente credentes, in
patria licet trepidi perstabant.

2 Tempore igitur interveniente aliquanto, cum recessissent domum
crudelissimi praedones, roborante deo reliquiae, quibus confugiunt
undique de diversis locis miserrimi cives, tam avide quam apes alveari
procella imminente, simul deprecantes eum toto corde et, ut dicitur,
innumeris 'onerantes aethera votis', ne ad internicionem usque delerentur,
3 duce Ambrosio Aureliano viro modesto, qui solus forte Romanae gentis
tantae tempestatis collisione occisis in eadem parentibus purpura
nimirum indutis superfuerat, cuius nunc temporibus nostris suboles
magnopere avita bonitate degeneravit, vires capessunt, victores pro-
vocantes ad proelium: quis victoria domino annuente cessit.

26 Ex eo tempore nunc cives, nunc hostes, vincebant, ut in ista gente
experiretur dominus solito more praesentem Israelem, utrum diligat eum
an non: usque ad annum obsessionis Badonici montis, novissimaeque
ferme de furciferis non minimae stragis, quique quadragesimus quartus
(ut novi) orditur annus mense iam uno emenso, qui et meae nativitatis
est.

2 Sed ne nunc quidem, ut antea, civitates patriae inhabitantur; sed
desertae dirutaeque hactenus squalent, cessantibus licet externis bellis,
sed non civilibus. Haesit etenim tam desperati insulae excidii insperatique

98

mentio auxilii memoriae eorum qui utriusque miraculi testes extitere: et
ob hoc reges, publici, privati, sacerdotes, ecclesiastici, suum quique   41

3   ordinem servarunt. At illis decedentibus cum successisset aetas
tempestatis illius nescia et praesentis tantum serenitatis experta, ita
cuncta veritatis ac iustitiae moderamina concussa ac subversa sunt ut
earum non dicam vestigium sed ne monimentum quidem in supra dictis
propemodum ordinibus appareat, exceptis paucis et valde paucis qui ob
amissionem tantae multitudinis, quae cotidie prona ruit ad tartara, tam
brevis numerus habentur ut eos quodammodo venerabilis mater ecclesia
in suo sinu recumbentes non videat, quos solos veros filios habet.

4   Quorum ne quis me egregiam vitam omnibus admirabilem deoque
amabilem carpere putet, quibus nostra infirmitas in sacris orationibus ut
non penitus conlabatur quasi columnis quibusdam ac fulcris saluberrimis
sustentatur, si qua liberius de his, immo lugubrius, cumulo malorum
conpulsus, qui serviunt non solum ventri sed diabolo potius quam Christo,
qui est benedictus in saecula deus, non tam disceptavero quam deflevero.
Quippe quid celabunt cives quae non solum norunt sed exprobrant iam
in circuitu nationes?

27   Reges habet Britannia, sed tyrannos; iudices habet, sed impios; saepe
praedantes et concutientes, sed innocentes; vindicantes et patrocinantes,
sed reos et latrones; quam plurimas coniuges habentes, sed scortas et
adulterantes; crebro iurantes, sed periurantes; voventes, sed continuo
propemodum mentientes; belligerantes, sed civilia et iniusta bella
agentes; per patriam quidem fures magnopere insectantes, sed eos qui
secum ad mensam sedent non solum amantes sed et munerantes;
eleemosynas largiter dantes, sed e regione inmensum montem scelerum
exaggerantes; in sede arbitraturi sedentes, sed raro recti iudicii regulam
quaerentes; innoxios humilesque despicientes, sanguinarios superbos
parricidas commanipulares et adulteros dei inimicos, si sors, ut dicitur,
tulerit, qui cum ipso nomine certatim delendi erant, ad sidera, prout
possunt, efferentes; vinctos plures in carceribus habentes, quos dolo sui
potius quam merito proterunt catenis onerantes, inter altaria iurando
demorantes et haec eadem ac si lutulenta paulo post saxa despicientes.

28   Cuius tam nefandi piaculi non ignarus est inmundae leaenae
Damnoniae tyrannicus catulus Constantinus. Hoc anno, post horribile
iuramenti sacramentum, quo se devinxit nequaquam dolos civibus, deo   42
primum iureque iurando, sanctorum demum choris et genetrice
comitantibus fretis, facturum, in duarum venerandis matrum sinibus,
ecclesiae carnalisque, sub sancti abbatis amphibalo, latera regiorum
tenerrima puerorum vel praecordia crudeliter duum totidemque

2   nutritorum — quorum brachia nequaquam armis, quae nullus paene
hominum fortius hoc eis tempore tractabat, sed deo altarique protenta in

die iudicii ad tuae civitatis portas, Christe, veneranda patientiae ac fidei
suae vexilla suspendent — inter ipsa, ut dixi, sacrosancta altaria nefando
ense hastaque pro dentibus laceravit, ita ut sacrificii caelestis sedem
purpurea ac si coagulati cruoris pallia attingerent.

3   Et hoc ne post laudanda quidem merita egit, nam multis ante annis
crebris alternatisque faetoribus adulteriorum victus legitima uxore contra
Christi magistrique gentium interdictum depulsa dicentium: 'quod Deus
4 coniunxit, homo non separet' et 'viri, diligite uxores vestras'. Amarissima
enim quoddam de vite Sodomorum in cordis sui infructuosa bono semini
gleba surculamen incredulitatis et insipientiae plantaverat, quod vulgatis
domesticisque impietatibus velut quibusdam venenatis imbribus irrigatum
et ad dei offensam avidius se erigens parricidii sacrilegiique crimen produxit
in medium. Sed nec adhuc priorum retibus malorum expeditus priscis
recentia auget malis.

29   Age iam (quasi praesentem arguo, quem adhuc superesse non nescio)
quid stupes, animae carnifex propriae? quid tibi flammas inferni voluntarie
accendis nequaquam defecturas? quid inimicorum vice propriis te
confodis sponte ensibus hastis? An ne ipsa quidem virulenta scelerum ac
2 si pocula pectus tuum satiare quiverunt? Respice, quaeso, et veni ad
Christum, siquidem laboras et inmenso pondere curvaris, et ipse te, ut
dixit, requiescere faciet; veni ad eum, qui non vult peccatoris mortem,
sed ut convertatur et vivat; dissolve secundum prophetam vincula colli
tui , fili Sion; redi, rogo, e longinquis licet peccatorum recessibus ad
piissimum patrem, qui despicienti porcorum sordidos cibos ac pertimescenti
dirae famis mortem et revertenti sibi laetus occidere consuevit vitulum
3 filio saginatum et proferre primam erranti stolam et regium anulum, et
tum spei caelestis ac si saporem praegustans senties quam suavis est
dominus. Nam si haec contempseris, scias te inextricabilibus   43
tenebrosisque ignium torrentibus iam iamque inferni rotandum
urendumque.

30   Quid tu quoque, ut propheta ait, catule leonine, Aureli Canine, agis?
Nonne eodem quo supra dictus, si non exitiabiliore parricidiorum
fornicationum adulteriorumque caeno velut quibusdam marinis irruentibus tibi voraris feraliter undis? nonne pacem patriae mortiferum ceu
serpentem odiens civiliaque bella et crebras iniuste praedas sitiens animae
2 tuae caelestis portas pacis ac refrigerii praecludis? Relictus, quaeso, iam
solus ac si arbor in medio campo arescens recordare patrum fratrumque
tuorum supervacuam fantasiam, iuvenilem inmaturamque mortem. Num
centennis tu ob religiosa merita vel coaevus Mathusalae exceptus paene
omni prole servaberis? nequaquam.
3   Sed nisi citius, ut psalmista ait, conversus fueris ad dominum, ensem
in te vibrabit in brevi suum rex ille qui per prophetam 'ego' inquit

'occidam et ego vivere faciam; percutiam et ego sanabo, et non est qui de manu mea possit eruere'. Quam ob rem 'excutere de faetido pulvere' tuo et convertere ad eum toto corde, qui creavit te, ut 'cum exarserit in brevi ira eius, beatus sis sperans in eum', sin alias, aeternae te manebunt poenae conterendum saeva continue et nequaquam absumendum tartari fauce.

31   Quid tu quoque, pardo similis moribus et nequitiis discolor, canescente iam capite, in throno dolis pleno et ab imis vertice tenus diversis parricidiis et adulteriis constuprato, boni regis nequam fili, ut Ezechiae Manasses, Demetarum tyranne Vortipori, stupide riges? quid te tam violenti peccatorum gurgites, quos ut vinum optimum sorbes, immo tu ab eis voraris, appropinquante sensim vitae limite non satiant? quid quasi culminis malorum omnium stupro, propria tua amota coniuge eiusdemque honesta morte, impudentis filiae quodam ineluctabili pondere miseram animam oneras?

  2   Ne consumas, quaeso, dierum quod reliquum est in dei offensam, quia nunc tempus acceptabile et dies salutis vultibus paenitentium lucet, in quo bene operari potes ne fiat fuga tua hieme vel sabbato. 'Diverte' secundum psalmistam 'a malo et fac bonum, inquire pacem bonam et sequere eam, quia oculi domini super te bona agentem et aures eius erunt in preces tuas et non perdet de terra viventium memoriam tuam. Clamabis et exaudiet te et ex omnibus tribulationibus tuis eruet te'. Cor siquidem contritum et humiliatum timore eius nusquam Christus   44 spernit. Alioquin vermis tortionis tuae non morietur et ignis ustionis tuae non extinguetur.

32   Ut quid in nequitiae tuae volveris vetusta faece et tu ab adolescentiae annis, urse, multorum sessor aurigaque currus receptaculi ursi, dei contemptor sortisque eius depressor, Cuneglase, Romana lingua lanio fulve? Quare tantum certamen tam hominibus quam deo praestas, hominibus, civibus scilicet, armis specialibus, deo infinitis sceleribus?

  2 Quid praeter innumerabiles casus propria uxore pulsa furciferam germanam eius, perpetuam deo viduitatis castimoniam promittentem, ut poeta ait, summam ceu teneritudinem caelicolarum, tota animi veneratione vel potius hebetudine [nympharum] contra interdictum apostoli denegantis posse adulteros regni caelestis esse municipes suspicis? Quid gemitus atque suspiria sanctorum propter te corporaliter versantium, vice immanis leaenae dentium ossa tua quandoque fracturae, crebris instigas iniuriis?

  3   Desine, quaeso, ut propheta ait, ab ira, et derelinque exitiabilem ac temetipsum maceraturum, quem caelo ac terrae, hoc est deo gregique eius, spiras, furorem. Fac eos potius mutatis pro te orare moribus, quibus suppetit supra mundum alligandi, cum in mundo reos alligaverint, et

4 solvendi, cum paenitentes solverint, potestas. Noli, ut ait apostolus,
superbe sapere vel sperare in incerto divitiarum, sed in deo, qui praestat
tibi multa abunde, ut per emendationem morum thesaurizes tibi fundamentum bonum in futurum et habeas veram vitam, perennem profecto, non
5 deciduam; alioquin scies et videbis etiam in hoc saeculo quam malum et
amarum est reliquisse te dominum deum tuum et non esse timorem eius
apud te et in futuro taetro ignium globo aeternorum te exuri nec tamen
ullo modo mori. Siquidem tam sceleratorum sint perpeti immortales igni
animae quam sanctorum laetitiae.

33   Quid tu enim, insularis draco, multorum tyrannorum depulsor tam
regno quam etiam vita supra dictorum, novissime stilo, prime in malo,
maior multis potentia simulque malitia, largior in dando, profusior in
peccato, robuste armis, sed animae fortior excidiis, Maglocune, in tam
vetusto scelerum atramento, veluti madidus vino de Sodomitana vite
2 expresso, stolide volutaris? Quare tantas peccaminum regiae cervici
sponte, ut ita dicam, ineluctabiles, celsorum ceu montium, innectis   45
moles? Quid te non ei regum omnium regi, qui te cunctis paene
Brittanniae ducibus tam regno fecit quam status liniamento editiorem,
3 exhibes ceteris moribus meliorem, sed versa vice deteriorem? Quorum
indubitatam aequanimiter conviciorum auscultato parumper adstipu-
lationem, omissis domesticis levioribusque, si tamen aliqua sunt levia,
palata solum longe lateque per auras admissa testaturam.

4   Nonne in primis adolescentiae tuae annis avunclum regem cum
fortissimis propemodum militibus, quorum vultus non catulorum leonis
in acie magnopere dispares visebantur, acerrime ense hasta igni oppressisti,
parum cogitans propheticum dictum', 'viri', inquiens, 'sanguinum et doli
5 non dimidiabunt dies suos'? Quid pro hoc solo retributionis a iusto iudice
sperares, etsi non talia sequerentur quae secuta sunt, itidem dicente per
prophetam: 'vae tibi qui praedaris, nonne et ipse praedaberis? et qui
occidis, nonne et ipse occideris? et cum desiveris praedari, tunc cades'?

34   Nonne postquam tibi ex voto violenti regni fantasia cessit, cupiditate
inlectus ad viam revertendi rectam, diebus ac noctibus id temporis,
conscientia forte peccaminum remordente, de deifico tenore monachor-
umque decretis sub dente primum multa ruminans, dein popularis aurae
cognitioni proferens, monachum sine ullo infidelitatis, ut aiebas,
2 respectu coram omnipotente Deo, angelicis vultibus humanisque, ruptis,
ut putabatur, capacissimis illis quibus praecipitanter involvi solent pingues
tauri moduli tui retibus, omnis regni auri argenti et quod his maius est
propriae voluntatis distentionibus ruptis, perpetuo vovisti, et tete, ac si
stridulo cavum lapsu aerem valide secantem saevosque rapidi harpagones
accipitris sinuosis flexibus vitantem ad sanctorum tibi magnopere fidas
speluncas refrigeriaque salubriter rapuisti ex corvo columbam?

3   O quanta ecclesiae matri laetitia, si non te cunctorum mortalium
hostis de sinu quodammodo eius lugubriter abstraxisset, foret! o quam
profusus spei caelestis fomes desperatorum cordibus, te in bonis
permanente, inardesceret! o qualia quantaque animam tuam regni
Christi praemia in die iudicii manerent, si non lupus callidus ille   46
agnum ex lupo factum te ab ovili dominico, non vehementer invitum,
4   facturus lupum ex agno sibi similem, rapuisset! o quantam exultationem
pio omnium patri deo sanctorum tua salus servanda praestaret, si non te
cunctorum perditorum infaustus pater, veluti magnarum aquila alarum
unguiumque, daemon infelici filiorum suorum agmini contra ius fasque
rapuisset!
5   Ne multa, tantum gaudii ac suavitatis tum caelo terraeque tua ad
bonam frugem conversio quantum nunc maeroris ac luctus ministravit ad
horribilem, more molossi aegri, vomitum nefanda reversio. Qua peracta
exhibentur membra arma iniquitatis peccato ac diabolo quae oportuerat
6   salvo sensu avide exhiberi arma iustitiae deo. Arrecto aurium auscultantur
captu non dei laudes canora Christi tironum voce suaviter modulante
neumaque ecclesiasticae melodiae, sed propriae, quae nihil sunt,
furciferorum referto mendaciis simulque spumanti flegmate proximos
quosque roscidaturo, praeconum ore ritu bacchantium concrepante, ita ut
vas dei quondam in ministerio praeparatum vertatur in zabuli organum,
quodque honore caelesti putabatur dignum merito proiciatur in tartari
barathrum.
35   Nec tamen tantis malorum offendiculis tuus hebetatus insipientiae
cumulo sensus velut quodam obice tardatur, sed fervidus ac si pullus,
amoena quaeque inperagrata putans, per extensos scelerum campos
2   inrevocabili furore raptatur, augendo priscis nova piaculis. Spernuntur
namque primae post monachi votum inritum inlicitae licet, tamen propriae
coniugis praesumptivae nuptiae, aliae expetuntur non cuiuslibet relictae,
sed viri viventis, non externi, sed fratris filii adamatae. Ob quod dura
cervix illa, multis iam peccaminum fascibus onerata, bino parricidali ausu,
occidendo supra dictum uxoremque tuam aliquamdiu a te habitam, velut
3   summo sacrilegii tui culmine de imis ad inferiora curvatur. Dehinc illam,
cuius dudum colludio ac suggestione tantae sunt peccatorum subitae
moles, publico et, ut fallaces parasitorum linguae tuorum conclamant,
summis tamen labiis, non ex intimo cordis, legitimo, utpote viduatam,
nostrae vero sceleratissimo adscivisti conubio.   47
4   Cuius igitur sancti viscera tali stimulata historia non statim in fletus
singultusque prorumpant? Quis sacerdos, cuius cor rectum deo patet,
non statim haec audiens magno cum ululatu illud propheticum dicat:
'quis dabit capiti meo aquam et oculis meis fontem lacrimarum? et
5   plorabo in die et nocte interfectos populi mei'. Heu! siquidem parum

auribus captasti propheticam obiurgationem ita dicentem: 'Vae vobis, viri impii, qui dereliquistis legem dei altissimi: et si nati fueritis, in maledictionem nascemini et si mortui fueritis, in maledictionem erit pars vestra. Omnia quae de terra sunt, in terram ibunt: sic impii a maledictione in perditionem': subauditur, si non revertantur ad deum

6 exaudita saltim tali admonitione: 'Fili, peccasti. Ne adicias ultra, sed et de pristinis tuis deprecare'; et iterum: 'Non tardes converti ad dominum neque differas de die in diem. Subito enim venit ira eius', quia, ut scriptura ait, 'rege audiente verbum iniquum omnes, qui sub illo sunt, scelesti sunt'. Nimirum 'rex', ut propheta dixit, 'iustus suscitat regionem'.

36   Sed monita tibi profecto non desunt, cum habueris praeceptorem paene totius Britanniae magistrum elegantem. Caveto igitur ne tibi quod a Salomone notatur accidat: 'quasi qui excitat dormitantem de gravi somno, sic qui enarrat stulto sapientiam: in fine enim narrationis dicet: quid primum dixeras?' 'Lava a malitia cor tuum', sicut dictum est,

2 'Hierusalem, ut salvus sis'. Ne contemnas, quaeso, ineffabilem misericordiam dei, hoc modo per prophetam a peccatis impios provocantis: 'repente loquar ad gentem et ad regnum, ut evellam et dissipem et destruam et disperdam'. Peccatorem hoc vehementer ad paenitentiam hortatur: 'et si paenitentiam egerit gens illa a peccato suo, paenitentiam et ego agam super malo quod locutus sum ut facerem ei'. Et iterum: 'quis dabit eis tale cor, ut audiant me et custodiant praecepta mea et

3 bene sit eis omnibus diebus vitae suae?' Itemque in cantico deuteronomii: 'Populus', inquit, 'absque consilio et prudentia: utinam saperent et intellegerent ac novissima providerent. Quomodo persequatur unus mille et duo fugent decem milia?' Et iterum in euangelio dominus: 'Venite ad me omnes, qui laboratis et onerati estis, et ego vos requiescere faciam. Tollite iugum meum super vos et discite a me, quia mitis sum et humilis corde, et invenietis requiem animabus vestris'.

4   Nam si haec surdis auribus audias, prophetas contemnas, Christum despicias, nosque, licet vilissimae qualitatis simus, nullius momenti   **48** ducas (propheticum illud sincera animi pietate servantes utcumque: 'si non ego implevero fortitudinem in spiritu et virtute domini, ut enuntiem domui Iacob peccata eorum et domui Israhel scelera eorum', ne simus 'canes muti non valentes latrare', et illud Salomonis ita dicentis: 'qui dicit impium iustum esse, maledictus erit populis et odibilis gentibus:

5 nam qui arguunt, meliora sperabunt', et iterum: 'non reverearis proximum in casum suum, nec retineas verbum in tempore salutis', itemque: 'erue eos qui ducuntur ad mortem et redimere eos qui interficiuntur ne parcas', quia 'non proderunt', ut idem propheta ait, 'divitiae in die irae: iustitia a morte liberat'; 'si iustus quidem vix salvus

6 sit, impius et peccator ubi parebit?'), ille profecto te tenebrosus tartari

torrens ferali rotatu undisque ac si acerrimis involvet semper cruciaturus
et numquam consumpturus, cui tunc erit sera inutilisque poenae oculata
cognitio ac mali paenitudo, a quo in hoc tempore accepto et die salutis ad
rectum vitae iter differtur conversio.

37   Hic sane vel antea concludenda erat, uti ne amplius loqueretur os
nostrum opera hominum, tam flebilis haec querulaque malorum aevi huius
historia. Sed ne formidolosos nos aut lassos putent quominus illud
Isaianum infatigabiliter caveamus: 'vae', inquiens, 'qui dicunt bonum malum
et malum bonum, ponentes tenebras in lucem et lucem in tenebras, amarum
in dulce et dulce in amarum', 'qui videntes non vident et audientes non

2 audiunt', quorum cor crassa obtegitur quadam vitiorum nube, libet quid
quantumque his supradictis lascivientibus insanisque satellitum Faraonis,
quibus eius periturus mari provocatur exercitus strenue rubro, eorumque
similibus quinque equis minarum prophetica inclamitent strictim edicere
oracula, quibus veluti pulchro tegmine opusculi nostri molimen, ita ut ne
certatim irruituris invidorum imbribus extet penetrabile, fidissime contegatur.

3   Respondeant itaque pro nobis sancti vates nunc ut ante, qui os
quodam modo dei organumque spiritus sancti, mortalibus prohibentes
mala, bonis faventes extitere, contumacibus superbisque huius aetatis
principibus, ne dicant nos propria adinventione et loquaci tantum

4 temeritate tales minas eis tantosque terrores incutere. Nulli namque
sapientium dubium est in quantis graviora sunt peccata huius temporis
quam primi, apostolo dicente: 'legem quis transgrediens duobus mediis
vel tribus testibus moritur: quanto putatis deteriora mereri supplicia qui
filium dei conculcaverit?'   49

38   En primus occurrit nobis Samuel iussu dei legitimi regni stabilitor,
deo antequam nasceretur dedicatus, a Dan usque Bersabee omni populo
Israhel veridicus propheta, signis indubitanter admirandis notus, ex cuius
ore spiritus sanctus cunctis mundi potestatibus intonuit, denuntiando
primo regi apud Hebraeos dumtaxat Sauli pro eo quod quaedam de
mandatis domini non compleverat, dicens: 'Stulte egisti nec custodisti
mandata domini dei tui quae praecepit tibi. Quod si non fecisses, iam
nunc pararet deus regnum tuum super Israhel in sempiternum: sed

2 nequaquam regnum tuum ultra consurget'. Quid ergo simile huius
temporis sceleribus? adulteriumne vel parricidium fecit? Nullo modo,
sed iussionis ex parte mutationem: quia, ut bene quidam nostrum ait,
non agitur de qualitate peccati, sed de transgressione mandati.

3   Itemque illum obiecta, velut putabat, purgantem et apologias, ut
generi humano moris est, sagaciter hoc modo adnectentem: 'immo
audivi vocem domini et ambulavi in via per quam misit me', tali
animadversione multavit. 'Numquid vult', inquit, 'dominus holocausta
aut victimas et non potius ut oboediatur voci domini? Melior est enim
oboedientia quam victimae, et audire magis quam offerre adipem

arietum, quoniam sicut peccatum ariolandi est repugnare et quasi scelus idolatriae nolle adquiescere. Pro eo ergo quod abiecisti sermonem

4 domini, abiecit et te, ne sis rex'. Et post pauca: 'Scidit', inquit, 'deus regnum Israhel a te hodie et dedit illud proximo tuo meliori te. Porro triumphator in Israhel non parcet et paenitudine non flectetur, neque enim homo est ut agat paenitentiam'; subauditur: super duris malorum praecordiis.

5 Notandum ergo est quod dixit scelus idolatriae esse nolle deo adquiescere. Non sibi scelerati isti, dum non gentium diis perspicue litant, subplaudant, siquidem conculcantes porcorum more pretiosissimas Christi margaritas idolatrae.

39 Sed licet hoc unum exemplum, ac si invictus adstipulator, ad corrigendos iniquos abunde sufficeret, tamen, ut in ore multorum testium omne comprobetur Brittanniae malum, transeamus ad cetera.

2 Quid David numerando populum evenit? dicente ad eum propheta Gaad: 'Haec dicit dominus: trium tibi optio datur: elige unum quod volueris ex his ut faciam tibi. Aut septem annis veniet tibi fames, aut tribus mensibus fugies adversarios tuos et illi te persequentur, aut   50

3 certe tribus diebus erit pestilentia in terra tua.' Nam artatus tali condicione et volens magis incidere in manus misericordis dei quam hominum, LXX milium populi sui strage humiliatur et, ni pro contribulibus apostolicae caritatis affectu ut illos plaga non tangeret mori optasset dicendo: 'Ego sum qui peccavi, ego pastor inique egi: isti qui oves sunt quid peccarunt? Vertatur, obsecro, manus tua contra me et contra domum patris mei', inconsideratam cordis elationem propria morte piaret.

4 Nam quid scriptura in consequentibus de filio eius narrat? 'Fecit', inquiens, 'Salomon quod non placuerat coram domino, et non adimplevit ut sequeretur dominum, sicut pater eius'. 'Dixit dominus ad eum: quia habuisti hoc apud te et non custodisti pactum meum et praecepta mea quae mandavi tibi, disrumpens scindam regnum tuum et dabo illud servo tuo'.

40 Quid duobus sacrilegis, aeque ut isti sunt, Israhel regibus Hieroboae et Baasae accidit audite: quibus sententia domini dirigitur per prophetam ita dicentis: 'Propter quod magnificavi te principem super Israhel, quia exacerbaverunt me in vanis eorum, ecce ego suscito post Baasam et post domum eius et tradam domum eius sicut domum Ieroboae Nabath. Qui mortuus fuerit de suis in civitate comedent eum canes, et mortuum corpus illius in campo comedent volatilia caeli'.

2 Quid illi quoque scelerato regi Israhel istorum conmanipulari, cuius colludio et uxoris dolo Naboth innocens propter paternam vineam oppressus est, sancto ore illius Heliae atque ignifero domini alloquio instructo minatur, ita dicente: 'Occidisti insuper et possedisti. Et post

haec addes: haec dicit dominus: in loco hoc in quo linxerunt canes sanguinem Naboth, lambent quoque tuum sanguinem'. Quod ita factum fuisse certissima ratione cognitum est.

3   Sed ne forte secundum supra dictum Achab 'spiritus mendax loquens vana in ore prophetarum vestrorum' seducat vos, [ne] sermones Michaeae prophetae audiatis: 'ecce permisit deus spiritum mendacii in ore omnium prophetarum tuorum qui hic sunt et dominus locutus est

4   contra te malum'. Nam et nunc certum est aliquos esse doctores contrario spiritu repletos et magis pravam voluptatem quam veritatem adserentes: quorum 'verba super oleum molliuntur et ipsa sunt iacula', qui dicunt: pax, pax, et non erit in peccatis permanentibus pax; ut alibi propheta dicit: 'non est gaudere inpiis, dicit dominus'.

41   Azarias quoque filius Obed Asae revertenti de caede decies centenum milium exercitus Aethiopum locutus est dicens: 'dominus vobiscum est, dum estis cum ipso et si exquisieritis eum invenietur a vobis et si   51 dereliqueritis eum derelinquet vos'.

2   Nam si Iosaphat ferens praesidium iniquo regi ita ab Ieu propheta Annaniae filio increpatur dicente: 'si peccatorem tu adiuvas aut quem dominus odit tu diligis, propterea ira dei est super te', quid illis qui propriis scelerum suorum criniculis compediuntur fiet? Quorum nos necesse est, si in acie dominica volumus dimicare, peccata odire, non animas, dicente psalmista 'qui diligitis dominum, odite malum'.

3   Quid ad supradicti Iosaphat filium currus et auriga Israhel propheta Helias, Ioram scilicet parricidam, qui egregios fratres suos ut pro ipsis regnaret spurius trucidavit, effatus est? 'Sic dicit', inquit, 'dominus deus patris tui David: eo quod non ambulaveris in via Iosaphat patris tui et in viis Asae regis Iuda et ambulasti in viis regum Israel et stuprose, ut gessit domus Achab, et fratres tuos filios Iosaphat meliores te interfecisti, ecce

4   dominus percutiet plaga magna te et filios tuos'. Et post pauca: 'et tu eris in magna valitudine in languore ventris tui, donec exeat venter tuus cum ipsa infirmitate de die ex die'.

5   Et ad Ioam regem Israhel ut vos derelinquentem dominum quid Zacharias filius Ioiadae vatis minatus sit adtendite, qui surgens populo dixit: 'Haec dicit dominus: quare praeteritis praecepta domini et non prosperamini? Quia dereliquistis dominum, et derelinquet vos',

42   Quid de auctore prophetarum Esaia dicam? qui prooemium profetiae suae vel visionem ita exorsus est dicens: 'Audite, caeli, et auribus percipite, terra, quoniam dominus locutus est. Filios enutrivi et exaltavi, ipsi autem spreverunt me. Cognovit bos possessorem suum et asinus praesepe domini sui, Israhel autem me non cognovit et populus meus non

2   intellexit'. Et post pauca minas meritas tantae insipientiae aptans: 'derelinquetur', inquit, 'filia Sion ut tabernaculum in vinea et sicut tugurium in cucumerario, sicut civitas quae vastatur'. Et principes

specialiter conveniens ait: 'audite verbum domini, principes Sodomorum; percipite legem domini, populus Gomorrhae'.

3 Notandum sane quod iniqui reges principes Sodomorum vocentur. Prohibens namque dominus sacrificia et dona sibi a talibus offerri (et nos inhiantes suscipimus quae deo abominationi sunt [non placita], eademque egenis et paene nihil habentibus distribui in perniciem nostram non sinimus) cum latis divitiis oneratis, sordibus peccatorum intentis ait: 'ne afferatis ultra sacrificium frustra; incensum abominatio est mihi'.

4 Itemque denuntiat: 'et cum extenderitis manus vestras, avertam oculos meos a vobis, et cum multiplicaveritis orationem, non exaudiam'. Et hoc quare facit ostendit: 'manus', inquiens, 'vestrae sanguine plenae sunt'. Simulque ostendens quomodo placaretur ait: 'lavamini, mundi estote, auferte malum cogitationum vestrarum ab oculis meis, quiescite agere perverse, discite benefacere, quaerite iudicium, subvenite oppresso,

5 iudicate pupillo'. Quasi placoris vicissitudinem adiungens ait: 'Si   52
fuerint peccata vestra ut coccinum, quasi nix dealbabuntur: et si fuerint rubra quasi vermiculus, velut lana alba erunt. Si volueritis et audieritis me, bona terrae manducabitis. Quod si nolueritis et me provocaveritis ad iracundiam, gladius devorabit vos'.

43 Accipite veracem publicumque adstipulatorem, boni malique vestri retributionem absque ullo adulationis fuco, non ut parasitorum venerata vestrorum venena in aures sibilant ora, testantem.

2 Itemque ad rapaces iudices sententiam dirigens ita effatur: 'Principes tui infideles, socii furum, omnes diligunt munera, sectantur retributiones, pupillo non iudicant, causa viduae non ingreditur ad· eos. Propter hoc ait dominus exercituum, fortis Israhel: heu consolabor super hostibus meis et vindicabor de inimicis meis': 'et conterentur scelerati et peccatores simul

3 et omnes, qui dereliquerunt dominum, consumentur'. Et infra: 'oculi sublimis hominis humiliabuntur et incurvabit altitudo virorum'. Et iterum: 'vae impio in malum, retributio enim manuum eius fiet ei'. Et post pauca: 'Vae qui consurgitis mane ad ebrietatem sectandam et ad potandum usque ad vesperam,ı ut vino aestuetis. Cithara et lyra et tympanum et tibia et vinum in conviviis vestris, et opus domini non respicitis et opera manuum eius non consideratis. Propterea captivus ductus est populus meus, quia non habuit scientiam, et nobiles eius interierunt fame et multitudo eius siti exaruit. Propterea dilatavit infernus animam suam et aperuit os suum absque ullo termino et descendent fortes

4 eius et populi eius et sublimes gloriosique eius ad eum'. Et infra: 'Vae qui potentes estis ad bibendum vinum et viri fortes ad miscendam ebrietatem, qui iustificatis impium pro muneribus et iustitiam iusti aufertis ab eo. Propter hoc sicut devorat stipulam lingua ignis et calor flammae exurit, sic radix eorum quasi favilla erit et germen eorum ut pulvis ascendet. Abiecerunt enim legem domini exercituum et eloquium sancti Israhel

despexerunt. In omnibus his non est aversus furor domini, sed adhuc
manus eius extenta'.

44   Et post aliquanta de die iudicii et peccatorum ineffabili metu
disceptans ait: 'Ululate, quia prope est dies domini' — si tunc prope erat,
quid nunc putabitur? — 'quia vastitas a deo veniet. Propter hoc omnes
manus dissolventur et omne cor hominis tabescet et conteretur, tortiones
et dolores tenebunt, quasi parturiens dolebunt. Unusquisque ad proximum
suum stupebit; facies combustae vultus illorum. Ecce dies domini veniet
crudelis et indignationis plenus et irae furorisque ad ponendam terram in
solitudinem et peccatores eius conterendos de ea, quoniam stellae caeli et
splendor earum non expandent lumen suum, obtenebrabitur sol in ortu
suo et luna non splendebit in tempore suo. Et visitabo super orbis mala
et contra impios iniquitatem ipsorum et quiescere faciam superbiam

2   infidelium et arrogantiam fortium humiliabo'. Et iterum: 'ecce dominus
dissipabit terram et nudabit eam et affliget faciem eius et disperget   53
habitatores eius, et erit sicut populus, sic sacerdos, et sicut servus, sic
dominus eius, sicut ancilla, sic domina eius, sicut emens, sic ille qui
vendit, sicut fenerator, sic ille qui mutuum accipit, sicut qui repetit, sic
qui debet. Dissipatione dissipabitur terra et direptione praedabitur.
Dominus enim locutus est verbum hoc. Luxit et defluxit terra, defluxit
orbis, infirmata est altitudo populi terrae et terra infecta est ab habitator-
ibus suis, quia transgressi sunt leges, mutaverunt ius, dissipaverunt foedus

45   sempiternum. Propter hoc maledictio vorabit terram'. Et infra:
'Ingemiscent omnes qui laetantur corde, cessabit gaudium tympanorum,
quiescet sonitus laetantium, conticescet dulcedo citharae, cum cantico
non bibent vinum, amara erit potio bibentibus illam. Attrita est civitas
vanitatis, clausa est omnis domus nullo introeunte. Clamor erit super
vino in plateis, deserta est omnis laetitia, translatum est gaudium terrae,
relicta est in urbe solitudo et calamitas opprimet portas, quia haec erunt
in medio terrae et in medio populorum'.

2   Et post pauca: 'Praevaricantes praevaricati sunt et praevaricatione
transgressorum praevaricati sunt. Formido et fovea et laqueus super te,
qui habitator es terrae. Et erit: qui fugerit a voce formidinis cadet in
foveam, et qui se explicuerit de fovea tenebitur laqueo: quia cataractae
de excelsis apertae erunt et concutientur fundamenta terrae.
Confractione confringetur terra, commotione commovebitur, agitatione
agitabitur sicut ebrius, et auferetur quasi tabernaculum unius noctis, et
gravabit eam iniquitas sua, et corruet et non adiciet ut resurgat. Et erit:
in die illa visitabit dominus super militiam caeli in excelso et super
reges terrae qui sunt super terram, et congregabuntur in congregationem
unius fascis in lacum et claudentur ibi in carcerem et post multos dies
visitabuntur. Et erubescet luna et confundetur sol cum regnaverit
dominus exercituum in monte Sion et in Ierusalem, et in conspectu

senum suorum fuerit glorificatus'.

46 Et post aliquanta, rationem reddens quam ob rem talia minaretur, ita ait: 'Ecce non est abbreviata manus domini, ut salvare nequeat, neque adgravata est auris eius, ut non exaudiat. Sed iniquitates vestrae diviserunt inter vos et deum vestrum, et peccata vestra absconderunt faciem eius a vobis, ne exaudiret. Manus enim vestrae pollutae sunt sanguine et digiti vestri iniquitate: labia vestra locuta sunt mendacium et lingua vestra iniquitatem fatur. Non est qui vocet iustitiam neque est qui iudicet vere, sed confidunt in nihil, et loquuntur vanitates et conceperunt

2 dolorem et pepererunt iniquitatem'. Et infra: 'Opera eorum inutilia et opus iniquitatis in manibus eorum. Pedes eorum in malum currunt, et festinant ut effundant sanguinem innocentem. Cogitationes eorum cogitationes inutiles, vastitas et contritio in viis eorum et viam pacis non cognoverunt et non est iudicium in gressibus eorum. Semitae eorum incurvatae sunt eis: omnis qui calcat in eis ignorat pacem. Propter hoc elongatum est iudicium a vobis et non apprehendit vos iustitia'.

3 Et post pauca: 'Et conversum est retrorsum iudicium et iustitia   54 longe stetit, quia corruit in platea veritas et aequitas non potuit ingredi. Et facta est veritas in oblivione, et qui recessit a malo praedae patuit. Et vidit dominus, et non placuit in oculis eius quia non est iudicium'.

47 Hucusque Esaiae prophetae pauca de multis dixisse sufficiat. Nunc vero illum qui priusquam formaretur in utero praescitus et priusquam exiret de vulva sanctificatus et in cunctis gentibus propheta positus est, Ieremiam scilicet, quid de populo insipiente rigidisque regibus pronuntiaverit parumper attendentes audite, hoc modo leniter verba

2 initiantem: 'Et factum est verbum domini ad me dicens: vade et clama in auribus Ierusalem et dices': 'audite verbum domini, domus Iacob et omnes cognationes domus Israhel. Haec dicit dominus: quid invenerunt in me patres vestri iniquitatis, qui elongati sunt a me et ambulaverunt post vanitatem et vani facti sunt et non dixerunt: ubi est qui ascendere

3 nos fecit de terra Aegypti?' Et post pauca: 'A saeculo confregisti iugum meum, rupisti vincula mea, dixisti: non serviam. Ego plantavi te vineam electam, omne semen verum. Quomodo ergo conversa es in pravum vinea aliena? Si laveris te nitro et multiplicaveris tibi herbam borith,

4 maculata es iniquitate tua coram me, dicit dominus'. Et infra: 'Quid vultis mecum iudicio contendere? Omnes me dereliquistis, dicit dominus. Frustra percussi filios vestros, disciplinam non receperunt. Audite verbum domini: Num quid solitudo factus sum Israhel aut terra serotina? Quare ergo dixit populus meus: recessimus, non veniemus ultra ad te? Num quid obliviscitur virgo ornamenti sui aut sponsa fasciae pectoralis suae? Populus vero meus oblitus est me diebus innumeris'. 'Quia stultus est populus meus, me non cognovit: filii insipientes sunt et vecordes: sapientes sunt, ut faciant mala, bene autem facere nescierunt'.

48   Tum propheta ex sua persona loquitur dicens: 'Domine, oculi tui respiciunt fidem. Percussisti eos et non doluerunt; attrivisti eos et renuerunt accipere disciplinam; induraverunt facies suas super petram et noluerunt reverti'.

2   Itemque dominus: 'Annuntiate hoc domui Iacob et auditum facite in Iuda dicentes: audi, popule stulte, qui non habes cor, qui habentes oculos non videtis et aures et non auditis. Me ergo non timebitis, ait dominus, et a facie mea non dolebitis? qui posui harenam terminum mari praeceptum sempiternum, quod non praeteribit; et commovebuntur et non poterunt, intumescent fluctus eius et non transibunt illud. Populo autem huic factum est cor incredulum et exasperans, recesserunt et abierunt, et non

3   dixerunt in corde suo: metuamus dominum deum nostrum'. Et iterum: 'Quia inventi sunt in populo meo impii insidiantes quasi aucupes, laqueos ponentes et pedicas ad capiendos viros. Sicut decipula plena avibus, sic domus eorum plenae dolo. Ideo magnificati sunt et ditati, incrassati sunt et inpinguati, et praeterierunt sermones meos pessime, causam pupilli non dixerunt et iudicium pauperum non iudicaverunt. Numquid super his non visitabo, dicit dominus, aut super gentem huiusmodi non ulciscetur anima mea?'

49   Sed absit ut vobis eveniat quod sequitur: 'loqueris ad eos omnia verba haec et non audient te et vocabis eos et non respondebunt tibi et dices ad eos: haec est gens quae non audivit vocem domini dei sui nec recepit   55 disciplinam; periit fides et ablata est de ore eorum'. Et post aliquanta: 'Numquid qui cadit non resurget et qui aversus est non revertetur? Quare ergo aversus est populus iste in Ierusalem aversione contentiosa? Apprehenderunt mendacium et noluerunt reverti. Attendi et auscultavi, nemo quod bonum est loquitur. Nullus est qui agat paenitentiam super peccato suo dicens: quid feci? Omnes conversi sunt ad cursum suum quasi equus impetu vadens in proelium. Milvus in caelo cognovit tempus suum, turtur et hirundo et ciconia custodierunt tempus adventus sui, populus meus non cognovit iudicium dei'.

2   Et tam vehementi sacrilegiorum caecitate et ineffabili ebrietate propheta conterritus et deflens eos qui se ipsos non deflebant, ut et nunc infelices tyranni agunt, optat sibi auctionem fletuum a domino concedi, hoc modo dicens: 'Super contritione filiae populi mei contritus sum: stupor obtinuit me. Numquid resina non est in Galaad aut medicus non est ibi? Quare ergo non obducta est cicatrix filiae populi mei? Quis dabit capiti meo aquam et oculis meis fontem lacrimarum? et plorabo die et nocte interfectos populi mei. Quis dabit mihi in solitudine diversorium viatorum? et derelinquam populum meum et recedam ab eis, quando omnes adulteri sunt, coetus praevaricatorum. Et extenderunt linguam suam quasi arcum mendacii et non veritatis: confortati sunt in terra, quia de malo ad malum egressi sunt et me non cognoverunt, dicit

3 dominus'. Et iterum: 'et dixit dominus: quia dereliquerunt legem meam, quam dedi eis, et non audierunt vocem meam et non ambulaverunt in ea, et abierunt post pravitatem cordis sui, idcirco haec dicit dominus exercituum deus Israhel: ecce ego cibabo populum istum absinthio et
4 potum dabo eis aquam fellis': et post pauca, quod etiam crebrius stilo propheta adiunxit, dicens ex persona dei: 'tu ergo noli orare pro populo hoc, et ne assumas pro eis laudem et orationem, quia non exaudiam in tempore clamoris eorum ad me et afflictionis eorum'.

50   Quid ergo nunc infausti duces facient? Illi pauci invenientes viam angustam amota spatiosa, prohibiti a deo ne preces pro vobis fundant perseverantibus in malis et tantopere incitantibus; quis e contrario ex corde ad deum repedantibus, deo nolente animam hominis interire, sed retractante ne penitus pereat qui abiectus est, vindictam non potuissent inducere, quia nec Ionas, et quidem cum multum concupiverit, Ninivitis propheta.

2   Sed omissis interim nostris audiamus potius quid prophetica tuba persultet: 'Quod si dixeris', inquiens, 'in corde tuo: quare venerunt mala haec? propter multitudinem iniquitatis tuae. Si mutare potest Aethiops pellem suam aut pardus varietates suas, et vos poteritis bene facere, cum
3 didiceritis malum'; subauditur, quia non vultis. Et infra: 'Haec dicit   56
   dominus populo huic, qui dilexit movere pedes suos et non quievit et domino non placuit: nunc recordabitur iniquitatum eorum et visitabit peccata eorum. Et dixit dominus ad me: Noli orare pro populo isto in bonum. Cum ieiunaverint, non exaudiam preces eorum, et si obtulerint holocausta et victimas non suscipiam ea'. Et iterum: 'et dixit dominus ad me: si steterit Moyses et Samuel coram me, non est anima mea ad populum istum: eice illos a facie mea et egrediantur'.
4   Et post pauca: 'Quis miserebitur tui, Ierusalem, aut quis contristabitur pro te aut quis ibit ad rogandum pro pace tua? Tu reliquisti me, dicit dominus, et retrorsum abisti, et extendam manum meam super te et
5 interficiam te'. Et post aliquanta: 'Haec dicit dominus: ecce ego fingo contra vos cogitationem: revertatur unusquisque a via sua mala et dirigite vias vestras et studia vestra. Qui dixerunt: desperamus, post cogitationes nostras ibimus et unusquisque pravitatem cordis sui mali faciemus. Ideo haec dicit dominus: Interrogate gentes: quis audivit talia horribilia quae fecit nimis virgo Israhel? Num quid deficiet de petra agri nix Libani aut velli possunt aquae erumpentes frigidae defluentes? quia oblitus est
6 me populus meus'. Et post aliquanta optione proposita loquitur dicens: 'Haec dicit dominus: Facite iudicium et iustitiam, et liberate vi oppressum de manu calumniatoris, et advenam et pupillum et viduam nolite contristare, neque opprimatis inique et sanguinem innocentem ne effundatis. Si enim facientes feceritis verbum istud, ingredientur per portas domus huius reges sedentes de genere David super thronum eius.

Quod si non audieritis verba haec, in memetipso iuravi, dicit dominus,
7 quia in solitudinem erit domus haec'. Et iterum, de rege enim scelesto
loquebatur: 'vivo ego, dicit dominus, quia si fuerit Iechonias anulus in
manu dextra mea, inde evellam eum et dabo in manu quaerentium animam
eius'.

51   Sanctus quoque Abacuc proclamat dicens: 'Vae qui aedificant
civitatem in sanguine et praeparant civitatem in iniquitatibus, dicentes:
nonne haec sunt a domino omnipotente? Et defecerunt populi multi in
igne, et gentes multae minoratae sunt'. Et ita prophetiam querulus
incipit: 'Usque quo clamabo et non exaudies? Vociferabor ad te, ut quid
mihi dedisti labores et dolores inspicere, miseriam et impietatem?
Contra et factum est iudicium et iudex accepit. Propter hoc dissipata est
lex et non perducitur ad finem iudicium, quia impius per potentiam
deprimit iustum. Propter hoc exiit iudicium perversum'.

52   Sed et beatus Osee propheta attendite quid loquatur de principibus
dicens: 'pro eo quod transgressi sunt pactum meum et adversus legem
meam tulerunt et exclamabant: cognovimus te quia adversum sis Israhel,
bonum ut iniquum persecuti sunt, sibi regnaverunt, et non per me:
tenuerunt principatum, nec me agnoverunt'.

53   Sed et sanctum Amos prophetam hoc modo minantem audite: 'In
tribus impietatibus filiorum Iuda et in quattuor non avertam eos   57
propter quod repulerunt legem domini et praecepta non custodierunt,
sed seduxerunt eos vana eorum. Et emittam ignem super Iudam et
comedet fundamenta Ierusalem. Haec dicit dominus: in tribus
impietatibus Israhel et in quattuor non avertam eos, propter quod
tradiderunt pecunia iustum et pauperem pro calciamentis, quae
calcant super pulverem terrae, et colaphis caedebant capita pauperum,
2 et viam humilium declinaverunt'. Et post pauca: 'quaerite dominum
et vivetis, ut non reluceat sicut ignis domus Ioseph et comedat eam, nec
erit qui extinguat'. 'Domus Israel odio habuerunt in portis redarguentem
et verbum iustum abominati sunt'.

3   Qui Amos prohibitus ne prophetaret in Israel absque adulationis
tepore respondens: 'Non eram', inquit, 'ego propheta nec filius
prophetae, sed eram pastor caprarius vellicans sycomoros, et suscepit me
dominus ab ovibus et dixit dominus ad me: vade et prophetiza in
plebem meam Israhel. Et nunc audi verbum domini'; regem namque
alloquebatur. 'Tu dicis: noli prophetare in Israel et non congreges turbas
in domum Iacob. Propter quod haec dicit dominus: uxor tua in civitate
meretricabitur et filii tui et filiae tuae gladio cadent et terra tua funiculo
metietur et tu in terra inmunda morieris; Israhel autem captivus ducetur
4 a terra sua'. Et infra:'audite itaque haec, qui contribulatis inmane
pauperem et dominationem exercetis in inopes super terram, qui dicitis:
quando transibit mensis ut adquiramus, et sabbata ut aperiamus thesauros?'

Et post pauca: 'iurat dominus contra superbiam Iacob, si obliviscetur in contemptione opera vestra et in his non conturbabitur terra et lugebit omnis qui commorabitur in ea et ascendet sicut flumen consummatio'.

5 'Et convertam dies festos vestros in luctum et miciam in omnem lumbum cilicium et in omne caput decalvationem et ponam eum sicut luctum dilecti et eos qui cum eo sunt sicut diem maeroris'. Et iterum: 'gladio morientur omnes peccatores populi mei, qui dicunt: non appropinquabunt neque venient super nos mala'.

54 Sed et sanctus Micheas vates attendite quid sit effatus: 'Audi', inquiens, 'tribus: et quid exornabit civitatem? numquid ignis? et domus iniquorum thesaurizans in thesauros iniquos et cum iniuria iniustitiam? Si iustificabitur in statera iniquus et in saccello pondera dolosa, ex quibus divitias suas in impietate repleverunt?'

55 Sed et Sophonias propheta clarus quas minas exaggerat audite: 'Prope est', inquit, 'dies domini magnus, prope et velox valde. Vox diei domini amara constituta est et potens. Dies irae dies ille, dies tribulationis et necessitatis, dies nubis et nebulae, dies tubae et clamoris, dies miseriae et exterminationis, dies tenebrarum et caliginis super civitates firmas et super angulos excelsos. Et contribulabo homines, et ibunt sicut caeci, quia domino peccaverunt, et effundam sanguinem sicut pulverem et carnes eorum sicut fimum boum, et argentum eorum et aurum non poterit eximere eos in die irae domini. Et in igne zeli eius consumetur omnis terra, quando consummationem et solitudinem faciet dominus super omnes commorantes in terram. Convenite et coniungimini, gens indisciplinata, priusquam efficiamini sicut flos praeteriens, priusquam veniat super vos ira domini'. 58

56 Et quid Aggaeus sanctus propheta dicat, attendite: 'haec dicit dominus: semel ego movebo caelum et terram et mare et aridum et avertam regnum et exterminabo virtutem regum gentium et avertam quadrigas et ascensores'.

57 Nunc quoque quid Zacharias filius Addo propheta electus dixerit intuemini, hoc modo prophetiam suam exordiens: 'revertimini ad me et revertar ad vos, dicit dominus, et nolite tales esse sicut patres vestri, quibus imputaverunt prophetae priores dicentes: haec dicit dominus omnipotens: avertite vos a viis vestris: et non intenderunt, ut ob-

2 audirent me'. Et infra: 'Et dixit ad me angelus: quid tu vides? Et dixi: falcem ego video volantem longitudinis cubitorum viginti. Maledictio, quae procedit super faciem totius terrae, quoniam omnis fur ex ea usque ad mortem punietur, et proiciam eam, dicit dominus omnipotens, et intrabit in domum furis et in domum iurantis in nomine meo mendacium'.

58 Sanctus quoque Malachias propheta dicit: 'ecce dies domini veniet succensa quasi caminus, et erunt omnes superbi et omnes facientes

114

iniquitatem ut stipula et inflammabit eos dies adveniens, dicit dominus exercituum, quae non relinquet ex eis radicem et germen'.

59   Sed et sanctus Iob attendite quid de principio impiorum et fine disceptaverit dicens: 'Propter quid impii vivunt? Et senuerunt inhoneste et semen eorum secundum desiderium eorum et filii eorum ante conspectum eorum et domus eorum fructuosae sunt et timor numquam nec plaga domini est super eos. Vacca eorum non abortivit et praegnans eorum pertulit partum et non erravit, sed permanent sicut oves aeternae, et pueri eorum gaudent et psalterium sumentes et citharam. Finierunt in

2   bonis vitam suam, in requiem inferorum dormierunt'. Num quid deus facta impiorum non respicit? 'Non ergo, sed lucerna impiorum extinguetur et superveniet eis eversio et dolores tamquam parturientis eos ab ira tenebunt. Et erunt sicut paleae a vento et sicut pulvis quem abstulit turbo. Deficiant filiis eius bona. Videant oculi eius occisionem suam, nec a domino resalvetur'.

3   Et post aliquanta de iisdem: 'qui gregem', inquit, 'cum pastore rapuerunt et iumentum orfanorum abduxerunt et bovem viduae pigneraverunt et declinaverunt impotentes a via necessitatis, agrum ante tempus non suum demessi sunt, pauperes potentium vineas sine mercede et sine cibo operati sunt, nudos multos dormire fecerunt sine vestimentis, tegmen animae eorum abstulerunt'.

4   Et post pauca, cum ergo sciret eorum opera, tradidit eos in tenebras: 'maledicatur ergo pars eius a terra, pareant plantationes eius aridae'. 'Retribuatur ergo illi sicut egit, contribuletur omnis iniquus sicut lignum sine sanitate. In iracundia enim surgens impotentem evertit. Propterea enim non credet de vita sua; cum infirmari coeperit, non   59 speret sanitatem, sed cadet in languorem. Multos enim laesit superbia eius et marcidus factus est sicut malva in aestu, velut spica cum de

5   stipula sua decidit'. Et infra: 'quod si multi fuerint filii eius, in occisionem erunt'; 'quod et si collexerit ut terram argentum et similiter ut lutum paraverit aurum, haec omnia iusti consequuntur'.

60   Quid praeterea beatus Esdras propheta ille bibliotheca legis minatus sit attendite, hoc modo disceptans: 'Haec dicit dominus meus: Non parcet dextera mea super peccantes nec cessabit romphaea super effundentes sanguinem innocuum super terram. Exibit ignis ab ira mea et devorabit fundamenta terrae et peccatores quasi stramen incensum. Vae eis qui peccant et non observant mandata mea, dicit dominus, non parcam illis. Discedite, filii apostatae, et nolite contaminare sanctificationem meam. Novit deus qui peccant in eum, propterea tradet eos in mortem et in occisionem. Iam enim venerunt super orbem terrarum mala multa'.

2   'Inmissus est gladius vobis ignis, et quis est qui recutiet ea? Num quid recutiet aliquis leonem esurientem in silva? aut num quid extinguet ignem, cum stramen incensum fuerit? Dominus deus mittet mala et quis

est qui recutiet ea? et exiet ignis ex iracundia eius et quis est qui extinguet eum? Coruscabit, et quis non timebit? tonabit, et quis non horrebit? Deus comminabitur, et quis non terrebitur a facie eius? Tremet terra et fundamenta maris fluctuantur de profundo'.

61   Ezechiel quoque propheta egregius quattuorque euangelicorum animalium mirandus inspector quid de sceleratis edixerit attendite, cui primum dominus miserabiliter plagam Israel deflenti ait: 'iniquitas domus Israel et Iuda invaluit nimis, quia impleta est terra populis multis et civitas impleta est iniquitate et inmunditia'. 'Ecce ego sum'. 'Non parcet oculus meus neque miserebor'. Et infra: 'Quoniam terra plena populis et civitas plena iniquitate est, et avertam impetum virtutis eorum et polluentur sancta eorum. Exoratio veniet et quaeret pacem et non

2 erit'. Et post aliquanta: 'Factus est', inquit, 'sermo domini ad me dicens: fili hominis, terra quae peccaverit mihi ut delinquat delictum, extendam manum meam in eam et conteram eius firmamentum panis et emittam in eam famem et tollam de ea hominem et pecora. Etsi sint tres viri isti in medio eius Noe Daniel et Iob, non liberabunt eam, sed ipsi in sua iustitia salvi erunt, dicit dominus. Quod si etiam bestias malas inducam super terram et puniam illam et erit in exterminium et non erit qui iter faciat a facie bestiarum et tres viri isti in medio eius sint, vivo ego, dicit dominus, si filii et filiae eius liberabuntur, sed ipsi soli salvi erunt, terra autem erit in interitum'.

3   Et iterum: 'Filius non accipiet iniustitiam patris neque pater accipiet iniustitiam filii. Iustitia iusti super ipsum erit. Et iniquus si avertat se ab omnibus iniquitatibus quas fecit et custodiat omnia mandata mea et faciat iustitiam et misericordiam multam, vita vivet et non morietur: omnia delicta eius quaecumque fecit, non erunt: in sua iustitia quam   **60** fecit vita vivet. Num quid voluntate volo mortem iniusti, dicit dominus, quam ut avertat se a via sua mala et vivat? Cum se autem converterit iustus a iustitia sua et fecerit iniquitatem secundum omnes iniquitates quas fecit iniquus, omnes iustitiae quas fecit non erunt in memoria: in

4 delicto suo quo excidit et in peccatis suis quibus peccavit morietur'. Et post aliquanta: 'Et scient omnes gentes quia propter peccata sua captivi ducti sunt domus Israel, eo quod reliquerunt me. Et averti faciem meam ab eis et tradidi eos in manus inimicorum eius et omnes gladio ceciderunt. Secundum immunditias suas et secundum iniquitates suas feci illis, et averti faciem meam ab eis'.

62   Haec de sanctorum prophetarum minis dixisse sufficiat: pauca tantum de sapientia Salomonis quae adhortationem vel denuntiationem exprimant regibus non minus quam minas huic opusculo inserere necessarium duxi, ne dicant me gravia et importabilia in humeros hominum verborum onera velle imponere, digito autem meo ea, id est consolatorio affatu, nolle movere. Audiamus itaque quid propheta dixit.

2   'Diligite' inquit 'iustitiam, qui iudicatis terram'. Hoc unum testimonium si toto corde servaretur, abunde ad corrigendum patriae duces sufficeret. Nam si dilexissent iustitiam, diligerent utique fontem quodammodo et originem totius iustitiae deum.

3   'Servite domino in bonitate et in simplicitate cordis quaerite eum'. Heu quis victurus est, ut quidam ante nos ait, quando ista a civibus perficiantur, si tamen usquam perfici possunt?

4   'Quoniam invenitur ab his qui non temptant illum, apparet autem eis qui fidem habent in eum'. Nam isti sine respectu temptant deum, cuius praecepta contumaci despectione contemnunt, nec fidem servant illi cuius oraculis blandis vel aliquantulum severis dorsum versant et non faciem.

5   'Perversae enim cogitationes separant a deo.' Et hoc in tyrannis nostri temporis perspicue deprehenditur.

6   Sed quid nostra mediocritas huic tam aperto sensui miscetur? Loquatur namque pro nobis, ut diximus, qui solus verax est, spiritus scilicet sanctus, de quo nunc dicitur: 'spiritus autem sanctus disciplinae effugiet fictum', et iterum: 'quoniam spiritus dei replevit orbem terrarum'.

7   Et infra finem malorum bonorumque oculato iudicio praetendens ait: 'Quoniam spes impii tamquam lanugo est quae a vento tollitur, et tamquam fumus qui a vento diffusus est, et tamquam spuma gracilis quae a procella dispergitur, et tamquam memoria hospitis unius diei praetereuntis, iusti autem in perpetuum vivent et apud deum est merces illorum et cogitatio eorum apud altissimum. Ideo accipient regnum decoris et diadema speciei de manu domini, quoniam dextera sua

8   proteget eos et brachio sancto suo defendet illos'. Dissimiles etenim qualitate sunt valde iusti et impii, nimirum, ut dixit dominus: 'eos qui honorant', inquiens, 'me, honorabo: et qui me spernunt, erunt ignobiles'.

63   Sed transeamus ad cetera: 'audite', inquit, 'omnes reges et   61 intellegite, discite, iudices finium terrae: praebete aures vos, qui continetis multitudines et placetis vobis in turbis nationum. Quoniam data est a deo potestas vobis et virtus ab altissimo, qui interrogabit opera vestra et cogitationes scrutabitur: quoniam cum essetis ministri regni illius, non recte iudicastis neque custodistis legem iustitiae neque secundum voluntatem eius ambulastis: horrende et celeriter apparebit vobis, quoniam iudicium durissimum his qui praesunt fiet. Exiguis enim conceditur misericordia, potentes autem potenter tormenta patientur. Non enim personas subtrahet, qui est omnium dominator: nec reverebitur magnitudinem cuiusquam, quoniam pusillum et magnum ipse fecit et aequaliter cura est illi pro omnibus. Fortioribus autem fortior instat cruciatio. Ad vos ergo, reges, hi sunt sermones mei, ut discatis sapientiam et non decidatis. Qui enim custodierint iusta iustificabuntur, et qui didicerint sancta sanctificabuntur'.

64 Hactenus cum regibus patriae non minus prophetarum oraculis
quam nostris sermonibus disceptavimus, volentes eos scire, quae
propheta dixerat: 'quasi' inquiens 'a facie colubri fuge peccata: si
accesseris ad illa, suscipient te; dentes leonis dentes eorum, interficientes
animas hominum', et iterum: 'quam magna misericordia domini et
2 propitiatio eius convertentibus ad se'. Et si non habemus in nobis illud
apostolicum, ut dicamus: 'optabam enim anathema esse a Christo pro
fratribus meis', tamen illud propheticum toto corde possimus dicere:
'heu quia anima perit!' et iterum: 'scrutemur vias nostras et quaeramus
et revertamur ad dominum: levemus corda nostra cum manibus ad deum
in caelo', sed et illud apostolicum: 'cupimus unumquemque vestrum in
visceribus Christi esse'.

65 Quam enim libenter hoc in loco ac si marinis fluctibus iactatus et in
optato evectus portu remis, si non tantos talesque malitiae episcoporum
vel ceterorum sacerdotum aut clericorum in nostro quoque ordine erigi
adversus deum vidissem montes, quos me secundum legem, ceu testes,
primum duris verborum cautibus, dein populum, si tamen sanctionibus
inhaeret, non ut corporaliter interficiantur, sed mortui vitiis vivant deo,
ne personarum arguar exceptionis, totis necesse est viribus lapidare,
2 verẹcundia interveniente quiescerem. Sed mihi quaeso, ut iam in
superioribus dixi, ab his veniam impertiri quorum vitam non solum laudo
verum etiam cunctis mundi opibus praefero, cuiusque me, si fieri possit,
ante mortis diem esse aliquamdiu participem optọ et sitio. Nostris iam
nunc obvallatis sanctorum duobus clipeis lateribus invictis, dorso ad
veritatis moenia stabilito, capite pro galea adiutorio domini fidissime   62
contecto,crebro veracium volatu volitent conviciorum cautes.

66 Sacerdotes habet Britannia, sed insipientes; quam plurimos ministros,
sed impudentes; clericos, sed raptores subdolos; pastores, ut dicuntur,
sed occisioni animarum lupos paratos, quippe non commoda plebi
providentes, sed proprii plenitudinem ventris quaerentes; ecclesiae
domus habentes, sed turpis lucri gratia eas adeuntes; populos docentes,
sed praebendo pessima exempla, vitia malosque mores; raro sacrificantes
2 et numquam puro corde inter altaria stantes; plebem ob peccata non
corripientes, nimirum eadem agentes; praecepta Christi spernentes et suas
libidines votis omnibus implere curantes; sedem Petri apostoli inmundis
pedibus usurpantes, sed merito cupiditatis in Iudae traditoris pestilentem
cathedram decidentes; veritatem pro inimico odientes et mendaciis ac si
carissimis fratribus faventes; iustos inopes immanes quasi angues torvis
vultibus conspicantes et sceleratos divites absque ullo verecundiae
3 respectu sicut caelestes angelos venerãntes; egenis eleemosynam esse
dandam summis e labiis praedicantes, sed ipsi vel obolum non dantes;
nefanda populi scelera tacentes et suas iniurias quasi Christo irrogatas
amplificantes; religiosam forte matrem seu sorores domo pellentes et

118

externas veluti secretiori ministerio familiares indecenter levigantes vel
potius, ut vera dicam licet inepta non tam mihi quam talia agentibus,

4 humiliantes; ecclesiasticos post haec gradus propensius quam regna
caelorum ambientes et tyrannico ritu acceptos defendentes nec tamen
legitimis moribus illustrantes; ad praecepta sanctorum, si aliquando
dumtaxat audierint, quae ab illis saepissime audienda erant, oscitantes
ac stupidos, et ad ludicra et ineptas saecularium hominum fabulas, ac si

5 iter vitae, quae mortis pandunt, strenuos et intentos; pinguedinis gratia
taurorum more raucos et ad illicita infeliciter promptos; vultus
arroganter in altum habentes et sensus conscientia remordente ad ima vel
tartarum demersos; uno sane perdito denario maestos et ad unum
inquisitum laetos; in apostolicis sanctionibus ob inscientiam vel
peccatorum pondus, ora etiam scientium obturantes, hebetes ac mutos

6 et in flexibus mundialium negotiorum mendacibus doctissimos; quorum
de scelerata conversatione multos sacerdotio irruentes potius vel illud   63
paene omni pecunia redimentes quam tractos et in eodem veteri
infaustoque intolerabilium piaculorum caeno post sacerdotalem
episcopatus vel presbyterii sedem, qui nec ibidem umquam sederunt,
utpote indigne porcorum more volutantes, rapto tantum sacerdotali
nomine nec tamen tenore, vel apostolica dignitate accepta, sed qui

7 nondum ad integram fidem sunt vel malorum paenitentiam idonei, quomodo ad quemlibet ecclesiasticum, ut non dicam summum, convenientes
et adepti gradum, quem non nisi sancti atque perfecti et apostolorum
imitatores et, ut magistri gentium verbis loquar, irreprehensibiles ·
legitime et absque magno sacrilegii crimine suscipiunt?

67   Quid enim tam impium tamque scelestum est quam ad similitudinem
Simonis magi, non intervenientibus licet interea promiscuis criminibus,
episcopatus officium vel presbyterii terreno pretio, quod sanctitate

2 rectisque moribus decentius adquiritur, quempiam velle mercari? Sed
in eo isti propensius vel desperatius errant, quo non ab apostolis vel
apostolorum successoribus, sed a tyrannis et a patre eorum diabolo
fucata et numquam profutura emunt sacerdotia: quin potius velut
culmen tectumque malorum omnium quoddam, quo non facile eis
improperentur a quoquam admissa prisca vel nova et cupiditatis
gulaeque desideria utpote praepositi multorum facilius rapiant, scelestae

3 vitae structurae superponunt. Nam si talis profecto coemptionis
condicio ab impudentibus istis non dicam apostolo Petro, sed cuilibet
sancto sacerdoti pioque regi ingesta fuisset, eadem responsa accepissent
quae ab apostolo auctor eorundem magus Simon dicente Petro:
'pecunia tua tecum sit in perditionem'.

4   Sed forte (heu!) qui ambitores istos ordinant, immo potius humiliant
atque pro benedictione maledicunt, dum ex peccatoribus non paenitentes,
quod rectius fuerat, sed sacrilegos et desperatos faciunt et Iudam

quodammodo in Petri cathedra domini traditorem ac Nicolaum in loco
Stephani martyris statuunt inmundae haereseos adinventorem, eodem
modo sacerdotio adsciti sunt: et ideo non magnopere detestantur in filiis,
quin immo venerantur, quod similiter ut patribus sibi evenisse
certissimum est.

5   Etenim eos, si in parochiam resistentibus sibi et tam pretiosum
quaestum denegantibus severe commessoribus huiuscemodi margaritam
invenire non possint, praemissis ante sollicite nuntiis transnavigare   64
maria terrasque spatiosas transmeare non tam piget quam delectat, ut
omnino talis species inaequiparabilisque pulchritudo et, ut verius dicam,

6 zabolica illusio vel venditis omnibus copiis comparetur. Dein cum magno
apparatu magnaque fantasia vel potius insania repedantes ad patriam ex
erecto erectiorem incessum fingunt et dudum summitates montium
conspicantes nunc recte ad aethera vel ad summa nubium vellera
luminum semidormitantes acies librant ac sese nova quaedam plasmata,
immo diabolica organa, ut quondam Novatus Romae, dominicae
mulcator margaritae, porcus niger, patriae ingerunt, violenter manus non
tam venerabilibus aris quam flammis inferni ultricibus dignas in tali
schema positi sacrosanctis Christi sacrificiis extensuri.

68   Quid tu, infelix popule, a talibus, ut dixit apostolus, bestiis ventris
praestolaris? Hisne corrigeris, qui se ipsos non modo ad bona non invitant,
sed secundum prophetae exprobrationem laborant ut inique agant?
Talibusne oculis illustraberis, qui haec tantum avide speculantur quae

2 proclive vitiis, id est Tartari portis, ducant? Vel certe secundum
salvatoris dictum, si non istos rapacissimos ut Arabiae lupos, ac si Loth
ad montem igneum Sodomorum imbrem praepropere fugeritis, caeci
educti a caecis pariter in inferni foveam cadetis.

69   Sed forsitan aliquis dicat: non ita omnes episcopi vel presbyteri, ut
superius comprehensi, quia non scismatis, non superbiae, non in-
munditiae infamia maculantur, mali sunt. Quod nec vehementer et nos
diffitemur. Sed licet sciamus eos castos esse et bonos, breviter tamen
respondebimus.

Quid profuit Heli sacerdoti quod solus non violaverit praecepta
domini, rapiendo in fuscinulis antequam adeps domino offerretur ex
ollis carnes, dum eadem mortis ira qua filii sunt multatur?

2 Quis rogo eorum ob invidiam melioris hostiae caelestique igni in
caelis evectae, ut Abel, occisus? qui etiam mediocris verbi aspernantur
convicium.

Quis perosus est consilium malignantium et cum impiis non sedit,
ut de eo veridice quasi de Enoch diceretur: 'ambulavit Enoch cum deo et
non inveniebatur', in mundi scilicet vanitate omnis post idola proclive id
temporis claudicare relicto deo insipientis?

3 Quis eorum salutari in arca, hoc est nunc ecclesia, nullum deo

adversantem, ut Noe diluvii tempore, non admisit, ut perspicue
monstraretur non nisi innoxios vel paenitentes egregios in dominica   65
domu esse debere?

Quis victoribus solum et in tricentenario numero, hoc est trinitatis
sacramento, liberato iusto regum quinque victriciumque turmarum
exercitus ferales vincentibus et nequaquam aliena cupientibus sacrificium
offerens, ut Melchisedech, benedixit?

4   Quis sponte proprium in altari capite caedendum, ut Habraham, deo
iubente optulit filium, ut simile quoddam huic impleret Christi mandatum
dicentis oculum dextrum scandalizantem evelli debere et prophetae
praecaveret se maledictum esse gladium et sanguinem prohibentem?

Quis memoriam malefacti de corde radicitus, ut Ioseph, evulsit?

5   Quis in monte cum domino locutus et nequaquam concrepantibus
tubis exinde perterritus duas tabulas cornutamque faciem aspectu
incredulis inhabilem et horrendam tropico sensu, ut Moyses, advexit?

Quis eorum pro peccatis populi exorans imo de pectore clamavit, ut
ipse, 'domine', inquiens, 'peccavit populus iste peccatum grande: quod
si dimittis eis, dimitte: alioquin dele me de libro tuo'?

70   Quis zelo dei accensus mirabili ad ultionem fornicationis sine
dilatione, sanando paenitentiae medicamine stupri affectum, ne ira populo
inardesceret, sicut Finees sacerdos, ut per hoc in aevo reputaretur illi
iustitia, strenue consurrexit?

Quis vero eorum vel in extirpationem usque ad internicionem de
terra repromissionis septem gentium morali intellegentia vel ad consta-
bilitionem spiritalis Israel pro eis Iesum Nave imitatus est?

2   Quis eorum populo dei finales terminos trans Iordanem, ut sciretur
quid cui tribui conveniat, sicut supradicti, Finees scilicet et Iesus,
sagaciter divisere, ostendit?

Quis ut adversariorum plebi dei innumera prosterneret gentium milia,
unicam filiam, quae propria voluptas intellegitur, imitans et in hoc
apostolum dicentem: 'non quaerens quod mihi utile est, sed quod multis,
ut salvi fiant', obviantem victoribus cum tympanis et choris, id est
carnalibus desideriis, in sacrificium votivae placationis, ut Iepte, mactavit?

3   Quis eorum ad conturbanda fuganda sternendaque superbarum
gentium castra, mysterii trinitatis, ut supra diximus, cum lagoenas viris
tenentibus egregias in manibus sonantesque tubas, id est propheticos et
apostolicos sensus, ut dixit dominus prophetae: 'exalta quasi tuba vocem
tuam': et psalmista de apostolis: 'in omnem terram exivit sonus eorum',
et lagoenas splendidissimo ignis lumine noctu coruscantes, quae
accipiuntur in sanctorum corporibus bonis operibus annexis et sancti   66
spiritus igni ardentibus, ut apostolus, 'habentes', inquit, 'thesaurum
istum in vasis fictilibus', post idolatriae luci, quod moraliter inter-
pretatum condensae et fuscae cupiditatis, succisionem silvae et evidentia

121

signa Iudaici velleris imbris caelestis expertis et gentilis rore sancti
spiritus madefacti fide non dubia, ut Gedeon, processit?

71   Quis eorum mori exoptans mundo et vivere Christo luxuriosos
gentium convivas laudantes deos suos, id est, sensus extollentes divitias,
ut apostolus 'et avaritia', inquit, 'quae est simulacrorum servitus',
concussis duabus virtute brachiorum columnis, quae intelleguntur in
voluptatibus nequam animae carnisque, quibus domus humanae omnis
nequitiae quodammodo pangitur ac fulcimentatur, tam innumerabiles, ut
Sampson, prostravit?

2   Quis orationibus holocaustoque lactantis agni Philistinorum metum
depellens insperatas tonitruorum voces nubiumque imbres concitans
absque adulatione regem constituens, eundem deo non placentem abiciens,
uncto pro illo meliore in regno, ut Samuel, valedicturus populo astabit
hoc modo dicens: 'Ecce praesto sum, loquimini coram domino et Christo
eius, utrum bovem cuiusquam tulerim an asinum, si quempiam calumniatus
sum, si oppressi aliquem, si de manu cuiusquam munus accepi'? Cui a
populo responsum est dicente: 'non es calumniatus nos neque oppressisti
neque tulisti de manu alicuius quippiam'.

3   Quis eorum, igne caelesti centum superbos exurens, quinquaginta
humiles servans et absque adulationis fuco, non deum per prophetas, sed
idolum Accaron consulenti, mortem imminentem iniquo regi annuntians,
omnes prophetas simulacri Baal, qui interpretati accipiuntur sensus humani
invidiae avaritiae, ut iam diximus, semper intenti, mucrone corusco, hoc
est verbo dei, ut Helias egregius vates, prostravit, et, zelo dei commotus,
iniquorum terrae imbres adimens aetherales, ac si fortissimo penurii
clustello tribus annis sexque mensibus obseratos, fame siti moribundus in
deserto conquestus est: 'domine', inquiens, 'prophetas tuos occiderunt et
altaria tua suffoderunt et ego relictus sum solus et quaerunt animam
meam'?

72   Quis eorum carissimum discipulum terrenis extra solitum ponderibus
oneratum, quae antea a se magnopere licet rogato ut acciperet despecta
fuissent, etsi non perpetua lepra, ut Helisaeus, saltim expulsione multavit?

2   Et quis ex illis puero in vitae desperatione aestuanti atque inproviso
super bellico hostium apparatu civitatem in qua erant obsidentium
tremefacto inter nos, ut ille, animae visus, ferventi exoratione ad deum
facta, ita ut intueri potuerit auxiliarium caelestis exercitus, armatorum
curruum seu equitum ignito vultu fulgentium montem plenum, patefecit,
et credere quin fortior esset ad salvandum quam inimici ad pugnandum?

     Et quis eorum corporis tactu mortui scilicet mundo, viventis autem
deo, alii diverso funere occubanti procul dubio mortuo deo, vitiis   67
vero viventi quasi supradictus proficiet, ita ut statim prosiliens Christo grates
pro sanitate agat cunctorum paene mortalium ore desperata?

3   Cuius eorum, carbone ignito de altari forcipe Cherubin advecto, ut

peccata sua delerentur humilitate confessionis, labia, ut Esaiae, mundata
sunt, et, efficaci oratione sibi adiuncta pii regis Ezechiae, supplantatione
centum octoginta quinque milia exercitus Assyriorum nullo apparente
vulneris vestigio angeli manu, ut supra dicti, prostrata sunt?

4   Quis eorum ob praecepta dei et minas caelitus datas veritatemque vel
non audientibus proferendam squalores pedoresque carcerum, ut
momentaneas mortes, ut beatus Ieremias excepit?

Et ne multa: quis eorum, ut magister gentium dixit, errare in montibus
et in speluncis et in cavernis terrae, lapidari, secari, totius mortis genere
pro nomine domini attemptari, sicut sancti prophetae, perpessus est?

73   Sed quid immoramur in exemplis veteribus, ac si non essent in novo
ulla? Audiant itaque nos qui absque ullo labore angustum hoc iter
Christianae religionis praetento tantum sacerdotali nomine intrare se
putant, carpentes paucos flores veluti summos de extento sanctorum novi
testamenti tironum amoenoque prato.

2   Quis vestrum, qui torpetis potius quam sedetis legitime in sacerdotali
sede, eiectus de consilio impiorum, post diversarum plagas virgarum, ut
sancti apostoli, quod dignus habitus est pro Christo vero deo contumeliam
pati toto corde trinitati gratias egit?

Quis ob testimonium verum deo ferendum fullonis vecte cerebro
percussus, ut Iacobus primus in novo dumtaxat episcopus testamento,
corporaliter interiit?

3   Quis gladio vestrum ab iniquo principe, ut Iacobus Iohannis frater,
capite caesus est?

Quis, ut protominister martyrque euangelicus, hoc solum criminis
habens, quod viderit deum, quem perfidi videre nequiverant, nefandis
manibus lapidatus est?

Quis inversis pedibus crucis affixus pro reverentia Christi patibulo,
quem non minus morte quam vita honoraturus, ut clavicularius ille
caelorum regni idoneus, extremum halitum fudit?

4   Quis ex vobis gladii ictu veridicantis pro confessione Christi post
vincula carceris, naufragia marum, virgarum caedem, post fluminum
latronum gentium Iudaeorum pseudoapostolorum continua pericula, post
famis ieiunii vigiliarum labores, post perpetem sollicitudinem omnium
ecclesiarum, post aestum pro scandalizantibus, post infirmitatem pro
infirmis, post admirabilem praedicando Christi evangelium orbis paene
circuitum, ut vas electionis magisterque gentium electus capite plexus
est?

74   Quis vestrum, ut sanctus martyr Ignatius Antiochiae urbis episcopus,
post admirabiles in Christo actus ob testimonium eius leonum molis   68
Romae confractus est? cuius verba cum ad passionem duceretur
audientes, si aliquando vultus vestri rubore confusi sunt, non solum in
comparatione eius vos non putabitis sacerdotes sed ne mediocres quidem

2   Christianos esse. Ait enim in epistola quam ad Romanam ecclesiam misit:
'A Syria usque Romam cum bestiis terra marique depugno, die ac nocte
conexus et colligatus decem leopardis, militibus dico ad custodiam datis,
qui ex beneficiis nostris saeviores fiunt. Sed ego eorum nequitiis magis
erudior, nec tamen in hoc iustificatus sum. O salutares bestias, quae
praeparantur mihi, quando venient? quando emittentur? quando eis frui
licebit carnibus meis? quas ego exopto acriores parari et invitabo ad
devorationem mei, et deprecabor ne forte, ut in nonnullis fecerunt,
timeant attingere corpus meum: quin immo, et si cunctabuntur, ego vim

3   faciam, ego me ingeram. Date, quaeso, veniam, ego novi quid expediat
mihi: nunc incipio esse Christi discipulus. Facessat invidia vel humani
affectus vel nequitiae spiritalis, ut Iesum Christum adipisci merear. Ignes,
cruces, bestiae, dispersiones ossium discerptionesque membrorum ac
totius corporis poenae et omnia in me unum supplicia diaboli arte
quaesita compleantur, dummodo Iesum Christum merear adipisci'.

4   Quid ad haec dormitantibus animae oculis aspicitis? quid talia surdis
sensuum auribus auscultatis? Discutite, quaeso, tenebrosam atramque
cordis vestri caliginem teporis, ut veritatis et humilitatis praefulgidum
lumen videre possitis. Christianus non mediocris sed perfectus, sacerdos
non vilis sed summus, martyr non segnis sed praecipuus dicit: nunc incipio
esse Christi discipulus.

5   Et vos, ac si Lucifer ille de caelo proiectus, verbis non potestate
erigimini, et quodammodo sub dente ruminatis et gestibus praetenditis
quae antea auctor vester depinxerat 'in caelum' inquiens 'conscendam et
ero similis altissimo': et iterum: 'ego fodi et bibi aquam et exsiccavi

6   vestigio pedum meorum omnes rivos aggerum'. Multo rectius oportebat
vos imitari illum et audire qui totius bonitatis et humilitatis vere
invictum exemplar est, dicentem per prophetam: 'ego autem sum vermis
et non homo, opprobrium hominum et abiectio plebis'. O mirabile
quoddam dixisse eum opprobrium hominum, cum omnis mundi opprobria
deleverit: et iterum in euangelio 'non possum ego a me ipso facere
quicquam', cum ipse coaevus patri ac spiritui sancto, communis
eiusdemque substantiae, caelum et terram cum omni eorum inaestimabili
ornamento fecerit, non alterius sed propria potestate; et vos arroganter
verba exaltasse, propheta dicente: 'quid superbit terra et cinis?'

75   Sed ad propositum revertar: quis, inquam, ex vobis, ut Smyrnensis
ecclesiae pastor egregius Polycarpus Christi testis, mensam humane   69
hospitibus ad ignem eum avide trahentibus apposuit et obiectus flammis
pro Christi caritate dixit: 'qui dedit mihi ignis ferre supplicium, dabit ut
sine clavorum confixione flammas immobiliter perferam'.

2   Unum adhuc praeter magnam verbis volans sanctorum silvam exempli
gratia ponam, Basilium scilicet Caesariensem episcopum, qui, cum ab
iniquo principe minae huiuscemodi intentarentur, quod nisi in crastinum

Arriano caeno, ut ceteri, macularetur esset omnino moriturus, dixisse fertur: 'ego sane ero cras, qui hodie sum: tu te utinam non mutares'. Et iterum: 'utinam haberem aliquid digni muneris quod offerrem huic qui maturius Basilium de nodo follis huius absolveret'.

3   Quis ex vobis apostolici sermonis regulam, quae ab omnibus semper sanctis sacerdotibus quibusque temporibus extantibus humanam suggestionem, praecipitanter ad nequitiam festinantem, recutientibus servata est, in concussione tyrannorum indirupte custodivit, hoc modo dicens: 'oboedire oportet magis deo quam hominibus'.

76   Igitur confugientes solito more ad domini misericordiam sanctorumque prophetarum eius voces, ut illi pro nobis oraculorum suorum iacula inperfectis pastoribus, ut antea tyrannis, quis compuncti sanentur, librent, videamus quid dominus per prophetas ad desides et inhonestos sacerdotes et non bene populum tam exempla quam verba docentes minarum loquatur.

2   Nam et Heli ille sacerdos in Silo pro eo quod non digno deo zelo severe in filios contemnentes deum ultus fuerat, sed molliter et clementer, utpote paterno affectu, admonuerat, tali animadversione damnatur, dicente ad eum propheta: 'haec dicit dominus: manifeste ostendi me ad domum

3 patris tui, cum essent in Aegypto servientes Pharaonis, et elegi domum patris tui ex omnibus tribubus Israel mihi in sacerdotio'. Et post pauca: 'Quare respexisti in incensum meum et in sacrificium meum improbo oculo et honorificasti filios tuos plus quam me, ut benediceres eos a primordio in omnibus sacrificiis coram me?' 'Et nunc sic dicit dominus: quoniam qui honorificant me, honorabo eos: et qui pro nihilo habent me, ad nihilum redigentur. Ecce dies venient et disperdam nomen tuum et

4 semen domus patris tui'. 'Et hoc tibi signum sit, quod veniet super duos filios tuos Ofni et Finees; in uno die morientur ambo in gladio virorum'. Si haec itaque patiuntur qui verbis tantum subiectos et non condigna ultione emendant, quid ipsis fiet qui ad mala hortantur peccando et trahunt?

77   Quid illi quoque perspicuum est vero vati post expletionem signi ab eodem praedicti et restitutionem aridae manus impio regi misso a   70 Iudaea prophetare in Bethel prohibitoque ne quid ibidem cibi gustaret ac decepto ab alio, ut dicebatur, propheta, ut parum quid panis et aquae

2 sumeret, obtigit, dicente ad eum suo hospite: 'Haec dicit dominus deus: quia inoboediens fuisti ori domini et non custodisti mandatum quod praecepit dominus deus tuus et reversus es et comedisti panem et bibisti aquam in hoc loco in quo mandaveram tibi ne manducares panem nec biberes aquam, non ponetur corpus tuum in sepulcro patrum tuorum. Et factum est', inquit, 'postquam manducavit panem et bibit aquam, stravit sibi asinam suam et abiit; et invenit eum leo in via et occidit eum'.

78   Esaiam quoque sanctum prophetam de sacerdotibus hoc modo loquentem audite: 'Vae impio in malum, retributio enim manuum eius

fiet ei. Populum meum exactores sui spoliaverunt et mulieres dominatae
sunt eius. Popule meus, qui beatum te dicunt ipsi te decipiunt et viam
gressuum tuorum dissipant. Stat ad iudicandum dominus et stat ad
iudicandos populos. Dominus ad iudicium veniet cum senibus populi sui
et principibus eius. Vos depasti estis vineam meam, rapina pauperis in
domo vestra. Quare atteritis populum meum et facies pauperum

2   commolitis? dicit dominus exercituum'. Et item: 'Vae qui condunt leges
iniquas et scribentes iniustitiam scripserunt, ut opprimerent in iudicio
pauperes et vim facerent causae humilium populi mei, ut essent viduae
praeda eorum et pupillos diriperent. Quid facietis in die visitationis et
calamitatis de longe venientis?' Et infra: 'Verum hi quoque prae vino
nescierunt et prae ebrietate erraverunt, sacerdotes nescierunt prae
ebrietate, absorpti sunt a vino, erraverunt in ebrietate, nescierunt
videntem, ignoraverunt iudicium. Omnes enim mensae repletae sunt

79 vomitu sordium, ita ut non esset ultra locus'. 'Propterea audite verbum
domini, viri illusores, qui dominamini super populum meum qui est in
Hierusalem. Dixistis enim: Percussimus foedus cum morte et cum inferno
fecimus pactum. Flagellum inundans cum transierit non veniet super nos,
quia posuimus mendacium spem nostram et mendacio protecti sumus'. Et
post aliquanta: 'et subvertet grando spem mendacii et protectionem aquae
inundabunt, et delebitur foedus vestrum cum morte et pactum vestrum
cum inferno non stabit: flagellum inundans cum transierit, eritis et in

2   conculcationem: quandocumque pertransierit, tollet vos'. Et iterum: 'Et
dixit dominus: eo quod appropinquat populus iste ore suo et labiis
glorificant me, cor autem eorum longe est a me: ideo ecce ego addam ut
admirationem faciam populo huic miraculo grandi et stupendo. Peribit
enim sapientia a sapientibus eius et intellectus prudentium eius abscondetur.
Vae qui profundi estis corde, ut a domino abscondatis consilium, quorum
sunt in tenebris opera et dicunt: Quis videt nos? et quis novit nos?

3 Perversa enim haec vestra cogitatio'. Et post aliquanta: 'Haec dicit
dominus: Caelum sedes mea et terra scabellum pedum meorum est. Quae
ista est domus quam aedificabitis mihi? et quis erit locus quietis meae?
Omnia haec manus mea fecit et facta sunt universa ista, dicit dominus.   71
Ad quem autem aspiciam nisi ad pauperculum et contritum spiritu et
trementem sermones meos? Qui immolat bovem quasi qui interficiat
virum: qui mactat pecus quasi qui excerebret canem: qui offert oblatio-
nem quasi qui sanguinem suillum offerat: qui recordatur thuris quasi qui
benedicat idolo. Haec omnia elegerunt in viis suis et in abominationibus
suis anima eorum delectata est'.

80   Hieremias quoque virgo prophetaque quid insipientibus loquatur
pastoribus, attendite: 'Haec dicit dominus: quid invenerunt patres vestri
in me iniquitatis, quia elongaverunt a me et ambulaverunt post vanitatem
et vani facti sunt?' Et paulo post: 'Et ingressi contaminastis terram meam et

hereditatem meam posuistis in abominationem. Sacerdotes non dixerunt:
ubi est dominus? et tenentes legem nescierunt me et pastores praevaricati
sunt in me. Propterea adhuc iudicio contendam vobiscum, ait dominus, et

2 cum filiis vestris disceptabo'. Item post aliquanta: 'Stupor et mirabilia
facta sunt in terra: prophetae praedicabant mendacium et sacerdotes
applaudebant manibus suis et populus meus dilexit talia. Quid igitur fiet in
novissimis eius?' 'Cui loquar et contestabor, ut audiat? Ecce incircumcisae
aures eorum et audire non possunt. Ecce verbum domini factum est illis in
opprobrium et non suscipiunt illud': 'quia extendam manum meam super
habitantes terram, dicit dominus. A minore quippe usque ad maiorem
omnes avaritiae student et a propheta usque ad sacerdotem cuncti faciunt
dolum. Et curabant contritionem filiae populi mei cum ignominia dicentes:
pax, pax, et non erit pax. Confusi sunt qui abominationem fecerunt: quin
potius confusione non sunt confusi et erubescere nescierunt. Quam ob
rem cadent inter ruentes, in tempore visitationis eorum corruent, dicit

3 dominus'. Et iterum: 'Omnes isti principes declinantium ambulantes
fraudulenter aes et ferrum universi corrupti sunt. Defecit sufflatorium in
igne, frustra conflavit conflator, malitiae autem eorum non sunt
consumptae. Argentum reprobum vocate eos, quia dominus proiecit illos'.

4 Et post pauca: 'Ego sum, ego sum, ego vidi, dicit dominus. Ite ad locum
meum in Silo, ubi habitavit nomen meum a principio, et videte quae
fecerim ei propter malitiam populi mei Israel. Et nunc quia fecistis omnia
opera haec, dicit dominus: et locutus sum ad vos mane consurgens et
loquens et non audistis, et vocavi vos et non respondistis, faciam domui
huic, in qua invocatum est nomen meum et in qua vos habetis fiduciam,
et loco, quem dedi vobis et patribus vestris, sicut feci Silo et proiciam vos a

81 facie mea'. Et iterum: 'Filii mei exierunt a me et non subsistunt, et non
est qui extendat ultra tentorium meum et erigat pelles meas, quia stulte
egerunt pastores et dominum non quaesierunt. Propterea non intellexerunt

2 et grex eorum dispersus est'. Et post aliquanta: 'Quid est quod dilectus
meus in domo mea facit scelera multa? Numquid carnes sanctae auferent
a te malitias tuas, in quibus gloriata es? Olivam uberem pulchram
fructiferam speciosam vocavit dominus nomen tuum. Ad vocem loquelae

3 grandis exarsit ignis in ea et combusta sunt fruteta eius'. Et iterum: 72
'Venite, congregamini, omnes bestiae terrae, properate ad devorandum.
Pastores multi demoliti sunt vineam meam, conculcaverunt partem meam,
dederunt portionem meam desiderabilem in desertum solitudinis'.
Itemque loquitur: 'Haec dicit dominus populo huic, qui dilexit movere
pedes suos et non quievit et domino non placuit. Nunc recordabitur

4 iniquitatum eorum et visitabit peccata illorum'. 'Prophetae dicunt eis:
non videbitis gladium et fames non erit in vobis, sed pacem veram dabit
dominus vobis in loco isto. Et dixit dominus ad me: Falso prophetae
vaticinantur in nomine meo, non misi eos et non praecepi eis, visionem

mendacem et divinationem et fraudulentiam et seductionem cordis sui prophetant vobis. Ideo haec dicit dominus: in gladio et fame consumentur prophetae illi, et populi quibus prophetaverunt proiecti erunt in viis

82 Hierusalem prae fame et gladio, et non erit qui sepeliat'. Et iterum: 'Vae pastoribus qui disperdunt et dilacerant gregem pascuae meae, dicit dominus. Ideo haec dicit dominus deus Israel ad pastores qui pascunt populum meum: Vos dispersistis gregem meum et eiecistis eos et non

2 visitastis illos. Ecce, ego visitabo super vos malitiam studiorum vestrorum, dicit dominus'. 'Propheta namque et sacerdos polluti sunt et in domu mea inveni malum eorum, dicit dominus: et idcirco via eorum erit quasi lubricum in tenebris, impellentur enim et corruent in ea, afferam enim super eos mala, annum visitationis eorum, dicit dominus. Et in prophetis Samariae vidi fatuitatem, et prophetabant in Baal et decipiebant populum

3 meum Israel. Et in prophetis Ierusalem vidi similitudinem adulterantium et iter mendacii: et confortaverunt manus pessimorum, ut non converterentur unusquisque a malitia sua: facti sunt mihi omnes Sodoma et habitatores eius quasi Gomorrha. Propterea haec dicit dominus ad prophetas: ecce ego cibabo eos absinthio et potabo eos felle. A prophetis enim Ierusalem est egressa pollutio super omnem terram. Haec dicit dominus exercituum: Nolite audire verba prophetarum, qui prophetant vobis et decipiunt vos: visionem enim cordis sui loquuntur, non de ore

4 domini. Dicunt enim his qui me blasphemant: Locutus est dominus: pax erit vobis: et omni, qui ambulant in pravitate cordis sui, dixerunt: Non veniet super eos malum. Quis enim affuit in consilio domini et vidit et

5 audivit sermonem eius? quis consideravit verbum illius et audivit? Ecce, turbo dominicae indignationis egreditur et tempestas erumpens super caput impiorum veniet: non revertetur furor domini usque dum faciat et usque dum compleat cogitationem cordis sui. In novissimis diebus intellegetis consilium eius'.

83 Parum namque cogitatis vel facitis quod sanctus quoque Ioel monens inertes sacerdotes ac deflens detrimentum populi pro iniquitatibus eorum edixit: 'Expergiscimini qui estis ebrii a vino vestro, et plorate et lamentamini omnes qui bibitis vinum in ebrietatem, quia ablata est ab ore vestro iucunditas et gaudium. Lugete, sacerdotes, qui deservitis altario, quia miseri facti sunt campi . Lugeat terra, quia miserum factum est frumentum et siccatum est vinum, diminutum est oleum, aruerunt agricolae. Lugete, possessiones, pro tritico et hordeo, quia periit vindemia ex agro, vitis arefacta est, ficus diminutae sunt: granata et palma et 73 malum et omnia ligna agri arefacta sunt, quoniam confuderunt gaudium filii hominum'.

2 Quae omnia spiritaliter intellegenda erunt vobis, ne tam pestilenti fame verbi dei animae vestrae arescerent.

3 Et iterum: 'flete, sacerdotes, qui deservitis domino, dicentes: parce,

domine, populo tuo et ne des hereditatem tuam in opprobrium et ne dominentur eorum gentes, uti ne dicant gentes: ubi est deus eorum?' Sed haec vos nequaquam auditis, sed omnia quibus propensius divini furoris indignatio inardescat admittitis.

84   Quid etiam sanctus Osee propheta sacerdotibus vestri moduli dixerit signanter attendite: 'audite haec, sacerdotes, et intendat domus Israel, et domus regis, infigite auribus vestris, quoniam ad vos est iudicium, quia laqueus facti estis speculationi et velut retiaculum extensum super Thabor, quod indicatores venationis confinxerunt.'

85   Vobis etiam a domino alienatio huiuscemodi intendatur per prophetam Amos dicentem: 'Odio habui et repuli dies festos vestros et non accipiam odorem in sollemnibus conventionibus vestris, quia etsi obtuleritis holocaustomata et hostias vestras, non accipiam ea. Et salutare declarationis vestrae non aspiciam. Transfer a me sonum cantionum tuarum, et psalmum organum tuorum non audiam'.

2   Famis etenim evangelici cibi (in) culina ipsa vestrae animae viscera excomedens grassatur in vobis, sicut supra dictus propheta praedixit: 'Ecce', inquiens, 'dies veniunt, dicit dominus, et inmittam famem in terram, non famem panis neque sitim aquae, sed famem in audiendo verbum dei. Et movebuntur aquae a mari usque ad mare, et ab aquilone usque ad orientem percurrent quaerentes verbum domini, et non invenient'.

86   Auribus quoque percipite sanctum Micheam ac si caelestem quandam tubam adversus subdolos populi principes concisius personantem: 'Audite nunc', inquiens, 'principes domus Iacob: nonne vobis est ut cognoscatis iudicium odientibus bona et quaerentibus maligna, rapientibus pelles eorum ab eis et carnes eorum ab ossibus eorum? quemadmodum comederunt carnes plebis meae et pelles eorum ab eis excoriaverunt, ossa eorum confregerunt et laniaverunt quasi carnes in

2   olla. Succlamabunt ad deum et non exaudiet eos et avertet faciem suam ab eis in illo tempore, propter quod malitiose gesserunt in adinventionibus suis super ipsos. Haec dicit dominus super prophetas qui seducunt populum meum, qui mordent dentibus suis et praedicant in eum pacem, et non est data in os eorum: excitavi in eum bellum. Propterea nox erit vobis ex visione et tenebrae vobis erunt ex divinatione, et occidet sol super prophetas et contenebrescet super eos dies, et confundentur videntes somnia et deridebuntur divini et obtrectabunt adversus omnes ipsi, quoniam non erit qui exaudiat eos: si non ego implevero fortitudinem in spiritu domini et iudicio et potestate, ut annuntiem domui Iacob

3   impietates suas et Israel peccata sua. Audite haec itaque, duces domus   74 Iacob, et residui domus Israel, qui abominamini iudicium et omnia recta pervertitis, qui aedificatis Sion in sanguine et Hierusalem in iniquitatibus: duces eius cum muneribus iudicabant et sacerdotes eius cum mercede respondebant et prophetae eius cum pecunia divinabant et in domino requiescebant dicentes: nonne dominus in nobis est? non venient super nos mala. Ideo propter vos Sion sicut ager arabitur et Hierusalem sicut specula pomarii erit et mons domus sicut locus silvae'.

4   Et post aliquanta: 'Heu me, quia factus sum sicut qui colligit stipulam in messe et sicut racemus in vindemia, cum non sit botrus ad manducandum primitiva: heu me, anima quia periit terrenis operibus, semper peccatorum reverentia exoritur reverens a terra, et qui corrigat inter homines non est. Omnes in sanguinem iudicio contendunt, et unusquisque proximum suum tribulatione tribulavit, in malum manus suas praeparat'.

87   Quid Sophonias etiam propheta egregius de vestris olim comessoribus disceptaverit attendite; de Hierusalem namque loquebatur, quae spiritaliter ecclesia vel anima intellegitur: 'o', inquiens, 'quae erat splendida et liberata civitas, confidens columba, non obaudivit vocem nec percepit disciplinam, in domino non confisa est et ad deum suum non accessit'.

2 Et id quare ostendit: 'Principes eius sicut leones rugientes, iudices sicut lupi Arabiae non relinquebant in mane, prophetae eius spiritum portantes viri contemptoris, sacerdotes eius profanabant sancta et impie agebant in lege. Dominus autem iustus in medio eius et non faciet iniustum: mane mane dabit iudicium suum'.

88   Sed et beatum Zachariam prophetam monentem vos in verbo dei audite: 'haec enim dicit omnipotens dominus: iudicium iustum iudicate, et misericordiam et miserationem facite unusquisque ad fratrem suum, et viduam et orfanum et advenam et pauperem per potentiam nolite nocere, et malitiam unusquisque fratris sui non reminiscatur in corde suo: et contumaces fuerunt, ne observarent, et dederunt dorsum stultitiae et aures suas degravaverunt, ut non audirent, et cor suum statuerunt insuadibile, ne audirent legem meam et verba quae misit dominus omnipotens in spiritu suo in manibus prophetarum priorum; et facta est

2 ira magna a domino omnipotente'. Et iterum: 'Quoniam qui loquebantur locuti sunt molestias, et divini visa falsa et somnia falsa loquebantur et vana consolabantur, propter hoc aridi facti sunt sicut oves, et afflicti sunt quoniam non erat sanitas. Super pastores exacervata est iracundia mea et

3 super agnos visitabo'. Et post pauca: 'Vox lamentantium pastorum, quia misera facta est magnitudo eorum. Vox rugientium leonum, quoniam miser factus est decursus Iordanis. Haec dicit dominus omnipotens: qui possidebant interficiebant, et non paenituit eos. Et qui vendebant eas dicebant: benedictus dominus, et ditati sumus et pastores earum nihil passi sunt in eis: propter quod non parcam iam super inhabitantes   75 terram, dicit dominus'.

89   Quid praeterea sanctus Malachias propheta vobis denuntiaverit audite, 'Vos' inquiens 'sacerdotes qui spernitis nomen meum, et dixistis:

in quo spernimus nomen tuum? Offerendo ad altare meum panes pollutos.
Et dixistis: in quo polluimus eos? In eo quod dixistis: mensa domini pro
nihilo est, et quae superposita sunt, sprevistis: quoniam, si adducatis
caecum ad victimam, nonne malum? si ammoveatis claudum aut languidum,
nonne malum? Offer itaque illud praeposito tuo, si suscipiet illud, si
accipiet personam tuam, dicit dominus omnipotens. Et nunc exorate
faciem dei vestri et deprecamini eum. In manibus vestris facta sunt haec. Si

2 accipiam ex vobis personas vestras?' Et iterum:'Et intulistis de rapina
claudum et languidum et intulistis munus. Numquid suscipiam illud de
manu vestra? dicit dominus. Maledictus dolosus, qui habet in grege suo
masculum et votum faciens immolat debile domino, quia rex magnus ego
sum, dicit dominus exercituum, et nomen meum horribile in gentibus. Et
nunc ad vos mandatum hoc, o sacerdotes; si nolueritis audire et ponere
super cor, ut detis gloriam nomini meo, ait dominus exercituum, mittam
in vos egestatem et maledicam benedictionibus vestris, quoniam non
posuistis super cor. Ecce ego proiciam vobis brachium et dispergam
super vultum vestrum stercus sollemnitatum vestrarum'.

3   Sed interea ut avidius organa nequitiae praeparetis ad bona, quid de
sancto sacerdote dicat, si quantulumcunque adhuc interni auditus in vobis
remanet, auscultate: 'Pactum meum', inquiens, 'fuit cum eo', de Levi
namque vel Moyse secundum historiam loquebatur, 'vitae et pacis, dedi
ei timorem, et timuit me, a facie nominis mei pavebat. Lex veritatis fuit
in ore eius et iniquitas non est inventa in labiis eius, in pace et in aequitate
ambulavit mecum et multos avertit ab iniquitate. Labia enim sacerdotis
custodient scientiam et legem requirent ex ore eius, quia angelus domini
exercituum est'.

4   Nunc item mutavit sensum et malos increpare non desinit, 'Vos'
inquiens 'recessistis de via et descandalizastis plurimos in lege et irritum
fecistis pactum cum Levi, dicit dominus exercituum. Propter quod et ego
dedi vos contemptibiles et humiles in omnibus populis, sicut non servastis
vias meas et accepistis faciem in lege. Numquid non pater unus omnium
nostrum? numquid non deus unus creavit nos? Quare ergo despicit

5 unusquisque fratrem suum?' Et iterum: 'Ecce veniet dominus exercituum:
et quis poterit cogitare diem adventus eius? et quis stabit ad videndum
eum? Ipse enim egredietur quasi ignis ardens et quasi poa laventium, et
sedebit conflans et emundans argentum, et purgabit filios Levi, et colabit

6· eos quasi aurum et quasi argentum'. Et post pauca: 'invaluerunt super me
verba vestra, dicit dominus, et dixistis: Vanus est qui servit deo, et quod
emolumentum quia custodivimus praecepta eius et quia ambulavimus
coram domino exercituum tristes? Ergo nunc beatos dicemus arrogantes,
si quidem aedificati sunt facientes iniquitatem; temptaverunt deum et
salvi facti sunt'.

90   Quid vero Ezechiel propheta dixerit attendite: 'Vae' inquiens 'super

131

vae veniet et nuntius super nuntium erit et quaeretur visio a propheta
et lex peribit a sacerdote et consilium de senioribus'. Et iterum: 'Haec   76
dicit dominus: eo quod sermones vestri sunt mendaces et divinationes
vestrae vanae, propter hoc ecce ego ad vos, dicit dominus, extendam
manum meam super prophetas qui vident mendacia et eos qui
loquuntur vana: in disciplina populi mei non erunt et in scriptura domus
Israel non scribentur et in terram Israel non intrabunt et scietis quia
ego dominus. Propterea populum meum seduxerunt dicentes: pax
domini, et non est pax domini. Hic struit parietem et ipsi ungunt eum
2 et cadet'. Et post aliquanta: 'vae his qui concinnant cervicalia subtus
omnem cubitum manus et faciunt velamina super omne caput universae
aetatis ad subvertendas animas. Animaeque subversae sunt populi mei et
animas possidebant et contaminabant me ad populum meum propter
manum plenam hordei et propter fragmentum panis ad occidendas animas
quas non oportebat mori, et ad liberandas animas quas non oportebat
3 vivere, dum loquimini populo exaudienti vana eloquia'. Et infra: 'Fili
hominis dic, tu es terra quae non compluitur neque pluvia facta est
super te in die irae, in qua principes in medio eius sicut leones rugientes
rapientes rapinas, animas devorantes in potentia et pretia accipientes, et
viduae tuae multiplicatae sunt in medio tui, et sacerdotes eius despexerunt legem meam et polluebant sancta mea. Inter sanctum et pollutum
non distinguebant et inter medium inmundi et mundi non dividebant, et
a sabbatis meis obvelabant oculos suos et polluebant in medio eorum'.
91 Et iterum: 'Et quaerebam ex eis virum recte conversantem et stantem
ante faciem meam omnino in tempora terrae, ne in fine delerem eam, et
non inveni. Et effudi in eam animum meum in igne irae meae ad
2 consumendum eos: vias eorum in caput eorum dedi, dicit dominus'. Et
post aliquanta: 'Et factus est sermo domini ad me dicens: fili hominis,
loquere filiis populi mei et dices ad eos: terra in quam ego gladium
superinducam, et acceperit populus terrae hominem unum ex ipsis et
dederit eum sibi in speculatorem et viderit gladium venientem super
terram et tuba canuerit et significaverit populo et audierit qui audit
vocem tubae et non observaverit, et venerit gladius et comprehenderit
eum, sanguis eius super caput eius erit: quia, cum vocem tubae audisset,
non observavit, sanguis eius in ipso erit: et hic, quia custodivit, animam
3 suam liberavit. Et speculator si viderit gladium venientem et non
significaverit tuba et populus non observaverit, et veniens gladius
acceperit ex eis animam, et ipsa propter iniquitatem suam capta est et
sanguinem de manu speculatoris requiram. Et tu, fili hominis,
speculatorem te dedi domui Israel et audies ex ore meo verbum, cum
dicam peccatori: morte morieris, et non loqueris, ut avertat se a via sua
impius, et ipse iniquus in iniquitate sua morietur, sanguinem autem eius
de manu tua requiram. Tu vero si praedixeris impio viam eius, ut avertat

se ab ea, et non se averterit a via sua, hic sua impietate morietur et tu animam tuam eripuisti'.

92   Sed sufficiant haec pauca de pluribus prophetarum testimonia, quis retunditur superbia vel ignavia sacerdotum contumacium, ne putent nos propria potius adinventione quam legis sanctorumve auctoritate eis talia denuntiare.

2   Videamus igitur quid euangelica tuba mundo personans inordinatis 77 sacerdotibus eloquatur: non enim de illis, ut iam diximus, qui apostolicam sedem legitime obtinent quique bene norunt largiri spiritalia conservis suis in tempore cibaria, si qui tamen multi in praesentiarum sunt, sed de pastoribus imperitis, qui derelinquunt oves et pascunt vana et non

3   habent verba pastoris periti, nobis sermo est. Evidens ergo indicium est non esse eum legitimum pastorem, sed ne mediocrem quidem Christianum, qui haec non tam nostra, qui valde exigui sumus, quam veteris novique testamenti decreta recusarit vel infitiatus fuerit, sicut bene quidam nostrorum ait: 'optabiliter cupimus ut hostes ecclesiae sint nostri quoque absque ullo foedere hostes, et amici ac defensores nostri non solum foederati sed etiam patres ac domini habeantur'.

4   Conveniant namque singuli vero examine conscientiam suam, et ita deprehendent an secundum rectam rationem sacerdotali cathedrae insideant. Videamus, inquam, quid salvator mundi factorque dicat.

5   'Vos estis', inquit, 'sal terrae: quod si sal evanuerit, in quo salietur? Ad nihilum valet ultra, nisi ut proiciatur foras et conculcetur ab

93 hominibus'. Hoc unum testimonium ad confutandos impudentes quosque abunde sufficere posset. Sed ut evidentioribus adhuc astipulationibus quantis semetipsos intolerabilibus scelerum fascibus falsi hi sacerdotes

2   opprimant verbis Christi comprobetur, aliqua annectenda sunt. Sequitur enim: 'Vos estis lux mundi. Non potest civitas abscondi supra montem posita, neque accendunt lucernam et ponunt eam sub modio, sed supra candelabrum, ut luceat omnibus qui in domo sunt'. Quis ergo sacerdotum huius temporis ita ignorantiae caecitate possessus ut lux clarissimae lucernae in aliqua domu cunctis noctu residentibus scientiae simul et bonorum operum lampade luceat? quis ita universis ecclesiae filiis tutum publicum conspicuumque refugium, ut est civibus firmissima forte in editi montis civitas vertice constituta, habetur?

3   Sed et quod sequitur: 'sic luceat lux vestra coram hominibus ut videant opera vestra bona et magnificent patrem vestrum qui in caelis est'; quis eorum uno saltim die potest implere? Quin potius densissima quaedam eorum nebula atraque peccaminum omni insulae ita incumbit nox ut omnes paene a via recta avertat ac per invios impeditosque scelerum calles errare faciat, quorum non modo pater caelestis non laudatur per opera sed etiam intolerabiliter blasphematur.

4   Velim quidem haec scripturae sacrae testimonia huic epistolae

inserta vel inserenda, sicut nostra mediocritas posset, omnia utcumque
94 historico vel morali sensu interpretari. Sed, ne in inmensum modum
opusculum hoc his qui non tam nostra quam dei despiciunt fastidiunt
avertunt proteletur, simpliciter et absque ulla verborum circuitione
congesta vel congerenda sunt.

2 Et post pauca: 'qui enim solverit unum de mandatis istis minimis
et docuerit sic homines, minimus vocabitur in regno caelorum'. Et
iterum: 'nolite iudicare, ut non iudicemini: in quo enim iudicio
iudicaveritis, iudicabitur de vobis'.

3 Quis, rogo, vestrum respiciet id quod sequitur? 'Quid autem vides',
inquit, 'festucam in oculo fratris tui et trabem in oculo tuo non
consideras? aut quomodo dicis fratri tuo: sine eiciam festucam de oculo
tuo et ecce, trabes in oculo tuo est?' Vel quod sequitur: 'nolite dare
sanctum canibus neque miseritis margaritas vestras ante porcos, ne forte
conculcent eas pedibus suis et conversi disrumpant vos', quod saepissime
vobis evenit.

4 Et populum monens ne a dolosis doctoribus, ut estis vos, seduceretur,
dixit: 'Attendite vobis a falsis prophetis, qui veniunt ad vos in vestimentis
ovium, intrinsecus autem sunt lupi rapaces. A fructibus eorum cognoscetis
eos. Numquid colligunt de spinis uvas aut de tribulis ficus? Sic omnis
arbor bona bonos fructus facit et mala malos'. Et infra: 'non omnis qui
dicit mihi: domine, domine, intrabit in regnum caelorum, sed qui facit
voluntatem patris mei, qui in caelis est, ipse intrabit in regnum caelorum'.

95 Quid sane vobis fiet, qui, ut propheta dixit, labiis tantum et non
corde deum adhaeretis? Qualiter autem impletis quod sequitur: 'ecce',
inquiens, 'ego mitto vos sicut oves in medio luporum', qui versa vice ut
lupi in gregem ovium proceditis? Vel quod ait: 'estote prudentes sicut
2 serpentes et simplices sicut columbae'? Prudentes quidem estis, ut
aliquem ore exitiabili mordeatis, non ut caput vestrum, quod est Christus,
obiectu quodammodo corporis defendatis, quem totis operum malorum
conatibus conculcatis. Nec enim simplicitatem columbarum habetis, quin
potius corvino assimilati nigrori ac semel de arca, id est ecclesia, evolitantes
inventis carnalium voluptatum fetoribus nusquam ad eam puro corde
revolatis.

3 Sed videamus et cetera: 'nolite', ait, 'timere eos qui occidunt corpus,
animam autem non possunt occidere, sed timete eum qui potest et
animam et corpus perdere in gehennam'. Quidnam horum feceritis
recogitate.

4 Quem vero vestrum sequens testimonium non in profunda cordis
arcana vulneret, quod de pravis antistitibus salvator ad apostolos
loquitur? 'Sinite illos, caeci sunt duces caecorum: caecus autem si caeco
ducatum praestet, ambo in foveam cadent'.

96 Egent sane populi, quibus praeestis vel potius quos decepistis, audire.

Attendite verba domini ad apostolos et turbas loquentis, quae et vos, ut audio, in medium crebro proferre non pudet. 'Super cathedram Moysi sederunt scribae et Pharisaei. Omnia ergo quaecumque dixerint vobis, servate et facite: secundum vero opera eorum nolite facere. Dicunt

2 enim et ipsi non faciunt'. Periculosa certe ac supervacua sacerdotibus doctrina est quae pravis operibus obfuscatur. 'Vae vobis, hypocritae, qui clauditis regnum caelorum ante homines, vos autem non intratis nec introientes sinitis intrare'. Non solum enim prae tantis malorum criminibus quae geritis in futuro sed etiam pro his qui vestro cotidie exemplo pereunt poenali poena plectemini: quorum sanguis in die iudicii de vestris manibus requiretur.

3 Sed quid mali quod servi parabola praetenderit inspicite, dicentis in corde suo: moram facit dominus meus venire. Qui pro hoc forsitan inceperat percutere conservos suos manducans et bibens cum ebriis. 'Veniet ergo', inquit, 'dominus servi illius in die qua non sperat, et hora qua ignorat, et dividet eum', a sanctis scilicet sacerdotibus, 'partemque eius ponet cum hypocritis', cum eis certe qui sub sacerdotali tegmine multum obumbrant nequitiae, 'illic', inquiens, 'erit fletus et stridor dentium', quibus in hac vita non crebro evenit ob cotidianas ecclesiae matris ruinas filiorum vel desideria regni caelorum.

97 Sed videamus, quid Christi verus discipulus magister gentium Paulus, qui omni ecclesiastico doctori imitandus est, sicut ipse hortatur: 'imitatores mei estote', inquiens, 'sicut et ego Christi', in tali negotio praeloquatur in prima epistola dicens: 'quia cum cognoverunt deum, non sicut deum magnificaverunt aut gratias egerunt, sed evanuerunt in cogitationibus suis et obcaecatum est insipiens cor eorum dicentes se esse sapientes, stulti facti sunt'. Licet hoc gentibus dici videatur, intuemini tamen quia competenter istius aevi sacerdotibus cum populis

2 coaptabitur. Et post pauca, 'qui commutaverunt', inquit, 'veritatem dei in mendacium et coluerunt et servierunt creaturae potius quam creatori, qui est benedictus in saecula, propterea tradidit illos deus in passiones

3 ignominiae'. Et iterum: 'et sicut non probaverunt deum habere in notitiam, tradidit illos deus in reprobum sensum, ut faciant quae non conveniunt, repletos omni iniquitate malitia impudicitia fornicatione avaritia nequitia, plenos invidia homicidio', scilicet animarum populi, 'contentione dolo malignitate, susurrones, detractores, deo odibiles, contumeliosos, superbos, elatos, inventores malorum, parentibus inoboedientes, insensatos, incompositos, sine misericordia, sine affectione, qui cum iustitiam dei cognovissent, non intellexerunt quoniam qui talia agunt digni sunt morte'.

98 Quisnam supra dictorum his omnibus in veritate caruit? Si enim esset, forte caperetur subiecto sensu, in quo ait: 'non solum qui faciunt ea sed etiam qui consentiunt facientibus', nullo scilicet hoc malo eorum

exstante immuni. Et infra: 'tu autem secundum duritiam tuam et cor impaenitens thesaurizas tibi iram in die irae et revelationis iusti   80
2 iudicii dei, qui réddet unicuique secundum opera sua'. Et iterum: 'Non est enim acceptio personarum apud deum. Quicumque enim sine lege peccaverunt, sine lege et peribunt: quicumque in lege peccaverunt, per legem iudicabuntur. Non enim auditores legis iusti sunt apud deum, sed
3 factores legis iustificabuntur'. Quid ergo severitatis ingruit his, qui non solum implenda non faciunt et prohibita non declinant, sed etiam ipsam verborum dei lectionem vel tenuiter auribus ingestam pro saevissimo angue refugiunt?

99   Sed transeamus ad sequentia. 'Quid ergo', inquit, 'dicemus? permanebimus in peccato, ut gratia abundet? Absit. Qui enim mortui sumus peccato, quomodo iterum vivemus in illo?' Et post aliquanta: 'Quis nos', ait, 'separabit a caritate Christi? Tribulatio? an angustia? an persecutio? an fames? an nuditas? an periculum? an gladius?' Quem vestrum, quaeso, talis intimo corde occupabit affectus, qui non modo pro pietate non laboratis, sed etiam ut inique agatis et Christum offendatis
2 multa patimini? Vel quod sequitur: 'Nox praecessit, dies autem appropinquavit. Abiciamus ergo opera tenebrarum et induamus arma lucis. Sicut in die honeste ambulemus, non in comessationibus et ebrietatibus, non in cubilibus et impudicitiis, non in contentione et aemulatione, sed induite dominum Iesum Christum et carnis curam ne feceritis in concupiscentiis'.

100   Et iterum ad Corinthios in prima epistola. 'Ut sapiens', inquit, 'architectus fundamentum posui, alter superaedificat. Unusquisque autem videat quomodo superaedificet. Fundamentum enim aliud nemo potest ponere praeter id quod est Iesus Christus. Si quis autem superaedificet super hoc aurum et argentum, lapides pretiosos, ligna, faenum, stipulam, unumquodque opus manifestum erit; dies enim domini declarabit illud, quia in igne revelabitur et uniuscuiusque opus quale sit, ignis probabit. Si cuius opus manserit quod superaedificaverit, mercedem accipiet. Si cuius opus arserit, detrimentum patietur. Nescitis quia templum dei estis et spiritus dei habitat in vobis? Si quis autem
2 templum dei violaverit, disperdet illum deus'. Et iterum: 'Si quis videtur apud vos sapiens esse in hoc saeculo, stultus fiat, ut sit sapiens. Sapientia enim huius mundi stultitia est apud deum'. Et post aliquanta: 'Non bona gloriatio vestra. Nescitis quia modicum fermentum totam massam corrumpit? Expurgate igitur vetus fermentum, ut sitis nova conspersio'. Quomodo expurgabitur vetus fermentum, id est peccatum, quod a diebus
3 in dies cunctis conatibus cumulatur? Et iterum: 'Scripsi vobis in epistola ne commisceamini fornicariis, non utique fornicariis huius mundi aut avaris aut rapacibus aut idolis servientibus: alioquin debueratis de hoc mundo exire. Nunc autem scripsi vobis non commisceri si quis nominatur

136

frater et est fornicator aut avarus aut idolis serviens aut maledicus aut ebriosus aut rapax, cum huiusmodi nec cibum quidem sumere'. Sed 81 latro nequaquam pro furto vel latrocinio furem alium damnat, quem potius optat tuetur amat utpote sui sceleris consortem.

101 Item in epistola ad Corinthios secunda: 'ideo', inquit, 'habentes hanc administrationem, iuxta quod misericordiam consecuti sumus, non deficiamus: sed abiciamus occulta dedecoris, non ambulantes in astutia neque adulterantes verbum dei', per malum exemplum scilicet et per

2 adulationem. In subsequentibus autem ita de malis doctoribus dicit: 'Nam eiusmodi pseudoapostoli, sunt operarii subdoli transfigurantes se in apostolos Christi. Et non mirum: ipse enim Satanas transfigurat se in angelum lucis. Non est magnum igitur si ministri eius transfigurentur ut angeli iustitiae; quorum finis erit secundum opera eorum'.

102 Attendite quoque quid ad Ephesios dicat. An nescitis vos pro hoc in aliquo reos teneri?'Hoc', inquiens, 'dico et testificor in domino, ut iam non ambuletis sicut gentes ambulant in vanitate sensus sui, tenebris obscuratum habentes intellectum, alienati a via dei per ignorantiam, quae est in illis propter caecitatem cordis eorum, qui desperantes semet ipsos tradiderunt impudicitiae in operationem omnis immunditiae et

2 avaritiae'. Et quis vestrum sponte expleverit id quod sequitur: 'propterea nolite fieri imprudentes, sed intellegentes quae sit voluntas dei, et nolite inebriari vino, in quo est luxuria, sed replemini spiritu sancto'?

103 Sed et quod ad Thessalonicenses dicit: 'Neque enim fuimus apud vos aliquando in sermone adulationis, sicut scitis, neque in occasione avaritiae, nec quaerentes ab hominibus gloriari neque a vobis neque ab aliis, cum possumus oneri esse ut ceteri apostoli Christi. Sed facti sumus sicut parvuli in medio vestrum vel tamquam si nutrix foveat parvulos suos; ita desiderantes vos cupide volebamus vobis tradere non solum euangelium sed etiam animas nostras'. Si hunc vos apostoli retinetis in omnibus affectum, eius quoque cathedrae legitime insidere noscatis.

2 Vel etiam quod sequitur: 'Scitis', inquit, 'quae praecepta dederim vobis. Haec est voluntas dei, sanctificatio vestra, ut abstineatis vos a fornicatione et sciat unusquisque vestrum vas suum possidere in honore et sanctificatione, non in passione desiderii, sicut et gentes quae ignorant deum. Et ne quis supergrediatur neque circumveniat in negotio fratrem suum, quoniam vindex est dominus de his omnibus. Non enim vocavit nos deus in inmunditiam sed in sanctificationem. Itaque qui haec spernit, non hominem spernit sed deum'.

3 Quis etiam vestrum circumspecte cauteque custodivit id quod sequitur: 'mortificate ergo membra vestra, quae sunt super terram, fornicationem immunditiam libidinem et concupiscentiam malam; propter quae venit ira dei in filios diffidentiae'? Videtis enim pro quibus peccatis ira dei potissimum consurgat.

104   Audite itaque quid de vobis prophetico spiritu sanctus idem
apostolus vestrisque consimilibus praedixerit, ad Timotheum aperte
scribens: 'Hoc enim scitote, quod in novissimis diebus instabunt
tempora periculosa. Erunt enim homines semet ipsos amantes, cupidi,
elati, superbi, blasphemi, parentibus inoboedientes, ingrati, scelesti,
sine affectione, incontinentes, inmites, sine benignitate, proditores,
protervi, tumidi, voluptatum amatores magis quam dei, habentes   82
quidem speciem pietatis, virtutem autem eius abnegantes. Et hos devita',
sicut et propheta dicit: 'odivi congregationem malignorum et cum impiis
non sedebo'.

2   Et post aliquanta, quod nostro tempore videmus pullulare, ait:
'Semper discentes, et numquam ad scientiam veritatis pervenientes:
quemadmodum enim Iamnes et Mambres restiterunt Moysi, ita et isti
resistunt veritati: homines corrupti mente, reprobi circa fidem, sed ultra
non proficient. Insipientia enim eorum manifesta erit omnibus, sicut et
illorum fuit'.

105   Etenim evidenter ostendit qualiter se exhibeant suo officio sacerdotes,
ita ad Titum scribens: 'te ipsum praebe exemplum bonorum operum, in
doctrina, in integritate, in gravitate, verbum sanum habens, irreprehensibile,
ut is qui ex adverso est vereatur, nullum malum habens dicere de nobis'.

2   Et iterum ad Timotheum: 'Labora', inquit, 'sicut bonus miles Christi Iesu.
Nemo militans deo implicat se negotiis saecularibus, ut placeat ei cui se
probavit. Nam et qui contendit in agone, non coronatur, nisi legitime
certaverit'.

3   Haec quidem bonorum adhortatio. Quod vero item comprehendit,
malorum hominum, ut vos quibusque intellegentibus apparetis,
denuntiatio est: 'si quis', inquiens, 'aliter docet et non adquiescit
sermonibus sanis domini nostri Iesu Christi et ei quae secundum pietatem
est doctrinae, superbus est, nihil sciens, sed languescens erga quaestiones
et pugnas verborum, ex quibus oriuntur invidiae , contentiones,
blasphemiae, suspiciones malae, conflictationes hominum mente
corruptorum, qui veritate privati sunt, existimantium quaestum esse
pietatem'.

106   Sed quid sparsim positis amplius utentes testimoniis sensuum ac (si)
diversorum undis in despecta ingenii nostri cymbula fluctuabimur?
Recurrere tandem aliquando usque ad lectiones illas quae ad hoc non
solum ut recitentur sed etiam adstipulentur benedictioni qua initiantur
sacerdotum vel ministrorum manus, eosque perpetuo doceant uti ne a
mandatis quae fideliter continentur in eis sacerdotali dignitate
degenerantes recedant, ex omni paene sanctarum scripturarum textu
merito excerptae sunt necessarium duximus; ut apertius cunctis pateat
aeterna supplicia mansura eos et non esse sacerdotes vel dei ministros

qui earum doctrinas atque mandata opere secundum vires suas non adimpleverint.

2 Audiamus ergo quid princeps apostolorum Petrus de tali negotio signaverit: 'benedictus', inquiens, 'deus et pater domini nostri Iesu Christi, qui per magnam misericordiam suam regeneravit nos in spem vitae aeternae per resurrectionem a mortuis domini nostri Iesu Christi in hereditatem incorruptibilem inmarcescibilem incontaminatam conservatam in caelis in vos qui in virtute dei custodimini'. Quare enim insipienter a vobis violatur talis hereditas, quae non sicut terrena decidua, sed inmarcescibilis atque aeterna est?

3 Et post aliquanta: 'propter quod succincti estote lumbos mentis vestrae, sobrii, perfecte sperantes in eam quae offertur vobis gratiam in revelatione Iesu Christi'. Rimamini namque pectoris vestri profunda, an sobrii sitis et perfecte sacerdotalem gratiam examinandam in domini revelatione conservetis. Et iterum dicit: 'Quasi filii benedictionis non 83 configurantes vos illis prioribus ignorantiae vestrae desideriis, sed secundum eum qui vos vocavit sanctos, et vos sancti in omni conversatione estote. Propter quod scriptum est: sancti estote, quia ego sum sanctus'. Quis rogo vestrum ita sanctitatem toto animi ardore sectatus est ut hoc, quantum in se est, avide festinaret implere?

4 Sed videamus quid in eiusdem secunda lectione contineatur: 'carissimi', inquit, 'animas vestras castificate ad oboediendum fidei per spiritum in caritate, in fraternitate, ex corde vero invicem diligentes perseveranter, quasi renati non ex semine corruptibili sed incorruptibili,

107 verbo dei vivi et permanentis in aeternum'. Haec quidem ab apostolo mandata et in die vestrae ordinationis lecta, ut ea indirupte custodiretis, sed nequaquam a vobis in iudicio impleta, sed nec multum cogitata vel intellecta sunt. Et infra: 'deponentes igitur omnem malitiam et omnem dolum et simulationem et invidiam et detractiones sic ut modo geniti infantes rationabile et sine dolo lac concupiscite, ut eo crescatis in salutem, quoniam dulcis est dominus'. Recogitate an haec quoque surdis

2 auribus a vobis audita crebrius conculcentur. Et iterum: 'vos autem genus electum: regale sacerdotium, gens sancta, populus in adoptionem, ut virtutes annuntietis eius qui de tenebris vos vocavit in illud tam admirabile lumen suum'. Non solum enim per vos virtutes dei non annuntiantur, sed etiam pravissimis vestris apud incredulos quosque despiciuntur exemplis.

3 Audistis forte in eodem die quod in lectione actus apostolorum lectum est, Petro in medio discipulorum surgente qui dixit: 'viri fratres, oportet scripturam impleri quam praedixit spiritus sanctus per os David de Iuda'. Et paulo post: 'hic itaque adquisivit agrum de mercede

4 iniquitatis'. Hoc securo vel potius hebeti corde, quasi non de vobis lectum fuisset, audistis. Quis, quaeso, vestrum non quaerit agrum de mercede

iniquitatis? Iudas namque loculos compilabat, vos ecclesiae donaria filiorumque animas eius vastatis. Ille adiit Iudaeos, ut deum venderet, vos tyrannos et patrem vestrum diabolum, ut Christum despiciatis. Ille triginta argenteis venalem habuit omnium salvatorem, vos vel uno obolo.

108   Quid plura? fertur vobis in medium Matthiae in confusionem vestram exemplum, [sanctorum quoque apostolorum] electione vel iudicio Christi non propria voluntate sortiti, ad quod caeci effecti non videtis quam longe a meritis eius distetis, dum in amorem et affectum Iudae traditoris sponte corruistis.

2   Apparet ergo eum qui vos sacerdotes sciens ex corde dicit non esse eximium Christianum. Sane quod sentio proferam. Posset quidem lenior fieri increpatio, sed quid prodest vulnus manu tantum palpare unguentove ungere quod tumore iam vel fetore sibi horrescens cauterio et publico ignis medicamine eget? si tamen ullo modo sanari possit aegro nequaquam medelam quaerente et ab hoc medico longius recedente.

3   O inimici dei et non sacerdotes, veterani malorum et non pontifices, traditores et non sanctorum apostolorum successores et non Christi ministri, auscultastis quidem secundae lectionis apostoli Pauli verborum sonum, sed in nullo modo monita virtutemque servastis, et simulacrorum modo, quae non vident neque audiunt, eodem die altari   84 astitistis, tunc et cotidie vobis intonantis: fratres, inquit, 'fidelis sermo est' et omni acceptione dignus. Ille dixit fidelem et dignum, vos ut infidelem et indignum sprevistis. 'Si quis episcopatum cupit, bonum opus desiderat'. Vos episcopatum magnopere avaritiae gratia, non spiritalis profectus obtentu cupitis et bonum opus illi condignum nequaquam

4 habetis. 'Oportet ergo huiusmodi irreprehensibilem esse'. In hoc namque sermone lacrimis magis quam verbis opus est, ac si dixisset apostolus eum esse omnibus irreprehensibiliorem debere. 'Unius uxoris virum'. Quod ita apud nos quoque contemnitur quasi non audiretur vel idem diceret et virum uxorum. 'Sobrium, prudentem'. Quis etiam ex vobis hoc

5 aliquando inesse sibi saltem optavit? 'Hospitalem': id si forte casu evenerit, popularis aurae potius quam praecepti gratia factum, non prodest, domino salvatore ita dicente: 'amen dico vobis, receperunt mercedem suam'. 'Ornatum, non vinolentum, non percussorem, sed modestum, non litigiosum, non cupidum'. O feralis inmutatio! o horrenda praeceptorum caelestium conculcatio! Nonne infatigabiliter ad haec expugnanda vel potius obruenda actuum verborumque arma corripitis, pro quis conservandis atque firmandis, si necesse fuisset, et poena ultro subeunda et vita ponenda erat?

109   Sed videamus et sequentia: 'domum', inquit, 'suam bene regentem, filios habentem subditos cum omni castitate'. Ergo imperfecta est patrum castitas si eidem non et filiorum adcumuletur. Sed quid erit ubi nec pater nec filius mali genitoris exemplo pravatus conspicitur castus? 'Si quis autem domui suae praeesse nescit, quomodo ecclesiae dei diligentiam adhibebit?' Haec sunt verba quae indubitatis effectibus approbantur.

2   'Diaconos similiter pudicos, non bilingues, non vino multum deditos, non turpe lucrum sectantes, habentes mysterium fidei in conscientia pura. Hi autem probentur primum et sic ministrent nullum crimen habentes'. His nimirum horrescens diu immorari unum veridice possum dicere, quin haec omnia in contrarios actus mutentur, ita ut clerici, quod non absque dolore cordis fateor, impudici, bilingues, ebrii, turpis lucri cupidi, habentes fidem et, ut verius dicam, infidelitatem in conscientia impura, non probati in bono sed in malo opere praesciti ministrantes et innumera crimini habentes sacro ministerio adsciscantur.

3   Audistis etiam illo die, quo multo dignius multoque rectius erat ut ad carcerem vel catastam poenalem quam ad sacerdotium traheremini, domino sciscitanti quem se esse putarent discipuli, Petrum respondisse: 'tu es Christus filius dei vivi', eique dominum pro tali confessione dixisse: 'beatus es, Simon Bar Iona, quia caro et sanguis non revelavit tibi, sed pater meus qui in caelis est'. Ergo Petrus a deo patre doctus recte Christum confitetur: vos autem moniti a patre vestro diabolo inique

4 salvatorem malis actibus denegatis. Vero sacerdoti dicitur: 'tu es Petrus et super hanc petram aedificabo ecclesiam meam': vos quidem assimilamini 'viro stulto qui aedificavit domum suam super arenam'. Notandum vero est quod insipientibus in aedificanda domo arenarum pendulae mobilitati dominus non cooperetur, secundum illud: 'fecerunt sibi reges et non per me'. Itidemque quod sequitur eadem sonat dicendo: 'et portae inferni non praevalebunt' [eiusque peccata intelleguntur]. De vestra quid exitiabili structura pronuntiatur? 'Venerunt flumina   85 et flaverunt venti et impegerunt in domum illam et cecidit et fuit ruina eius magna'.

5   Petro eiusque successoribus dicit dominus: 'et tibi dabo claves regni caelorum': vobis vero: 'non novi vos, discedite a me, operarii iniquitatis', 'ut separati sinistrae partis cum haedis eatis in ignem aeternum'. Itemque omni sancto sacerdoti promittitur: 'et quaecumque solveris super terram, erunt soluta et in caelis: et quaecumque ligaveris super terram, erunt ligata et in caelis'. Sed quomodo vos aliquid solvetis, ut sit solutum et in caelis, a caelo ob scelera adempti et immanium peccatorum funibus compediti, ut Salomon quoque ait: 'criniculis peccatorum suorum

6 unusquisque constringitur'? Quaque ratione aliquid in terra ligabitis quod supra mundum etiam ligetur, praeter vosmetipsos, qui ita ligati iniquitatibus in hoc mundo tenemini ut in caelis nequaquam ascendatis, sed infaustis tartari ergastulis, non conversi in hac vita ad dominum, decidatis?

110   Nec sibi quisquam sacerdotum de corporis mundi solum conscientia supplaudat, cum eorum quis praeest si qui propter eius imperitiam vel

desidiam seu adulationem perierint, in die iudicii de eiusdem manibus, veluti interfectoris, animae exquirantur: quia nec dulcior mors quae infertur a bono quoque homine quam malo; alioquin non dixisset apostolus velut paternum legatum suis successoribus derelinquens: ' Mundus ego sum ab omnium sanguine. Non enim subterfugi quo minus annuntiarem vobis omne mysterium dei'.

2   Multumque nam usu ac frequentia peccatorum inebriati et incessanter irruentibus vobis scelerum cumulatorum ac si undis quassati unam veluti post naufragium in qua ad vivorum terram evadatis paenitentiae tabulam toto animi nisu exquirite, ut avertatur furor domini a vobis misericorditer dicentis: 'nolo mortem peccatoris, sed ut convertatur et vivat'.

3   Ipse omnipotens deus totius consolationis et misericordiae paucissimos bonos pastores conservet ab omni malo et municipes faciat subacto communi hoste civitatis Hierusalem caelestis, hoc est, sanctorum omnium congregationis, pater et filius et spiritus sanctus, cui sit honor et gloria in saecula saeculorum. Amen.

EPISTULARUM GILDAE
DEPERDITARUM FRAGMENTA

1   De excommonicatione dicit Gildas: Non Noe Cham filium suum   86
magicae artis scribam aut arca aut mensae communione voluit arcere.
Non Abraham Aner et Heschol in debellatione quinque regum exhorruit.
Non Loth Sodomitarum convivia execratus est. Non Isaac mensae
participationem Abimelech et Ocazat et Phicol duci militum negat, sed
post cibum et potum iuraverunt sibi mutuo. Non Iacob extimuit
communicare filiis suis, quos novit venerari idola. Non Ioseph rennuit
Faraoni mensae et scypho participari. Non Aaron sacerdotis idolorum
Madian mensam reppulit. Nec non Moyses simul cum Iethro hospitium et
convivium pacificum init. Non dominus noster Iesus Christus publicanorum
convivia devitabat, ut omnes peccatores et meretrices salvaret.

2   Gildas dicit de abstinentia ciborum: Abstinentia corporalium ciborum
absque caritate inutilis est. Meliores sunt ergo qui non magno opere ieiunant
nec supra modum a creatura dei se abstinent, cor autem intrinsecus nitidum
coram deo sollicite servantes, a quo sciunt exitum vitae, quam illi qui
carnem non edunt nec cibis saecularibus delectantur, neque vehiculis
equisque vehuntur, et pro his quasi superiores ceteris se putantes; quibus
mors intravit per fenestras elevationis.

3   Gildas in epistolis suis de novissimis diebus: 'Instabunt tempora pessima
et erunt homines sui amatores, avari, adrogantes, superbi, blasphemi,
parentibus inoboedientes, ingrati, inpuri, sine adfectione, sine pace,
accusatores, intemperantes, crudeles, odio habentes bonum, proditores,
temerarii, inflati, voluptatum amatores magis quam dei, habentes formam
pietatis et virtutem eius abnegantes'. Multi peribunt agentes mala, ut ait
apostolus: 'habentes zelum dei, sed non secundum scientiam, ignorantes
dei iustitiam et suam quaerentes statuere, iustitiae dei non sunt subiecti'.
Omnes fratres culpantes sunt qui suas secum adinventiones et praesumptiones
non fecerunt. Hi dum pane ad mensuram utuntur, pro hoc sine mensura
gloriantur: dum aqua utuntur, simul odii poculo potantur: dum siccis
ferculis, simul et detractationibus fruuntur: dum vigilias extendunt, aliquos
somno demersos notant, pedibus et membris dicentes ceteris: si non caput
fueris, ut ego sum, ad nihili te conputabo: quod non tam pro   87
dilectionis causa promittitur quam despectus. Dum principalibus decretis

meditantur, servos dominis, vulgus regibus, auro plumbum, argento ferrum, (vineae) ulmum praeferunt. Ita ieiunium caritati, vigilias iustitiae, propriam adinventionem concordiae, clausulam ecclesiae, severitatem humilitati, postremo hominem deo anteponunt: non intendentes quod euangelium sed quod voluntas iubet; quid apostolus sed quid superbia doceat; non intendentes statum siderum in caelo inaequalem esse et angelorum officia inaequalia. Hi ieiunant, quod nisi propter alias virtutes adsectantur nihil prodest. Illi caritatem, quae summa plenitudo legis est, intentione perficiunt a deo docti, cum spiritus sancti citharae dicunt 'quasi pannus menstruatae omnes iustitiae nostrae'. Hi autem folles diaboli dicunt forsitan melioribus, quorum vident angeli faciem patris: recedite a nobis, quia immundi estis. Quo respondit dominus: 'isti fumus erunt in furore meo et ignis ardens cotidie'. Non spernentes fratres dicit dominus [pauperes] beatos esse, sed pauperes; non animosos, sed mites; neque invidiosos, sed lugentes vel propria vel aliorum peccata; qui esuriunt et sitiunt non aquam cum ceterorum despectu, sed iustitiam; nec pro nihilo alios ducentes, sed misericordes; non qui superbo, sed mundo corde; non alis severi, sed pacifici; non qui inferunt bella, sed qui persecutionem patiuntur propter iustitiam, habituri videlicet regnum caelorum.

4   Gildas ait de monachis qui veniunt de loco viliore ad perfectiorem: Quorum abbas ita degeneravit ab opere dei ut mereatur ad mensam sanctorum non recipi, sed et fornicationis crimine, non suspectionis sed mali evidentis, onerari, — suscipite sine ullo scrupulo monachos tales ad vos de flamma inferni confugientes, nequaquam eorum consulto abbate. Illos vero quorum abbatem de mensa sanctorum propter infamiam non arcemus, non debemus illo nolente suscipere. Quanto magis venientes a sanctis abbatibus et nullo alio modo suspectis nisi quod habent pecora et vehicula vel pro consuetudine patriae vel sua infirmitate, quae minus laedunt habentes, si cum humilitate et patientia, quam aratra trahentes et suffossoria figentes terrae cum praesumptione et superbia. Quicquid autem monacho de rebus saecularibus superabundat, ad luxurias et divitias debet referri, et quod necessitate, non voluntate habere compellitur, ut non penuria cadat, non illi ad malum reputabitur. Capitibus namque praecipua corporis ornamenta delata non debent inferiora despicere et manuum cotidiana commoda superbire superioribus fas non est. Nonne haec nec illa possunt sibi mutuo dicere: 'operam vestram non necesse habemus', quae ad communem eiusdem corporis pertinent utilitatem? Haec diximus ut sciant summi sacerdotes quod, sicut non debent inferiores clerici eos despicere, ita et illi nec clericos, sicut nec caput quidem cetera membra.

5   Gildas ait: Abbas districtioris regulae non admittat monachum alterius abbatis paulo remissioris: et qui remissior est, non retineat

monachum suum ad districtiora tendentem. Habent quippe
sacerdotes et episcopi terribilem iudicem, cui pertinet, non nobis, de
illis in utroque saeculo iudicare.

6   Gildas: 'Maledictus qui transfert terminos vel proximi sui.'
'Unusquisque permaneat in eo in quo vocatus est apud deum', ut nec
primarius nisi voluntate mutetur subiectorum neque subiectus sine
senioris consilio locum prioris obtineat. 'Quae sunt honesta nostra, his
honorem abundantiorem circumdamus'. Iudicare ergo satis salubre est
subiectos episcopis abbatibusque, quorum sanguinem, si eos non bene
regnant, de manibus requiret dominus: inoboedientes vero patribus sint
sicut gentiles et publicani; et omnibus hominibus tam bonis quam malis
praeter suos subiectos illud apostoli: existimantes omnes homines, rel.

Pervenit illud iudicium pro incerto exitu vitae, legentes in scriptura
apostolum perditum cupiditate et latronem confessione in paradisum
translatum.

7   Item: Conepiscopos autem et conabbates nec non consubiectos non
iudicare melius est. Faetentes vero alicuius nequam famae pedore nullo
modo ad integrum arguant, sed leniter increpent cum patientia: quos
pro conscientia ut possint, debent quasi suspectos vitare nec tamen ut
reos veros excommunicare et mensa vel pace arcere, (nisi) cum ratio
aliqua necessitatis aut conventus vel locutionis exegerit; sed illis
denuntietur, quod non recte agant, quia non possumus eos pro hoc
damnare: dum communicant illi indigne, forte nos per cogitationes
malas daemonibus communicamus. Quos vero scimus sine ulla
dubitatione esse fornicatores, nisi legitimo ordine paeniteant, a pace et
mensa, cuiuscumque ordinis legitime fuerint, arcemus: ut est illud: si
quis frater nominatur et est fornicator, rel. Et propter principalium
vitiorum causas evidenter probatas, nulla alia ratione debemus fratres
a communicatione altaris et mensae cum tempus poposcerit arcere.

8   Gildas: Veritas sapienti nitet, cuiuscumque ore fuerit prolata.

FRAGMENTA DUBIA

9   Gildas: Adsentiente Aaron in culpando Moyse propter uxorem
Aethiopissam lepra Maria damnatur: quod nobis timendum qui bonis
principibus detrahimus propter mediocres culpas.

10   Item: Navi fracta, qui potest natare natet.

INCIPIT PRAEFATIO GILDAE DE POENITENTIA

1   Praesbiter aut diaconus faciens fornicationem naturalem siue sodomitam praelato ante monachi uoto .iii. annis peniteat. Ueniam omni hora roget, superpos(s)itionem faciet in una quaque hebdomada exceptis .l. diebus post passionem; pane sine mensura et ferculo aliquatenus butero inpinguato die dominico, caeteris uero diebus paxmati panis mensura et misso parum inpinguato, horti holeribus, ouis paucis, Britannico formello utatur, himina Romana lactis pro fragilitate corporis istius eui, tenuclae uero uel battuti lactis sextario Romano sitis gratia et aquae talimpulo, si operarius est; lectum non multo feno instructum habeat; per .iii. xlmas superaddat aliquid prout uirtus eius admiserit. Semper ex intimo corde defleat culpam suam; obedientiam prae omnibus libentissime excipiat. Post annum et dimedium eucharistiam summat, ad pacem ueniat, psalmos cum fratribus canat, ne penitus anima tanto tempore caelestis medicinae (ieiuna) intereat.

2   Si quis inferiore gradu possitus monachus, .iii. annis poeniteat, sed mensura grauetur panis. Si operarius, sextarium de lacte Romanum et alium de tenucla et aquam quantum sufficiat pro sitis ardore summat.

3   Si uero sine monachi uotu presbiter aut diaconus peccauerit, sicut
4   monachus sine gradu sic peniteat. Si autem peccatum uoluerit monachus facere, anno et dimedio. Habet tamen abas huius rei moderandae facultatem, si oboedientia eius placita fuerit Deo et abati suo.

5   Antiqui patres .xii. presbitero et .vii. diacono poenitentiae statuere.

6   Monachus furatus uestem uel aliquam rem .ii. annis ut supra poeniteat, si iunior est; si senior, anno integro. Si uero monachus non fuerit eque anno et maxime in .iii. xlsimis.

7   Si monachus exundante uentre euomerit sacrificium in die, cenam suam non praesummat; et si non infirmitatis causa, vii. superpossitionibus,
8   si infirmitatis et non uoracitatis,.iiii. superpossitionibus deleat culpam. Si autem non sacrificium, diei superpossitione et multa increpatione plectatur.

9   Si casu neglegens quis sacrificium aliquod perdat, per .iii. xlmas, relinquens illud feris et alitibus deuorandum.

10   Si quis autem ebrietatis causa psallere non potest, stupens elinguis, caena priuatur.

11   Peccans cum pecode anno; si ipse solus, .iii. xlmas deluat culpam.

12   Qui communicauerit a suo abate excommunicato, xl.

13   Manducans morticinam inscius, xl.

14   Sciendum est tamen quod quanto quis tempore moratur in peccatis tanto ei augenda penitentia est.

15   Si cui inponitur opus aliquod et contemptus gratia illud non fecerit,

16   cena careat. Si uero obliuione, demedium cotidiani uictus. Si autem summat alterius opus, illud notum faciat abati cum reuerentia, excepto eo nullo audiente, et sic peragat, si iubetur.

18   Offensus quis ab aliquo debet hoc indicare abati, non tamen

17   accussantis sed medentis afectu, et abas decernat. Nam qui iram corde multo tempore retinet, in morte est.

Si autem confitetur peccatum, xl ieiunet, et si ultra in peccato persistat, .ii. xl, et si idem fecerit, abscidatur a corpore sicut membrum putredum, quia furor homicidium nutrit.

19   Qui non occurrit ad (secundi psalmi) consummationem, canat .viii. in ordine psalmos. Si excitatus ueniat post misam, quicquid cantauerunt replicet ex ordine fratres. Si uero ad secundam uenerit, caena careat.

20   Si quis errans commotauerit aliquid de u(e)rbis ubi periculum adnotatur, triduanum aut .iii. superpositiones faciat.

21   Si sacrum terra tenus neglegendo ceciderit, caena careat.

22   Qui uoluntate obsceno liquore maculatus fuerit dormiendo, si ceruisa et carne habundat cenubium, .iii. noctis horis stando uigilet, si sane uirtutis est. Si uero pauperem uictum habet, xxviii. aut .xxx. psalmos canet stando suplex aut opere extraordinario pendat.

23   Pro bonis regibus sacra debemus offerre, pro malis nequaquam.

24   Presbiteri uero pro suis episcopis non prohibentur offerre.

25   Qui arguitur pro aliquo delicto et quasi inconsultans refrenatur, cena careat.

26   Qui sarculum perfrangit et ante fracturam non habuit, aut illud extraordinario opere restituat aut superponat.

27   Qui uiderit aliquem ex fratribus abatis transgredi praecepta, debet abatem non caelare; sed ante admoneat peccantem ut solus quod male agit confiteatur abati. Non tam dilator quam ueritatis regulae exsecutor inueniatur.

HUCUSQUE GILDAS

In this penitential, and occasionally elsewhere (85.2; 106.1; frg. 3 and 7), letters or words added against the evidence of the manuscripts are given in round brackets.

N O T E S

by JM, unless marked MW.

ABBREVIATIONS

J. Th. Stud... *Journal of Theological Studies.* MGH... *Monumenta Germanice Historica;* AA... *Auctores Antiquissimi;* Epp... *Epistulae;* SRM... *Scriptores Rerum Merovingicarum.* VSBG... *Vitae Sanctorum Britanniae et Genealogiae.* A.W. Wade-Evans, University of Wales Press, 1944.

1.14   GOVERNORS. *Rector* is the late Roman technical term for governor, as in 6.1;14.1 below; see also note 23.5 below.

3.1   ISLAND OF BRITAIN. Gildas apparently quotes from a late Roman geographer, comparable with Marcianus of Heraclea, who totted up the headlands, estuaries, cities, etc., which Ptolemy named. Nennius and perhaps Orosius used the same source. Ptolemy named 58 'cities' in Britain, 38 of them south of Hadrian's Wall. The xxviii reproduced by Gildas and Nennius is perhaps a scribal error for xxxviii.

4.3   PORPHYRY. A third century anti-Christian Neo-Platonist, listed with others as *rabidi canes,* Jerome *de Viris Illustribus,* praef.
FERTILE OF TYRANTS. The quotation is from Jerome Ep. 133,9, not Porphyry; but Jerome mentions Porphyry earlier in the same paragraph.

5.1   KINGS. Often used of emperors in late Roman writers.

6.1   LIONESS. Boudicca, who rebelled against the Romans in 60-61 A.D.

10.2   PARTITION. Located by the sixth century graves and villages of the pagan English, in four large but separated regions, Surrey, Kent and the Tilbury district; Norfolk and its borders; Lincolnshire and its borders, east of the Trent; and the East Riding; with several much smaller districts about Dunstabl and Abingdon, and in Hampshire and East Sussex. See also 92,3 note. The English areas did not include either Verulamium or Caerleon.

AARON AND JULIUS. Otherwise remembered only in local tradition.

11.1   THAMES. Gildas clearly did not know the district.

12.3   ARIAN. The major heresy of the fourth century.

13.1   MAXIMUS. Rebelled in Britain, acknowledged in the west 383-388, killed Gratian in Gaul and expelled Valentinian II from Italy.

13.2   AQUILEIA. So Prosper, Orosius, and others. Gildas had access to
written histories of the Roman Empire, but not of fifth century Britain;
see 4.4.

14.1   SCOTS. The late Roman name for the Irish, not used of northern Britain
before the ninth century.

PICTS. 'Painted' or 'tattoed' peoples, north of the Forth.

15.3   WALL..TURF..STONE. Gildas accurately describes the two northern walls
(see also 18.2), and probably saw them, for he was *Arecluta..regione oriundus,
patre Cauuo*, 'a native of the Clydeside region, son of Cauuos' (Rhuys Life
of Gildas, 1...Mommsen p. 91, Williams p. 322, misreading *Cauno*). The
spellings of the proper names 'clearly belong to the sixth century' and 'can
only come from contemporary manuscripts' (K.H.Jackson *Language and History
in Early Britain* 42, cf. 306-307).

16.1   GREEDY. An early Gallic people whose appetite for plunder made their name
a by-word (Festus pp. 15-16, Lindsay); here used as an adjective, as in Nennius
(63, cf. 57) and Aldhelm (pp. 239.14; 241.13, Ehwald). (MW)

19.1   CORACLES. *Curuca* and *cyula*, keel (23.3), accurately distinguish the native
British and English words for their ships. *Cyula* here is probably the earliest
surviving word of written English.

20.1   AETIUS. Consul for the third time in 446, the fourth time in 453, the first
consul III, other than an emperor, for more than 300 years. The MSS use 'g'
for the 'y' sound of the dipthong, as later in Fredegarius, in Old English and
other Germanic dialects, but Bede, quoting Gildas, used the normal spelling,
Aëtius. The letter provides the only date, 446/452, in Gildas' narrative. But
he misplaced it; at that date, the barbarian enemy were the English (24.1 and
23.1 notes). The letter should have been inserted at the end of ch. 24, but
Gildas had no means of learning the point at which he should insert it into his
otherwise timeless narrative. The mistake misled Bede, who did not know the
evidence that corrects Gildas. In his Chronicle, in 725, he entered the letter
among the events of the 430s, since Gildas had placed it after the end of the
Roman rule of Britain, but long before the coming of the English. By the time
he wrote his History, in 731, Bede had discovered Aëtius' date (1.13), but
had to retain its place in the narrative, condensing Gildas' next few chapters
into a few years. The Chronicle was also corrected, and all surviving MSS
insert the date 446 against the entry which is placed in the 430s.

20.3   PHILO. A Jewish writer, of the earlier first century A.D.

21.2   NO PREVIOUS AGE. *Nulla..retro aetas* might also mean 'no age remembered
the possession of such afterwards', as Williams. (MW)

23.1   PROUD TYRANT. Vortigern. A variety of calculations (Nennius 66) place his accession in 425; for his death, see 25.1 note.

      SAXONS. Used by Roman writers as a general term for barbarians beyond the Franks. In Britain they preferred the term *Engle*; though some districts and a few writers adopted Roman usage as a collective term, no individual settled or born in Britain is known to have called himself a 'Saxon'.

      LET INTO THE ISLAND. The calculations of Nennius 66 give the date 428; the archaeological evidence does not admit a significantly later date; see 24.1 note

      PEOPLES OF THE NORTH. The 'old enemies', Picts as well as Scots, were 'overseas nations' (14.1) who came by sea, with 'oars' and 'sails' (16.1); this time they threatened not raiding, but settlement (22.1). The siting of the earliest known English settlements protected the Humber, Wash, Thames and perhaps the Southampton area.

23.3   THREE KEELS. So also Nennius (31), naming Hengest as their leader, as does Bede, and Thanet as their settlement. It is quite possible that the first invitation was limited to this number, and to Thanet.

23.5   SUPPLIES. *Annonae, Epimenia, Hospites* are late Roman technical terms for the billeting of federate allies.

24.1   FIRE..DEVASTATED. A contemporary in northern Gaul (MGH AA ix = *Chronica Minora* i, pp. 652 ff.) wrote in 452 that ten years before, in 441/2, 'Britain passed under the control of the Saxons (*in dicionem Saxonum*)'. The event, that seemed to him as decisive as the control of Goths, Burgundians and others in Gaul, cannot have been other than the initial success of the revolt which Gildas describes. He could not know that in the future the British would fight back. Gildas and Nennius agree that further contingents followed the first over a period of years before the revolt; the first settlement was therefore some time before 441; see 23.1 notes.

25.1   SURVIVORS. Gildas telescopes prolonged fighting (Nennius 43 ff.), to which the Saxon Chronicle allots twelve years, ending with the expulsion of the English from Thanet, followed by their subsequent return, further fighting, and a peace conference, where Hengest treacherously assassinated 'all King Vortigern's three hundred Elders', by definition the leading aristocracy. Similar tales are told in legend, but also in Xenophon's *Anabasis* and in Ammianus Marcellinus in the fourth century A.D.

      BEYOND THE SEA. The migration is located, in northern and central Gaul, and dated by Sidonius *Ep.* 3.9; Jordanes *Getica* 45; Gregory of Tours *Historia Francorum* 2, 18. The signature of Mansuetus, 'Bishop of the British', among many territorial Bishops, in 461 (Mansi 7, 941), suggests that the migration was then recent, not yet absorbed into normal dioceses. The British were said to number 12,000 fighting men, implying a total population of around 50,000. The likeliest occasion is after massacre of the aristocracy. Since the emigrants took with them whatever books survived (4.4 above), they are likely to have included a large proportion of the literate and well-to-do survivors.

25.3   AMBROSIUS AURELIANUS. The only fifth century person named by Gildas, presumably named in order to spotlight the inferiority of his living descendants.

CERTAINLY. The Latin might alternatively mean 'his parents, who had certainly worn purple'. (MW)

PURPLE. *Purpuram sumere* is the late empire technical term for to 'become emperor'; *induere* carries a slight suggestion of 'assume without adequate qualification'. Ambrosius, who is said to have opposed Vortigern in the 430s (Nennius 31, cf. 66) was probably too old to be the same man, but might have been his imperial father.

26.1   BADON HILL. A hill near a place called Badon. The name is normal Celtic, cf. Vaubadon, near Bayeux, *Vallis Badonis* in the 11th century (Domesday Book, Herts. 1.13; *Val Badon* Kent and Northants; and *Dictionnaire Topographique du Calvados* 292, in 1180). It was in the west, since the Welsh Annals record a second battle of Badon in 665. The earliest spelling of Bath in the Saxon Chronicle at 577, in an entry whose other proper names survive in one MS in the spelling of the late sixth century, is *Badan*. This spelling was not then English, but it persists beside the normal English, *aet Hatum Bathum*. The contents table (ch. 68) prefixed to a MS of Nennius, without reference to the battle, places the Hot Baths in the lower Severn region at *Badon*. There is no other record of the British name of Bath.
Any or all of the numerous English places named Badbury or the like might linguistically derive from a Celtic *Badon;* but since several are in regions where no other comparable Welsh names survive, they more probably derive from the personal name Bada, common in English place names; but without need to suppose a 'folk-hero'.

THE YEAR. The battle was fought in the year of Gildas' birth, about 43 years before he wrote. He wrote before the death of Maelgwn, in the mid sixth century Justinian plague, in or before 550 (33.1 note); and before the monasticism became a mass movement, in the 540s (65.2 note). The date should therefore be in the 490s. The Welsh Annals date Badon to 516 and Camlann to 537; but these are the only British entries in the first century of their record, inserted into a framework of extracts from Irish Annals, with nothing to suggest that the Annalist had any guidance as to where they should be inserted. As with the other early Annals entries, the interval between events is likely to rest on an older tradition than the absolute dates.

26.2 KINGS. Traditions dating back to the sixth century name Arthur as the victor of Badon, and the Welsh Annals credit him with twenty years life thereafter. Gildas does not name him, or any other of his time, but held that orderly government endured for about a generation after Badon.

26.4 WORTHY LIVES..ADMIRE. Gildas may mean monks, as Williams supposed; of 'caves of the saints' (34.2). In the west as in the east, monasticism had by the end of the fifth century 'fallen into torpor and sterility' (C. de Montalembert *Les Moines d'Occident* 1,288 = English translation 1,514). In Gildas' lifetime, Benedict of Nursia founded a dozen houses besides Monte Cassino in Italy, and there were also a few new foundations in Gaul; but no vigorous large scale movement developed in Europe until the next century, except in Brittany and on its borders, see 65.2 note.

27.1 KINGS...TYRANTS. These words, and *duces,* are used of the same persons.

IF CHANCE. A strange phrase, apparently reiterating 'so far as they can' above. (MW)

28.1 CONSTANTINE. Not to be confused with numerous other rulers of the same name.

DUMNONIA. Devon, Cornwall and part of Somerset.

WHO TRUSTED. This parenthesis is difficult to follow. It was surely the royal youths who trusted in God and the rest. The holy men should be the clergy present in the church at the time of the murder, the mother their own. This may be a relic of a first draft, inefficiently worked into a new context. (MW

30.1 CANINUS. Evidently a pun on the Welsh name Conan, Kynan. Since the other kings are listed in geographical order, south to north, he may have ruled in the Gloucester region.

31.1 GOOD KING. Named Aircol Llauhir (Agricola Longhand) in Welsh genealogies.

VORTIPOR. Probably identical with 'Voteporix Protector', whose memorial stone, now in Caermarthen Museum (Nash-Williams *Early Christian Monuments of Wales* 138), is inscribed in Latin and Irish.

DEMETAE. Of Dyfed, south-west Wales.

32.1 BEAR'S STRONGHOLD. Gildas' Latin literally translates 'Din Eirth'. Of several strongholds so named, the best known is Dinarth near Llandudno, three miles from Deganwy, traditionally Maelgwn's fortress. If this place were meant, Cuneglasus at one time mastered much of Maelgwn's land.

CUNEGLASUS. In the genealogies, cousin of Maelgwn.

RED BUTCHER does not translate Cuneglasus; more easily 'blue (or grey) dog'.

32.2　THE POET SAYS. Who the poet was is unknown, and what he meant is unclear. (MW)

33.1　MAGLOCUNUS. In the genealogies, great-grandson of Cunedda, who was held
　　　　to have reduced the Irish colonists in most of Wales in the earlier fifth century.
　　　　Later tradition regarded Maelgwn and his son Rhun as the most powerful rulers
　　　　of mid sixth century Britain. The Welsh Annals, at 547, transcribe an Irish
　　　　record of plague deaths, at about 550, substituting Maelgwn for the Irish names.

33.4　KING YOUR UNCLE. In the genealogies, Eugen, father of Cuneglasus.

34.5　CONVERSION. To monasticism, as in Columbanus (Letter 4, note, below).

36.1　REFINED MASTER. Perhaps intending Illtud of Llanilltud Fawr (Llantwit
　　　　Major) in Glamorgan, where also Gildas, Samson and Paul Aurelian are said to
　　　　have been schooled.

38.2　ONE OF US. Gildas quotes from *de Virginitate* 6 (Patrologia Latina 30,162 =
　　　　18,77 = 20,273 = 103,671). The author was a Pelagian, contemporary and
　　　　sympathiser of the early fifth century Sicilian Briton (J.Th.S. 16,1965,26 ff),
　　　　and may well have been British himself, the obvious interpretation of 'one
　　　　of us'.   The work evidently still circulated in Britain a hundred years after
　　　　publication. Like other British and Irish writers from the 5th to the 8th
　　　　centuries, Gildas was not a 'Pelagian heretic'; his writing shows no sign that
　　　　he was aware of the views of Augustine, of his controversy with Pelagius, or
　　　　even of his existence.

65.1　MY ORDER. Probably meaning monks.

65.2　SAINTS. Regularly used of monks. The medieval literature, chiefly in the
　　　　form of Saints' Lives, is immense, much of it preserved only in late and grossly
　　　　corrupt versions. The essence of its story is however confirmed in a number
　　　　of contemporary and near contemporary writings, notably the works of
　　　　Columbanus of Luxeuil (ed. G.S.M. Walker *Scriptores Latini Hiberniae* 2
　　　　Dublin 1957; also MGH *Epp.* 3) and his Life by Jonas (MGH SRM 4,1);
　　　　Adomnan's Life of Columba of Iona; and the earliest Life of Samson, written
　　　　about 600, a generation after his death. Several of the ninth century Lives
　　　　of Breton saints also reproduce extracts from sixth century texts, recognisable
　　　　from the spellings of proper names. These texts by themselves amply attest a
　　　　sudden large scale growth before the plague years of the later 540s, and a
　　　　rapid acceleration thereafter, simultaneously in South Wales, Ireland, Cornwall
　　　　and Brittany, where very many hundreds of new monasteries entailed a
　　　　massive shift of population; the impact was noticeable but less in north Wales

and northern Britain, and in northern Gaul, from Normandy to Belgium.
The impetus of the reforming monks was brought to Burgundy in the 590s by
Columbanus, and there erupted into an extensive movement in the 640s.
In the 630s the Irish brought monasticism to the Northumbrians, then dominant
over most of the English, and thenceforth increasing numbers of English and
Irish monks founded or inspired monasteries in northern and central Europe,
culminating in the conversion of most of the Germans and some Slavs in the
eighth century. The early texts give not only facts and dates, but also express
the singleminded sincerity, whose appeal gave the movement its strength,
size and endurance.

66.4 SPORTS. Or 'shows' ? (MW)

67.3 SIMON MAGUS. Perhaps the passage cited by Columbanus to Gregory I
shortly before 600 (MGH Epp. 3. 156), *Simoniacos et Giltas auctor pestes
scripsit* (the eminent Gildas also wrote that Simoniacs are pests); but Gildas
may have dealt with Simoniacs more largely in a lost letter.

74.5 YOUR PATTERN. i.e. Lucifer. Cf. 67.3 'Simon Magus, their original'. (MW)

89.4 CHANGED HIS SENSE. From the historical, or literal sense to the moral.
For the contrast, cf. 93.4; and, in general, B. Smalley, *The Study of the Bible
in the Middle Ages* (1952),ch.1. (MW)

92.3 NO KIND OF ALLIANCE. *Absque ullo foedere..foederati* suggests
technical terms. Later emperors in Europe often employed Germanic
foederati against other Germans, or native rivals; and many were criticised
for so doing. The sentence seems to mean that we should have no pagan anti-
Christian *foederati*, but that our proper allies should be Christian rulers who
are defenders of the faith. The context is unclear, but seems to rebuke the
Bishops who favour anti-Christian *foederati*. The districts where the first pagan
English burials appear to date from the earlier sixth century are few; it is
possible that some of them derived from the employment of English *foederati*
by British rulers.

The LETTERS, preserved in Irish MSS, were probably written during or
after Gildas' visit to Ireland in 565.

Letters 2 - 4. MELIORES. The 'better', or stricter monks. The austere Rule
that Gildas condemns is summarised in Ricemarcus (Rhygyfach), Life of
David, VSBG 150 ff. David's rule was termed the 'Life of Water' (*aquatica vita*)
because it eschewed meat and wine, and confined the diet to the fish, that
lives in water, with bread, vegetables and water. (ch.2. VSBG 150). The Rule
(ch. 21-31 VSBG 157-8) forbids the use of animals, even for pulling the plough;
condemns all property and wealth, including the 'gifts of the wicked' to
monasteries, and categorically bans all personal possessions by monks, even

prescribing penance for the use of the words 'my book'. Ricemarcus' citation from the rule, *iugum ponunt in humeris; suffossoria vangasque invicto brachio terrae defigunt* is close to Gildas' *aratra trahentes et suffosoria figentes terrae.* The similarity suggests that both drew on a common source, the Rule of David, as published in his lifetime; it is not probable that Ricemarcus knew or recognised Gildas' strictures on David, or turned Gildas' disapproval to praise of his own hero, David.

Letter 4. AD PERFECTIOREM.   This is perhaps the letter cited by Columban of Luxeuil, in a letter written to Pope Gregory the Great in the late 590s (MG. *Epp.* 3, 156 ff.)
quid faciendum est de monachis illis, qui..vitae perfectioris desiderio accensi primae conversionis loca relinquunt..invitis abbatibus..Vennianus auctor Giltam de his interrogavit, et elegantissime ille rescripsit.
('What is to be done about those monks who are inspired by a desire for a more perfect life, and leave the monastery where they were first converted, against their abbots' will? The eminent Finnian asked Gildas about them; and Gildas wrote him a most judicious reply'). Finnian was perhaps the abbot of Moville, Co. Down (Irish national grid J 57), who died about 580.

INDEX OF BIBLICAL QUOTATIONS

Biblical references are given from the Vulgate, but names of books appear
in their familiar English form, with abbreviations as employed in the
OXFORD DICTIONARY OF THE CHRISTIAN CHURCH.
Non-biblical references have the author in capitals.

// 37.1 woe to those...Is.5.20 seeing do not see...Mt.13.13 // 37.2 the retinue of Pharaoh...cf.Exod.14.23, 15.19 // 37.4 anyone breaking...Heb.10.28-9 // 38.1 you have been...1 Sam.13.13-14 // 38.2 one of us...ANON., De Virginitate 6 = Patr.Lat.30.167 // 38.3 but I listened...1 Sam.15.20 does the Lord...1 Sam.15.22-3 // 38.4 God has torn...1 Sam.15.28-9 // 39.2 the Lord says this...2 Sam.24.12-13 // 39.3 it is I...2 Sam.24.17 // 39.4 Solomon acted...1 Kgs.11.6 the Lord said...1 Kgs.11.11 // 40.1 because I exalted...1 Kgs.16.2-4 // 40.2 further...1 Kgs.21.19 // 40.3 a lying spirit... 1 Kgs.22.22 behold, God...1 Kgs.22.23 // 40.4 their words...Pss.54.22 these men...cf.Jer.6.14, 8.11 there is no joy...Is.48.22, 57.21 // 41.1 the Lord is with you...2 Chron.15.2 // 41.2 if you help...2 Chron.19.2 you who love...cf.Pss.96.10 // 41.3 these are the words...2 Chron.21.12-14 // 41.4 your stomach...2 Chron.21.15 // 41.5 these are the words...2 Chron.24.20 // 42.1 hear, heavens...Is.1.2-3 // 42.2 the daughter...Is.1.8 hear the word... Is.1.10 // 42.3 bring me...Is.1.13 // 42.4 and when you...Is.1.15 your hands...Is.1.15 wash...Is.1.16-17 // 42.5 if your sins...Is.1.18-20 // 43.2 your princes...Is.1.23-24 the wicked...Is.1.28 // 43.3 the eyes...Is.2.11 woe to the wicked...Is.3.11 woe to those...Is.5.11-14 // 43.4 woe to you... Is.5.22-5 // 44.1 howl...Is.13.6-11 // 44.2 behold...Is.24.1-6 // 45.1 all who rejoice...Is.24.7-13 // 45.2 the sinners...Is.24.16-23 // 46.1 behold... Is.59.1-4 // 46.2 their works...Is.59.6-9 // 46.3 and judgement...Is.59.14-15 // 47.1 one who was known...cf.Jer.1.5 // 47.2 the Lord said...Jer.2.1-2 hear the word...Jer.2.4-6 // 47.3 of old...Jer.2.20-22 // 47.4 why do you want... Jer.2.29-32 for my people...Jer.4.22 // 48.1 Lord, your eyes...Jer.5.3 // 48.2 announce this...Jer.5.20-24 // 48.3 for there are found...Jer.5.26-9 // 49.1 you will speak...Jer.7.27-8 shall the fallen...Jer.8.4-7 // 49.2 I am hurt...Jer. 8.21-9.3 // 49.3 and the Lord said...Jer.9.13-15 // 49.4 do not, then...Jer. 11.14 (cf. 7.16 and 14.11, to which Gildas alludes in his parenthesis) // 50.1 the prophet Jonah...cf.Jon.3 // 50.2 if you say...Jer.13.22-3 // 50.3 this is what...Jer.14.10-12 and the Lord...Jer.15.1 // 50.4 who will pity...Jer.15.5-6 // 50.5 this is what...Jer.18.11-15 // 50.6 the Lord says...Jer.22.3-5 // 50.7 as I live...Jer.22.24-5 // 51 woe to those...Hab.2.12-13 how long...Hab.1.2-4 // 52 they have broken...Hos.8.1-4 // 53.1 after three...Am.2.4-7 // 53.2 seek the Lord...Am.5.6 the house...Am.5.10 // 53.3 I was not...Am.7.14-17 // 53.4 hear this...Am.8.4-5 the Lord swears...Am.8.7-8 // 53.5 and I shall turn... Am.8.10 by the sword...Am.9.10 // 54 hear...Mic.6.9-12 // 55 the great day...Zeph.1.14-2.2 // 56 the Lord says...Hag.2.22-3 // 57.1 return to me... Zech.1.3-4 // 57.2 and the angel...Zech.5.2-4 // 58 behold...Mal.4.1 // 59.1 why do the wicked...Job.21.7-13 // 59.2 surely...Job 21.16-20 // 59.3 they have seized...Job 24.2-7 // 59.4 let his portion...Job 24.18 let him be...Job 24.20-24 // 59.5 but be his sons...Job 27.14 but if...Job 27.16-17 // 60.1 my Lord says...2 Esd.15.21-7 // 60.2 a sword of fire...2 Esd.16.3-12 // 61.1 his vision...cf.Ezek.1.5 seq. the wickedness...Ezek.9.9 behold...Ezek.5.8 my eye...Ezek.5.11 (cf.9.10) since the earth...Ezek.7.23-5 // 61.2 the Lord said...Ezek.14.12-16 // 61.3 the son...Ezek.18.20-24 // 61.4 and all the nations...Ezek.39.23-4 // 62.1 heavy and unbearable burdens... cf.Mt.23.4 // 62.2 love justice...Wisd.1.1 // 62.3 serve the Lord...Wisd.1.1 one of my predecessors...unidentified // 62.4 for he is found...Wisd.1.2 // 62.5 for perverse thoughts...Wisd.1.3 // 62.6 the holy spirit...Wisd.1.5 since the spirit...Wisd.1.7 // 62.7 the hope...Wisd.5.15-17 // 62.8 I will honour... 1 Sam.2.30 // 63 hear...Wisd.6.2-11 // 64.1 flee from sins...Ecclus.21.2-3 how great...Ecclus.17.28 // 64.2 I could wish...Rom.9.3 alas...Mic.7.2? (cf. Gildas 86.4) let us scrutinise...Lam.3.40-1 we wish...Phil.1.8 // 65.1 as the

157

law...cf.Deut.17.5-7 // 66.7 irreproachable...1 Tim.3.2 // 67.3 to hell...Acts 8.20 // 67.4 Nicolas...v.RUFINUS, Hist.Eccl. 3.29 // 67.6 Novatus...v. RUFINUS, Hist.Eccl. 6.43 // 68.1 beasts of the belly...Tit. 1.12 labour to do ill...Jer.9.5 // 68.2 Lot...cf.Gen.19.17 the blind... Mt.15.14 // 69.1 the priest Eli...1 Sam.2.12 seq. // 69.2 Abel...Gen. 4.5 seq. hated the counsel...Pss.25.5 Enoch walked...Gen.5.24 // 69.3 Noah...Gen.6.11 seq. Melchizedek...Gen.14.14 seq. // 69.4 Abraham... Gen.22.1 seq. one's right eye...Mt.5.29 prophet...Jer.48.10 Joseph... Gen.50.15 seq. // 69.5 Moses spoke..Exod.19.16, 34.29 Lord, this people... Exod.32.31-2 // 70.1 Phinehas...Num.25.1-8 Joshua...cf.Jos.24.11 // 70.2 the wise division...Jos.21-22 Jephthah...Jgs.11.30 seq. not seeking... 1 Cor.10.33 // 70.3 Gideon...Jgs.7.9 seq. raise your voice...Is.58.1 their sound...Pss.18.5 having this treasure...2 Cor.4.7 felling of the trees... Jgs.6.25 seq. clear signs...Jgs.6.36 seq. // 71.1 Sampson...Jgs.16.25 seq. and avarice...Col.3.5 // 71.2 Samuel dispelled...1 Sam.7.7-10 aroused... 1 Sam.12.18 appointed...1 Sam.10.1 seq. rejected...1 Sam.15.28 seq.,16.13 behold...1 Sam.12.2-4 // 71.3 burned up...2 Kgs.1.9 seq. all the prophets... 1 Kgs.18.40 showers from heaven...Jas.5.17 Lord, they have...1 Kgs.19.10 // 72.1 leprosy...2 Kgs.5.27 // 72.2 opened the eyes...2 Kgs.6.17 the touch of his body...2 Kgs.4.32 seq. // 72.3 lips cleansed...Is.6.6-7 tripped up...Is.37.36 // 72.4 prison...e.g.Jer.20.2 wandering...Heb.11.37-8 // 73.2 cast out...Acts 16.23-5 James...v.RUFINUS, Hist.Eccl.2.23.3 // 73.3 James, brother of John...Acts 12.2 first martyr...Acts 7.58 // 74.2 from Syria...RUFINUS, Hist.Eccl.3.36.7-9 // 74.5 I shall ascend...Is.14.13-14 I dug...Is.37.25 // 74.6 but I am a worm...Pss.21.7 I can do...Jn.5.30 why do earth...Ecclus.10.9 // 75.1 Polycarp...RUFINUS, Hist.Eccl.4.15.31 // 75.2 Basil...RUFINUS, Hist.Eccl.11.9 // 75.3 one must obey...Acts 5.29 // 76.2 the Lord says...1 Sam.2.27-8 // 76.3 why have you looked...1 Sam.2.29 and now...1 Sam.2.30-1 // 76.4 and the sign...1 Sam.2.34 // 77.2 the Lord God says...1 Kgs.13.21-24 // 78.1 woe to the wicked...Is.3.11-15 // 78.2 woe to those...Is.10.1-3 but these...Is.28.7-8 // 79.1 therefore...Is.28.14-15 and hail...Is.28.17-19 // 79.2 and the Lord...Is.29.13-16 // 79.3 the Lord says...Is.66.1-3 // 80.1 the Lord says...Jer.2.5 and when...Jer.2.7-9 // 80.2 astonishing miracles...Jer.5.30-1 to whom...Jer.6.10 for I will...Jer.6.12-15 // 80.3 all these...Jer.6.28-30 // 80.4 I am...Jer.7.11-15 // 81.1 my sons...Jer. 10.20-21 // 81.2 why is it...Jer.11.15-16 // 81.3 come, gather...Jer.12.9-10 this is what...Jer.14.10 // 81.4 the prophets...Jer.14.13-16 // 82.1 woe to the shepherds...Jer.23.1-2 // 82.2 for prophet...Jer.23.11-20 // 83.1 awake... Joel 1.5,9-12 // 83.3 weep...Joel 2.17 // 84 hear this...Hos.5.1 // 85.1 I hated...Am.5.21-23 // 85.2 behold...Am.8.11-12 // 86.1 listen...Mic.3.1-12 // 86.4 woe is me...Mic.7.1-3 // 87.1 o what...Zeph.3.1-2 // 87.2 her princes...Zeph.3.3-5 // 88.1 the almighty Lord...Zech.7.9-12 // 88.2 those who spoke...Zech.10.2-3 // 88.3 the voice...Zech.11.3-6 // 89.1 it is you... Mal.1.6-9 // 89.2 and you have...Mal.1.13-2.3 // 89.3 my covenant...Mal. 2.5-7 // 89.4 you have strayed...Mal.2.8-10 // 89.5 behold...Mal.3.1-3 // 89.6 your words...Mal.3.13-15 // 90.1 woe upon woe...Ezek.7.26 the Lord says...Ezek.13.8-10 // 90.2 woe to those...Ezek.13.18-19 // 90.3 say, son of man...Ezek.22.24-6 // 91.1 and I looked...Ezek.22.30-1 // 91.2 and the Lord... Ezek.33.1-9 // 92.3 we greatly desire...unidentified // 92.5 you are the salt... Mt.5.13 // 93.2 you are the light...Mt.5.14-15 // 93.3 let your light...Mt.5.16 // 94.2 for whoever...Mt.5.19 do not judge...Mt.7.1-2 // 94.3 why do you... Mt.7.3-4 do not give...Mt.7.6 // 94.4 beware...Mt.7.15-17 not everyone... Mt.7.21 // 95.1 behold...Mt.10.16 // 95.2 be prudent...Mt.10.16 // 95.3

do not fear...Mt.10.28 // 95.4 let them be...Mt.15.14 // 96.1 in the
seat...Mt.23.2-3 // 96.2 woe to you...Mt.23.13 // 96.3 my master...Mt.
24.48-51 // 97.1 imitate me...1 Cor.11.1 when they came...Rom.1.21-22
// 97.2 they changed...Rom.1.25-6 // 97.3 and as they...Rom.1.28-32 //
98.1 not only those...Rom.1.32 but as a result...Rom.2.5-6 // 98.2 there
is no...Rom.2.11-13 // 99.1 what shall we say...Rom.6.1-2 who will
separate...Rom.8.35 // 99.2 the night...Rom.13.12-14 // 100.1 like a
wise...1 Cor.3.10-17 // 100.2 if any man...1 Cor.3.18-19 your boasting...
1 Cor.5.6-7 // 100.3 I wrote...1 Cor.5.9-11 // 101.1 as we have...2 Cor.
4.1-2 // 101.2 for such men...2 Cor.11.13-15 // 102.1 this I say...Eph.
4.17-19 // 102.2 therefore...Eph.5.17-18 // 103.1 we never used...1 Thess.
2.5-8 // 103.2 you know...1 Thess.4.2-8 // 103.3 therefore...Col.3.5-6
(though Gildas seems to imply that this too is from 1 Thess.) // 104.1 know...
2 Tim.3.1-5 I hated...Pss.25.5 // 104.2 always learning...2 Tim.3.7-9 //
105.1 show yourself...Tit.2.7-8 // 105.2 labour...2 Tim.2.3-5 // 105.3 if
any man...1 Tim.6.3-5 // 106.2 blessed be God...1 Pet.1.3-5 // 106.3 so
gird...1 Pet.1.13 as sons...1 Pet.1.14-16 // 106.4 dearest...1 Pet.1.22-3 //
107.1 therefore laying...1 Pet.2.1-3 // 107.2 you are...1 Pet.2.9 // 107.3
brothers...Acts 1.15-16 and so...Acts 1.18 // 108.1 Matthias...Acts 1.26 //
108.3-5 brothers (and the succeeding quotations)...1 Tim.3.1-3 // 108.5 indeed
I say... Mt.6.2 // 109.1-2 one who rules (and the succeeding quotations)...1 Tim.
3.4-5, 8-10 // 109.3 when the Lord asked...Mt.16.15-17 // 109.4 you are
Peter...Mt.16.18 the foolish man...Mt.7.26 they have made kings...Hos.8.4
and the gates of hell...Mt.16.18 the rivers came...Mt.7.27 // 109.5 and I
shall...Mt.16.19. I do not know...Lk.13.27: cf.Mt.25.32-3,41 and whatever...
Mt.16.19 each man...Prov.5.22 // 110.1 I am clean...Acts 20.26-27 // 110.2
I do not...Ezek.33.11 // frg.1 Noah...Gen.7.13 Abraham...Gen.14.24 Lot...
Gen.19 Isaac...Gen.26.26, 30-31 Jacob...Gen.42 Joseph...Gen.41 Aaron...
Exod.18.12 Moses...ibid. our Lord...Mt.9.10: cf.21.31 // frg.2 death has
entered...cf. Jer.9.21 // frg.3 the worst of times...2 Tim.3.1-5 having zeal...
Rom.10.2-3 all our righteousness...Is.64.6 whose angels...Mt.18.10 they
will be...Is.65.5 the Lord calls...Mt.5. 3 seq. // frg.4 we have no need...1 Cor.
12.21 // frg.6 cursed is he...Deut.27.17 let each ...1 Cor.7.24 those parts...
1 Cor.12.23 count all men...cf.Phil.2.3 an apostle...Mt.26.15 a thief...Lk.
23.41-3 // frg.7 if any man...1 Cor.5.11 // frg.9 Miriam...Num.12

VARIANTS FROM MOMMSEN'S TEXT

References are by chapter and section. Asterisks indicate that the new reading appears in at least one manuscript (or early edition). Daggers indicate changes made with no manuscript support to conform with the Vulgate and/or Septuagint. The reading printed in this edition is given first; Mommsen's reading follows.

1.1-2 putet. Quia] putet, quia // 1,9 *Abraham et Isaac] Abraham, Isaac // 1.14 ininterrupte (Bulhart)] interrupte // 1.14 protractum? Serves....taceas.] protractum serves....taceas? // 1.16 autem] enim atque // 2 *reliquiis] reliquis // 3.2 *munitionibus] molitionibus // 7 *experte] experte relicta // 17.2 rotantium] rotarum // 21.2 *obducitur, fame....pullulante.] obducitur. Fame....pullulante, //21.6 *errare] errore // 25.2 alveari] alvearii // 27 sed eos] et eos // 28.1 *iuramenti sacramentum] sacramentum iuramenti // 32.1 *urse....ursi] Urse....Ursi // 32.2 hebetudine] hebetudine nympharum // 36.1 *cum habueris] tum habueris // 37.1 *dicunt] dicit // 40.3 *sermones] ne sermones // 40.3 *Michaeae] Michae // 42.3 abominationi sunt (Grosjean)] ab omni natione sunt non placita // 43.4 *lingua ignis et] ignis et ligna // 44.2 *hoc. Luxit] hoc: luxit // 44.2 †infecta] interfecta // 45.1 *citharae, cum cantico non] citharae cum cantico, non // 45.2 †fovea et laqueus] foveae et laqueus // 45.2 *quia cataractae] qui cataractae // 50.3 *huic, qui....placuit:] huic: qui....placuit, // 51 *impietatem? Contra et] impietatem contra: et // 53.1 calcant] calciant // 55 *vox diei] vox dei // 57.2 †proiciam eam] proiciam eum // 57.2 †domum furis (cf. Williams)] domum furoris // 57.2 †domum iurantis] domum iurationis // 59.1 *permanent] permanet // 59.3 *impotentes] imponentes // 59.4 *pareant] pariant // 59.5 *paraverit] raraverit // 61.1 *quaeret] quaerent // 61.2 †manum meam in eam] manum meam // 62.8 *qualitate sunt] sunt qualitate, sunt // 64.1 †te; dentes] te dentes // 66.6 *umquam] usquam // 66.7 *paenitentiam] paenitentia // 67.4 *sibi evenisse] subinde venisse // 67.6 *fingunt] pingunt // 72.1 *antea] ante ea // 72.2 potuerit (Grosjean)] poterit // 72.2 *seu] ceu // 72.2 *fortior] fortior forma // 74.3 *ut Iesum] ut in Iesum // 74.3 *merear. Ignes....bestiae] merear ignes....bestias // 74.3 *compleantur] complentur // 74.5 *auctor] actor // 81.2 *grandis] grandes // 82.3 †adulterantium] adulterium // 85.2 in culina] culina // 86.3 *iudicabant] iudicant // 86.4 *manducandum primitiva:] manducandum: primitiva, // 87.2 *leones] leo // 88.3 *passi] parsi // 93.2 *in editi] ut editi // 94.1 *ulla....circuitione] ullo....circuitio // 95.2 *revolatis] revolastis // 99.2 †lucis. Sicut] lucis sic ut // 100.1 *manserit quod] manserit, qui // 103.1 †oneri (Williams)] honori // 106.1 si diversorum] diversorum // 107.1 *rationabile] rationabilis // 108.1 exemplum,] exemplum, sanctorum quoque apostolorum // 108.1 *affectum] effectum // 108.4 diceret] dicere // 109.4 praevalebunt'] praevalebunt' eiusque peccata intelleguntur // 109.6 *supra mundum] supra modum // frg.3 despectus. Dum....meditantur,] despectus, dum....meditantur. vineae ulmum (cf. Williams)] ulnum *omnes iustitiae] omnis iustitiae fratres dicit dominus beatos esse, sed pauperes; non] fratres: dicit dominus pauperes beatos esse, sed pauperes non // frg.4 monachis qui veniunt de loco viliore ad perfectiorem. Quorum] monachis. Qui veniunt de loco viliore ad perfectiorem, quorum illa possunt (Williams)] ille possunt // frg.7 nequam famae pedore (cf. Mommsen's note)] nequam fama putare arcere, nisi] arcere, legitime fuerint] legitime fuerunt

160

INDEX OF PROPER NAMES

Biblical names are not indexed. Names not in the text are bracketed.